Relevant Linguistics

Relevant Linguistics

An Introduction to the Structure and Use of English for Teachers

Paul W. Justice

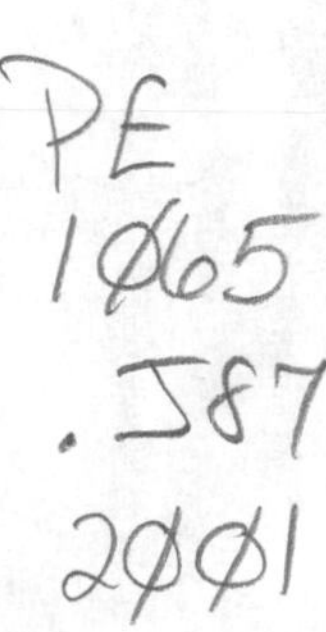

CSLI PUBLICATIONS
Center for the Study of Language and Information
Stanford, California

Center for the Study of Language and Information
Leland Stanford Junior University
Printed in the United States
05 04 03 5 4

Library of Congress Cataloging-in-Publication Data
Justice, Paul W., 1966–
Relevant linguistics : an introduction to the structure and use of English for teachers / Paul W. Justice.
p. cm. – (CSLI lecture notes ; no. 137)
Includes bibliographical references and index.

ISBN 1-57586-358-8 (pbk. : alk. paper)

1. English language – Study and teaching.
2. English language – Grammar.
3. English language – Syntax.
4. English language – Usage.
5. Linguistics. I. Title. II. Series.

PE1065 .J87 2001 428'.0071'1–dc21
2001047924

∞ The acid-free paper used in this book meets the minimum requirements of the American National Standard for Information Sciences – Permanence of Paper for Printed Library Materials, ANSI Z39.48-1984.

CSLI was founded early in 1983 by researchers from Stanford University, SRI International, and Xerox PARC to further research and development of integrated theories of language, information, and computation. CSLI headquarters and CSLI Publications are located on the campus of Stanford University.

CSLI Publications reports new developments in the study of language, information, and computation. In addition to lecture notes, our publications include monographs, working papers, revised dissertations, and conference proceedings. Our aim is to make new results, ideas, and approaches available as quickly as possible. Please visit our web site at http://cslipublications.stanford.edu/ for comments on this and other titles, as well as for changes and corrections by the author and publisher.

Contents

Preface

To the Student

As more and more institutions of higher learning realize the importance of linguistics in teacher preparation programs, linguistics courses are becoming a more integral part of their curriculum. You're reading this book because you're in a linguistics class, and you're probably in a linguistics class because your school feels that an understanding of language will help you be a better teacher. Unfortunately, you probably haven't taken a linguistics class before, so you probably have no idea what linguistics is all about or how it will help you be a better teacher. Hopefully, by the end of the term, this will change.

For many first time students of linguistics, the subject is inaccessible, boring, and seemingly irrelevant. The purpose of this textbook is to make linguistics more accessible, more interesting and more obviously relevant to you. It has been written with future teachers in mind. While it's not a teaching handbook, it does highlight areas of linguistics that are most relevant to teachers, occasionally even making specific suggestions for applications of the material to classroom teaching. In most cases, however, the specific applications will be up to you, the creative teacher, to identify.

For those neither in, nor pursuing, a career in education, this book will hopefully provide an accessible introduction to linguistic study, which will give you valuable insight into human language and prepare you for future study in the field.

To the Instructor

This textbook is based on many semesters of tried and true methods and materials. Every semester at San Diego State University there are seven or more sections of an introductory class that is populated largely by current and future elementary and secondary school teachers. Our goal is to teach them about the structure and use of language, with an emphasis on English, the language of instruction in most of their classrooms. The various instructors of this class have tried many different textbooks and have received repeated complaints from students about all of them. Some students say the books are incomprehensible; others say they are filled with an excessive amount of jargon, and others still don't see the connection between the material in the book and their chosen profession. The aim of this book is to eliminate, or at least reduce, these complaints by making linguistics more accessible and relevant. This text does not claim to be better than those currently in use; it merely claims to be more appropriate (and effective) for a particular group of students.

The approach this book takes is, of course, very descriptive in nature. The goal is to impress upon students the systematic nature of language and the scientific nature of linguistic inquiry. The text is data driven, with copious examples provided throughout. The idea is to lead students through descriptive analyses and help them really "see" the concepts as well as to provide them with reference materials that they can refer to when studying for tests or, better yet, preparing their own lessons or deciding how to address a classroom situation.

The data and examples used are mostly from English. When foreign language data is used, it is for the purpose of illustrating the differences between English and other languages. The purpose of these comparisons is to make students aware that there is nothing inherently "normal" about the way English works and that students from non-English speaking backgrounds have difficulty with English for very understandable reasons—the same reasons native English speakers have difficulty with other languages. Also, this focus on English tends to make the material seem more relevant to the students and, therefore, captures their attention better.

One issue to keep in mind when using this textbook is what can be referred to as the struggle between completeness and simplicity. That is, as teachers, we want to present our students with complete information about the structure and use of language, but at the same time, because language is so amazingly complex, we are sometimes forced to simplify it to make it more comprehensible to our students. At times, this text does this. Also at times, the sharper students catch the oversimplifications. Rather than apologize for it, an instructor can explain to them why the material has been simplified and invite them to continue searching for more "complete" answers to their questions.

Many of these oversimplifications appear in Chapter Six. Students tend to get overwhelmed by the sheer volume of material in a study of syntax, the result being that difficult choices must be made regarding how detailed the approach should be. Because of this, the approach to syntax in this chapter is greatly simplified in places. For example, in the presentation of phrase structure, certain kinds of words are not included at all. A quick glance reveals that adverbs, while covered at the beginning of the chapter, do not make an appearance in the phrase structure sections. Also in this section, the approach to constituents is simplified. For example, noun phrases are represented with the simplified structure det+adj+N, rather than a structure that indicates grouping at different hierarchical levels. This is one of several simplifications that have been made with regard to phrase structure. Another feature that has been simplified is the treatment of "that" as a relative pronoun. While this word is generally regarded as a complementizer, not a relative pronoun, among linguists, such a presentation does not work well with the student population this book is written for. The philosophy behind this text is to teach as much about the structure and use of English as possible without going so far that students tune out.

On a related note, while this text walks students through the basics of linguistic analysis in a very thorough way, you will find that it does not always delve as deeply as possible into some issues. That is, many of the gray areas of linguistics are not dealt with. For example, in the chapter on morphology, compounding is dealt with in a brief paragraph, while the topic could easily be discussed over several pages. The intended audience of this book often complains that detailed discussions serve only to confuse them and erect barriers between them and the material. This book *does* cover these gray areas, to a certain extent, because they are an essential part of the discipline, but not completely because some of the details are probably better dealt with in class. In fact, one of the main benefits of this book is, hopefully, that it will free up class time to discuss these complex issues by covering the basics in the text in a comprehensible way.

Also, while the chapters are presented in a particular order, from the smallest units of language to larger ones, there is a certain amount of flexibility in terms of the order in which the chapters can be used. For example, the chapter on morphology could be covered before the chapters on phonetics and phonology. Another possibility that has been effective in the past is to handle phonology and morphophonology together, after both the phonetics and morphology chapters. However, given the way the information on word classes is split between the morphology and syntax chapters, it's probably best to cover syntax later, as the syntax chapter assumes knowledge of the material covered in the morphology chapter. Also, the final chapter on language variation assumes knowledge of all of the material presented earlier. It serves to introduce important new concepts while reviewing familiar ones. Thus, it is most effective when covered at the end of the term.

Finally, understanding the pedagogical plan behind the book can help instructors decide how best to work with it. The philosophy behind this curriculum is that students learn best in class when they have a foundation of knowledge and skills to work with. Thus, it's recommended that students be assigned readings to be completed *before* the class session that will cover that particular area. Also important for establishing this foundation is completion of the quick exercises and data analyses in the text of each chapter. These can be used to lead into class discussions and involve students in those discussions. The other two components of the pedagogical philosophy are a thorough exploration of each area during class and independent practice through the completion of the end of chapter exercises *after* class. No solutions to these exercises are provided in the book, so instructors who want to use them as graded exercises can do so. For those instructors who do not want to use them as graded exercises, solutions are available via the Web and can be distributed to students. Only instructors who adopt the text will have access to these solutions. To obtain access, please contact the publisher by email at pubs@csli.stanford.edu or by FAX at 650-725-2166. Please provide proof of text adoption and make your request on university letterhead.

The graphic below illustrates the pedagogical philosophy.

Step 1		Step 2		Step 3
Students read text and complete in-text exercises and analyses independently	⇒	Class discussion adds to depth of understanding	⇒	Students complete end of chapter exercises independently to solidify understanding

Acknowledgments

I'd like to thank all the people who helped make this project possible. First, I'm grateful to my family for providing me the best educational opportunities from a young age and for stressing the importance of education throughout my life.

I'd also like to thank Dikran Karagueuzian of CSLI, who encouraged me to pursue the project in the first place. Also very helpful throughout the writing and editing process was Tony Gee of CSLI.

Several people who devoted valuable time to read and comment on earlier versions of the work are also due heartfelt thanks. My colleague and mentor at San Diego State University, Jeff Kaplan, provided invaluable linguistic insights in virtually every area, vastly improving the accuracy of the content. Bridget de la Garza from San Diego City Schools read a draft with the keen eye of a curriculum specialist and made many suggestions to improve the clarity of the presentation. Colleen Christiansen, the consummate copy editor, provided feedback in nearly every area, particularly style and presentation. Had I followed all of their suggestions, I'd probably have a better finished product.

Finally, I'd like to thank all the students over the years in my Linguistics 420 classes at San Diego State University, especially those early on, who had to endure horribly organized versions of my materials. Their comments and suggestions have been of tremendous use.

Any errors and limitations that managed to survive this barrage of constructive feedback are mine.

Paul Justice
San Diego State University

1

What is Linguistics?

In this chapter, we'll examine the discipline of linguistics to prepare you for the term. In addition to defining what linguistics *is*, we'll examine what it is *not*. In the process of doing this, we'll identify some of the more common, and important, misconceptions about linguistics.

Some specific goals of this text are the following:

- To encourage you to reevaluate your own beliefs and attitudes about language.
- To make you aware of the complexity of language and able to articulate this awareness.
- To make you aware of some of the similarities and difference among languages.
- To expose you to the "core" sub-fields of linguistics (phonetics, phonology, morphology and syntax).
- To introduce you to linguistic analysis, and to encourage you to think scientifically about language
- To provide you with some tools that you can apply in subsequent study of linguistics or professional settings.

Some important fundamental concepts of linguistics are stated below (adapted from Department of Linguistics, pp. 2–3):

- Every language is amazingly complex.
- Despite this complexity, all languages are highly systematic, though their systematicity is not transparent to native speakers of those languages.
- It is not easy for speakers of a language to think about or talk about their language use; although our speech is completely rule governed, we are not consciously aware of these rules.
- Speech is the primary mode of language; writing is only a secondary one. For proof of this, just think about the age at which you started speaking and the age at which you started reading and writing.
- Although most children learn their first language fluently by the age of five, they're not explicitly taught it; instead, they naturally acquire the rules of their language from the language use they hear around them.
- Linguists are interested in describing the similarities and differences among languages; this is especially important when trying to teach someone a second language.

What Do Linguists Do?

When people meet a teacher of linguistics, the first question they generally ask is "how many languages do you speak?" This question perfectly illustrates the fact that most people have very little idea what linguistics is all about. It also illustrates one of the most pervasive misconceptions about the discipline:

<u>Misconception #1:</u> Linguistics is the study of specific languages with the goal of learning to read, write or speak them.

If this were true, every linguist would speak a variety of languages fluently; otherwise, they'd be pretty poor linguists. Imagine the surprise, however, when people meet a linguist who speaks only a single language. This does *not* mean, however, that such individuals are linguistically deficient. While these linguists don't speak any languages other than English, they know a fair amount *about* many other languages. Put another way, they don't know them (i.e., speak them), but they do know about them. This is an important distinction to make. It also leads us to a working definition of linguistics:

Clarification #1: Linguistics is the scientific study of the phenomenon of human language.

There are some important, yet seemingly subtle, points wrapped up in this definition. First, note the form of the word "language." If it were to read "languages," then the misinformed souls referred to earlier would be correct. Rather than studying specific languages, linguists study the "phenomenon" of language, in terms of its structure and use. We use this word "phenomenon" in our definition not to make it unnecessarily wordy, but to clarify and reconfirm the notion of the larger issue of human language, rather than specific languages, as the primary focus of linguistics. You can think of human language as one big system, with each individual language being a specific part of the system. This concept is illustrated in Figure 1.1.

Figure 1.1: Human Language

Also important is the use of the word "scientific" in the definition. Throughout our exploration of the phenomenon of language, we will employ a scientific approach, similar to the "scientific method" you learned in grade school. That is, we will *observe* real language, we will make *hypotheses* about it, and then we will *test* our hypotheses to see if they're accurate. In the end we will describe "laws" of language in much the same way a physicist describes laws of nature. We'll explore the nature of language "laws" (i.e. rules) in more detail shortly.

A final note to make here is the *mode* of language that we will be dealing with primarily. At all times, unless otherwise specified, when we discuss language, it will be *spoken* language that we are referring to. The *written* mode will also be covered, but when this is the case, a special note will be made.

What is the Nature of Language?

Now that we have defined linguistics as the scientific study of language, we need to spend some time discussing what language is. This is not as simple as one might think. Most people, when asked to define language, focus on the concept of communication. They come up with definitions for language such as "a way to communicate thoughts and ideas." It's true that language is a tool for communication, but to offer such a simple definition would be misleading. The fact of the matter is that language is far more complex than most people realize. Consider the following example:

(1) Jimmy says to Joey: "Hey, what's up?"

What thoughts or ideas have actually been communicated to Joey? Most people agree that the idea communicated by questions is a request for information. For example, if someone asks you "What time is it?" they're communicating to you that they would like some information, namely the time of day. In (1), however, do you think Jimmy really wants information from Joey? How do you think he will react if Joey really starts to tell him what's up (generally understood to mean what's happening in his life)? If Jimmy is like most people, he'll get bored rather quickly. He'll also probably make a mental note never to ask Joey that kind of question again. Instead, he'll probably just say something like (2) and keep on walking.

(2) "Hey, Joey, good to see you."

And why is this statement an easy substitute for the question in (1)? The answer is simple: because (2) conveys essentially the same "information and ideas" as (1), namely a greeting. In some cases, we use language not to express ideas or communicate information, but to perform social functions such as greetings. Expressions like the question in (1) are intended solely to perform social functions and do not really contain any other "meaning." Performing a social function is not the same as "conveying information."

To further dismiss the simplified communication-oriented definition of language, consider example (3):

(3) Man says to woman at a bar: "You look lovely tonight."

Now, presumably it's possible that he merely wants to express an idea in his head, give her that information and be done with the interaction. However, most people would probably suspect that this man has an ulterior motive, and that by telling her she looks lovely, he may be able to influence her actions. In fact, it's entirely possible that he doesn't really believe this "idea" that he's expressed to her, yet he expresses it anyway. Why? Perhaps he believes a compliment is going to help him achieve some other purpose (we'll leave the exact nature of that purpose to your imagination). So, we see that in the case of some compliments, the use of language goes beyond the desire to "convey information."

The important point to get out of the preceding discussion is that language is far more complex than we realize. In fact, it's so complex that it's difficult to provide a nice, neat, concise definition of it. Instead of *defining* language, then, we'll *describe* it. We can describe language as a complex system involving ideas and expressions. Stated another way, when we use language, we put thoughts (ideas) into words (the expressions). Thought this might seem straight-forward at first, upon closer inspection, we'll see that it's actually more complicated.

Let's begin with the link between ideas and expressions. Is it always as tight as we'd like it to be? In other words, do we always say exactly what we mean? Certainly not. Any teenager who has ever planned a telephone call to an admired boy or girl knows this well. No matter how much they rehearse exactly what they want to say, it never seems to come out as they had hoped. This problem connecting ideas and expressions is what leads countless teenagers (and adults) to jot down notes before making important phone calls to line up dates.

To further illustrate the complexity of language, we have to consider the situation in which utter expressions. The fact of the matter is that a single set of expressions can have multiple meanings depending on the situation in which utter them. In other words, the ideas (or meaning) represented by our words is, at least to a certain extent, context specific. Consider (4) and (5):

(4) Teacher asks students in the back of a large lecture hall: "Is Zoe there?"
(5) X says to Y, who has just answered X's telephone call: "Is Zoe there?"

In (4), the teacher is expressing his desire for information, specifically whether a certain person is present in the classroom or not. If the students reply "yes," then the questioner is satisfied and the discussion moves on to other matters. In (5), however, if Y answers "yes" and hangs up, X won't be as satisfied as the teacher. This is because the expressions in (5), though identical to the expressions in (4), are used to express a different meaning (i.e. there is a different idea behind it). In (5), the meaning goes beyond a request for information about the presence of a person and includes a request to actually speak with the person. Thus, we see that, in some cases, the situation in which an expression is uttered can change its meaning. This is, indeed, complicated.

Focus on Expressions: The Nature of Words

An important point to raise when discussing language is the nature of the words we use to express ideas. The words we use are **signs** of our meaning, but what is it about them that makes their meaning clear? Consider the words in 6:

(6) water, agua, su

Even if you don't recognize the third word, you can probably guess what it means based on the other two words. All three of these words are used to represent the meaning of H_20 in different languages —"agua" is the Spanish word for water, and "su" is the Turkish word for water. Notice, however, that while they have the same meaning behind them, the words are completely different on the surface. That is, they don't sound alike at all. If there were some inherent connection between the words we use and their meanings, then every language would use the exact same words. This, however, is certainly not true. There is nothing inherent in the sounds w-a-t-e-r or a-g-u-a that indicates the meaning of these words. Instead, English's use of w-a-t-e-r, Spanish's use of a-g-u-a, and Turkish's use of s-u are completely *arbitrary*. This is illustrated by the fact that these different languages have different words for H_20, yet all three of the words represent the same meaning to speakers of the languages. Our understanding of "water" as H_20 is based only on our agreement, as English speakers, that we will use the sign "water" to represent this meaning. People who do not speak a word of English, however, are not in on this agreement, and cannot connect the sign word with the meaning H_20. The point here is that most words are completely arbitrary.

While the overwhelming majority of words in any language are completely arbitrary signs, like the words in (6), there are some words that do, at least in some way, indicate their meaning. The most obvious examples are like those in (7):

(7) meow, moo

The words we use to represent animal noises generally sound somewhat, though not exactly, like the actual noises. Thus, unlike the words in (6), there is some inherent connection between the words in (7) and their meanings. It is not an arbitrary choice to use "meow" for a cat's noise and "moo" for a cow's. Instead, the choice is based on something real in the world. Specifically, the pronunciation of the word is similar to its meaning, the sound it represents. Words like the ones in (7) are examples of **onomatopoeia**. Onomatopoeic words are ones that do, in some way, indicate their meaning. These words, therefore, are *not* completely arbitrary signs.

Further evidence for onomatopoeic words not being completely arbitrary comes from other languages. For example, if you ask people who speak other languages what the word for a cat's noise is in their language, chances are that the word will be similar to the English "meow." This makes sense, because the word is, after all, onomatopoeic. Table 1.1 provides cross-linguistic examples of onomatopoeia.

meaning	English word	Arabic	Chinese	Japanese
cat's sound	meeyow	mowmow	mayow	neeyow
rooster's sound	cockadoodledoo	keekeekees	coocoo	kohkaykoko

Table 1.1: Onomatopoeic Words (adapted from the Department of Linguistics, p. 16)

What you should notice is that the words, while similar across all the languages, are not identical. In fact, it's impossible to find a word that is universal to all languages. If one were to exist, it would be a completely non-arbitrary sign, and such signs simply do not exist in human language. In other words, there are no completely non-arbitrary words in language. For completely non-arbitrary signs, we need to look to nature. For example, the presence of smoke is a completely non-arbitrary sign that there is fire in some form. No language, however, has such signs.

So, you're probably wondering at this point how a system with so much arbitrariness can work. The answer lies in the word "system." Language is not just a bunch of words thrown together; instead, it's very *systematic*, and when native speakers of a language speak their own language, they unconsciously follow a set of complicated rules. This set of rules is often referred to as **grammar**, a word that often evokes painful memories for some people. In the next section, we will explore the nature of these grammar rules.

The Nature of Grammar Rules: Prescriptivism vs. Descriptivism

Perhaps one of the reasons people have negative feelings toward grammar is the approach to grammar that is generally taken in schools. Specifically, grammar is presented as a set of rigid rules that must be followed by anyone who wants to be considered a "good" or "correct" speaker of a language. Naturally, any approach of this nature sets people up for failure if they do not conform exactly to the standard that's been set. It's no wonder, then, that many people grow up disliking grammar. No doubt, people's early experiences with grammar have contributed significantly to the second misconception:

Misconception #2: Linguistics is concerned with trying to get people to speak "properly".

Linguistics teachers hear this from students all the time. Often students report that by taking a linguistics class they hope to learn to speak "better" English. Their assumption is that this is the purpose of a linguistics course. This is certainly not the case. Rather than *prescribe* to students how they should speak a language, linguistics is mainly concerned with *describing* how people actually speak. This distinction is generally referred to as **prescriptivism** vs. **descriptivism**.

Prescriptivism

As the term suggests, someone who subscribes to a prescriptive approach to grammar, believes that there is a prescribed (written before, or ahead of time) list of rules to which all speakers of a language must conform. Those who do not conform are said to be speaking "incorrectly" and in some cases are labeled "linguistically deficient." It's understandable that many people take this view of grammar. After all, this is the approach taken in most language instruction. A quick glance at any foreign language textbook confirms this. Chapters usually begin with the statement of a rule. This prescribed rule is then modeled using a variety of examples. After that, there are exercises for the students to practice the rule that they've learned. This is clearly a prescriptive approach.

Prescriptivism is not, however, limited to the foreign language classroom. You've probably learned many prescriptive rules of English during the course of your education, most of them in English or composition classes. The "rules" in (8) represent two of the more common prescriptive rules of English.

(8) a. It's ungrammatical to end a sentence with a preposition.
b. It's ungrammatical to split an infinitive.

If you violate these rules, as we have in the sentences in (9), you have, in the eyes of a prescriptivist, spoken ungrammatical English.

(9) a. Linguistics is what I live for.
b. Captain Kirk wants to boldly go where no man (or woman) has gone before.

The problem for prescriptivists, however, is that these sentences sound perfectly good to nearly all native English speakers and sentence just like these are spoken regularly by native English speakers. We'll address this "problem" in the next section.

Descriptivism

What you will soon see, hopefully, is that prescriptivism ignores reality. First, while formal foreign language instruction is, as has been noted, generally prescriptive, first language acquisition is clearly not. Every person reading this book learned a language fluently by the age of five, and with very few, if any, exceptions, none of you read or heard any grammar rules during this time. This list of prescribed rules that the prescriptivist adheres to did not play a role in your acquisition of your first language. In fact, most of you probably never encountered a stated grammar rule until you were at least 12 or 13 years old.

Consider also the fact that nearly every single one of you reading this book violates the rules in (8) on a regular basis. In fact, the examples in (9) that violate these rules probably sound just fine to nearly all of us. If native speakers of English end sentences with prepositions and split infinitives regularly, who are these prescriptivists to claim that such English speakers don't know how to speak the language? This is something that we should all take exception with (note the sentence final preposition).

To further illustrate the absurdity of prescriptivism, consider the origin of prescriptive rules, in particular the prescriptive rule prohibiting the splitting of infinitives. In the eighteenth-century there was a movement among grammarians to standardize English, and when questions arose about which forms should be deemed "correct," they were often answered by using classical languages, Greek and Latin, as models[1]. In Latin, infinitive forms consist of a single word. Examples are the verbs "vocare" (to call) and "vertere" (to turn). Thus, in Latin, it is impossible to split an infinitive. In English, however, infinitives consist of "to" plus the verb (as in "to turn" and "to call"), giving rise to the possibility of splitting an infinitive, such as the infinitive "to go" that's split in (9b). To attempt to make the rules of one language, English, conform to the rules of another, Latin, can only be described as absurd.

<u>Clarification #2:</u> Linguists are concerned with describing how people actually speak.

Rather than trying to prescribe how people *should* speak, linguists are interested in describing how they actually *do* speak. Descriptive grammar does not judge linguistic production as correct or incorrect; instead it observes what people say and describes it. Such an approach also involves surveying native speakers of a language to test their intuitions regarding what "sounds good" or "sounds bad" to them. The approach taken by a descriptivist is that whenever a native speaker of a language speaks, he or she is following a set of grammar rules. In other words, aside from the occasional slip of the tongue, all native speaker linguistic production *is 100% rule governed.* The descriptive linguist is well aware, however, that not all native speakers are following the exact same set of rules. Consider the sentences in (10).

(10) a. We love linguistics classes.
b. *Love we classes linguistics.
c. ?If I were you, I would take lots of linguistics classes.
d. ?If I was you, I would take lots of linguistics classes.

No doubt you find (10a) perfectly grammatical, but you find (10b) wholly ungrammatical, and would never expect to hear any native speaker of English uttering such a sentence (an asterisk before a sentence, as in (10b), indicates ungrammaticality). It's difficult to imagine any native speaker of English disagreeing with you. What this proves is that we all share some (in fact, many) of the same rules. There is certain to be disagreement, however, among native English speakers regarding the grammaticality of (10c) and (10d) (a question mark before a sentence indicates questionable grammaticality). For some of you, (10c) is grammatical, while (10d) is ungrammatical; for others, the exact opposite is true; for others still, both are grammatical. Does this mean that some of us are right and others are wrong? If so, who's right? To a descriptive linguist, because sentences like both (10c) and (10d) are spoken regularly by native speakers of English, they are both grammatical for the people who speak them. (10c) and (10d) prove that while all native speakers of English share certain rules, we do not share *all* rules. In fact, there is a tremendous amount of linguistic diversity among the speakers of any language. We will revisit this issue in more detail at the end of the book.

What this lack of consensus regarding grammaticality tells us is that to judge certain speakers as incorrect or deficient because they don't conform to a standard laid out by certain individuals, such as the eighteenth-century grammarians described earlier, is misguided. Linguists do not judge; they merely observe and describe. We will see that the *correct vs. incorrect* distinction is more useful than *the appropriate vs. inappropriate* distinction. That is, when speaking with people who prefer (10c) to (10d), it would be more

---

[1] See Barry (1998), pp. 4–5, for a more detailed discussion.

appropriate to use (10c), and while speaking with people who prefer (10d) to (10c), it would be more appropriate to use (10d).

Much of what we do in this textbook is describe rules of English. Notice, however, the use of the word "describe." Our rules will be based on observation of real linguistic data, meaning real language. In some cases, we will use data already gathered, and in other cases we will generate our own. The important point, however, is that everything we do will be based on observation of real language, not a rule prescribed by some language "authority." In some cases, we might even feel the need to disagree with a dictionary. This is fine as long as we base our conclusions on real data.

You'll see that the process of linguistic inquiry that we employ is a very scientific one that should remind you of your first junior high school science class. Specifically, we will use a "scientific method" of investigation. Just as in a physical science class we will follow certain steps, as illustrated in (11).

(11) step 1: observe (we will gather real language data and analyze it)
step 2: hypothesize (based on our observations, we will hypothesize a rule)
step 3: test (we will gather additional data to test our hypothesis)
step 4: conclude (we will write a final rule based on our observations and tests)

Notice that it's not until the very end that we will write our rules. This is a true *descriptive*, as opposed to *prescriptive*, process.

Descriptivism and the Language Arts Curriculum

At this point, you may be wondering how descriptivism fits into language arts instruction. If whatever native speakers say regularly is grammatical, what are we supposed to teach? To begin with, many of the students in US classrooms today are not native speakers of English. For these students, even the native speaker consensus that is illustrated in (10a) and (10b) is not necessarily shared. Much of their early English production might not be governed by a set of rules. Instead, it might be constructed partially through guessing; or it might be influenced partially by rules of the students' native languages. Therefore, rules like the ones governing (10a) and (10b) that we discover through a descriptive process sometimes need to be explicitly taught.

Next, for native speakers of English, the concept of appropriateness mentioned earlier is important when determining the relevance of descriptive grammar to classroom instruction. While all varieties of English are inherently equal, some are more appropriate in certain contexts. For people to be successful in our society, knowing how to speak the **standard** variety of English, meaning the one that's accepted in formal contexts, is of tremendous importance. The descriptive linguist realizes this, and, while being careful not to judge **non-standard** production as incorrect, works to teach his or her students the systematic differences between the two and how to produce the standard variety in the appropriate contexts.

To illustrate the concept of standard vs. non-standard, we can return to the questionable examples in (10). For some native speakers of English, (10c) is "correct" while for others (10d) is preferable. Only one of these, however, is considered standard (decide on your own which one you think is standard). In some cases, native speakers need to be taught the standard form if the non-standard one is what they've internalized. This must be done carefully, though. Imagine being told that what sounds right to you, what you've grown up with your whole life, is just plain *wrong*. For many of you, this will be easy, because while many of you prefer (10d), in fact, (10c) is considered standard. If this is hard for you to swallow, you can relate to what many students of non-standard speaking backgrounds go through when learning the standard variety.

Narrowing the Focus: English and other Languages

Up to this point, we have focused on the study of language in general. Now, let's shift our attention to specific languages, English in particular. An important point to keep in mind when studying language is that not all languages are structured the same way; nor are there "better" or "worse" ways for languages to be structured. While it's true that there are certain **universals**, or shared features, across human languages (in fact, language universals are the subject of a great deal of linguistic inquiry currently), there are also many differences among languages. What you, as a native English speaker, consider to be "normal" or "logical" in language might be completely foreign and unfamiliar to someone whose first language is not English. Conversely, what seems completely "normal" or "logical" to a speaker of another language might be foreign to you. This is part of what makes learning a second language so difficult. It is essential for teachers working with non-native speakers of English to understand this. Throughout this text, we will examine differences between English and other languages to make this point clear and to help you appreciate some of the difficulties your non-native speaking students face.

English: an Ideal Language?[2]

English seems to function just fine as a human language, but is it perfect? Like every natural human language, English is somewhat less than ideal. An ideal language would be one that is 100% clear or 100% efficient. Clearly, English is not 100% clear, as is illustrated by the amount of **lexical ambiguity** in language. Lexical ambiguity describes a situation in which a word could have multiple meanings. A common example used in linguistics classes is the sentence in (12).

(12) I'll meet you at the bank.

Does "bank" refer to a financial institution or the side of a river? It's not clear from this sentence; we would need more context to determine the answer to this question. Two words, such as "bank" and "bank," that are pronounced the same but have different meanings are called **homonyms**. English has many homonyms. Related to homonyms are **homophones**, words that are pronounced the same but have different meanings *and* different spellings. Examples of homophones are "pray" and "prey." An ideally clear language would have no homonyms or homophones; instead, each word would have exactly one meaning, and for every meaning there would be just a single word.

Just as English is not ideally clear, it is not ideally efficient. If it were, we would have a *single* word, for example, "suff," to express *every* meaning. While this would make learning vocabulary easy, it would not facilitate communication. Unfortunately, communication in an ideally efficient language would require powers of telepathy, which we do not have. How else would we know which of the countless meanings of "suff" a speaker intends? If he says only "suff" when he greets you, "suff" when he wants a drink and "suff" when he tells you happened to him at work yesterday, how will you know which of these three "meanings" he intends?

Though English, like every other natural language, is not ideal, we shouldn't be too quick to condemn it. It is, in fact, a compromise between the two "ideal" extremes described above. Think about the number of words you would have to learn if there were no homonyms in English; one word for every meaning would mean a whole lot of words to know. Instead, the language has sacrificed some clarity for efficiency. Ideal clarity would also take some of the fun out of life. Imagine a world without puns (plays on words) such as the one in (13). Pretty dull, to be sure.

(13) Q: Why is the baby ant confused?
A: All his uncles are ants [aunts].

Q: Why is a moon rock tastier than an earth rock?
A: It's a little meteor [meatier].

Q: Did you hear about the butcher who backed into the meat grinder?
A: He got a little *behind* in his work.

Also, in an ideally clear language, the humorous (but real) newspaper headlines in (14) wouldn't be humorous at all, and wouldn't that be a shame? What makes the examples in (13) and (14) humorous, assuming you find them humorous, is precisely the lack of clarity in English that we've been discussing. Specifically, it's the lexical ambiguity that creates the humor. In each headline, there is a word or words that can have multiple meanings, and one of these meanings is clearly inappropriate for the context. One might say, then, that a lack of linguistic clarity adds a little spice to life.

---

[2] Ideas adapted from Finegan (1999), pp. 4–5.

(14) a. Iraqi Head Seeks Arms
b. Is There A Ring Of Debris Around Uranus?
c. Prostitutes Appeal To Pope
d. Safety Experts Say School Bus Passengers Should Be Belted
e Red Tape Holds Up New Bridge
f. Kids Make Nutritious Snacks

And, of course, imagine the confusion that would result from an ideally efficient language (one with just a single word). We would never know what people were trying to say. By having more than just one word, the language sacrifices some efficiency for clarity. English is, then, a compromise between clarity and efficiency.

So, while English might not be ideal, it works; and as future educators who will be using English as the language of instruction, it will important for you to have a conscious awareness of how it works. That is the focus of this book.

Tying It All Together: The Relevance of Linguistics

Before we begin our exploration of English, and language in general, we need to stop and consider the relevance of linguistics to classroom teachers. Frequently, students complain that they don't see the point in studying linguistics. Many of them are already classroom teachers, they argue, and have been for several years, so why do they need to learn something new? This attitude leads us to our final misconception of the chapter:

Misconception #3: Linguistics is not relevant for primary and secondary school teachers.

Nothing could be further from the truth. While the students' complaints are, on one level, legitimate, they are very misguided on another. What this mean is that while it's true that no one *needs* linguistics to be a teacher, we would argue that to be the *best* teachers they can be requires a great deal of knowledge, including linguistic knowledge. To use a confusing, but accurate, saying, "we don't always know what we don't know." One of the goals of this textbook is to help you see what you didn't previously know about language, and to encourage you to use your newly found knowledge in your classrooms.

Clarification #3: Linguistics is highly relevant for primary and secondary school teachers.

Regardless of the subject or subjects you teach, language is involved. While language obviously plays a larger role in language arts than in other areas, it is certainly not limited to language arts. If you're teaching history, language is involved. If you're teaching math, language is involved. Because you will be using and responding to language in your classroom, having a greater awareness of it will make you a more effective teacher. You're probably having a difficult time seeing exactly how right now, but hopefully, by the end of the term, it will be clear to you. Remember, the usefulness of linguistics depends to a great extent on the creativity of the teacher. You need to be active in your application of linguistic knowledge in your classroom.

Summary

In this chapter we previewed the course by learning about what linguistics is and is not, uncovering some of the most common misconceptions about the field. We studied language as a general phenomenon and took a look at English in particular. We also investigated the nature of linguistic rules. Finally, we considered the relevance of linguistics to education professionals, specifically primary and secondary school teachers.

Misconceptions	**Clarifications**
#1: Linguistics is the study of specific languages with the goal of learning to read, write or speak them.	#1: Linguistics is the scientific study of the phenomenon of human language.
#2: Linguistics is concerned with trying to get people to speak "properly".	#2: Linguists are concerned with describing how people actually speak.
#3: Linguistics is not relevant for primary and secondary school teachers.	#3: Linguistics is highly relevant for primary and secondary school teachers.

Exercises

English Homophones

As you know, English (along with every other natural human language) is not an ideal language. Part of what makes English less than ideal is the significant amount of **homonymy** in the language. Homonymy refers to the relationship between words that have the same sounds, but different meanings. The term **homophone** is often used to refer to homonyms that have different spellings, as well as different meanings. Homonyms and homophones can be a particularly troublesome area for English Language Learner (ELL) students, for obvious reasons. Below is an exercise that should give you an idea of the extent of homonymy in English.

For each word given below, think of a *homophone*. Whenever possible, try to think of two homophones for each word. The first one has been done for you.

to	too	two
do		
pair		
raise		
air		
there		
right		
sight		
weigh		
need		
praise		

2

Phonetics: The Sounds of English

Phonetics is the study of the sounds of language. Our goals in this chapter will be the following:

- to identify the organs used in the production of speech
- to describe the features of linguistic sounds
- to represent linguistic sounds using phonetic **orthography** (writing symbols)

Phonetics: Its Relevance to Classroom Teachers

Often students ask why they need to study phonetics. One response to this question is that you never know when or how phonetics, or any other area of linguistics, will be useful in a classroom. As we noted in Chapter 1, much of this depends on the creativity of the individual teacher. In addition to this, we can easily identify some specific applications. First, nearly all teachers must pass a series of standardized tests to receive their credential. Some of these tests, including the RICA (Reading Instruction Competency Assessment) test, which is given to many teacher candidates in the state of California, include material from phonetics. They require candidates to have a working knowledge of terms such as "phoneme" and concepts such as "phonemic awareness," because these are concepts that have direct applications in instruction, particularly reading instruction. Learning the terms and concepts required to pass standardized tests is reason enough to study phonetics.

Beyond simply helping a candidate qualify for a teaching position, however, phonetics can be invaluable to teachers as they practice their trade. This is particularly true in the case of reading instruction. Over the years, literacy professionals have gone back and forth regarding the best method to teach reading. In the 1980s and early 1990s, a theory called **Whole Language** gained favor. According to this theory, students would naturally acquire the ability to read by being exposed to "quality" literature. The results of this approach alone, however, were mixed, with many students reading at a level far below their grade. This led to a return to a **phonics**-based approach, in which students were encouraged to sound words out as they read them. As you may have guessed, phonics and phonetics are closely related. Because current preferences in the school systems favor a combination of *both* whole language and phonics, anyone who intends to teach reading would do well to understand phonetics.

This is true not only of reading specialists at the elementary school level, but also of teachers of a variety of subjects at the secondary level. Unfortunately, not all students enter high school reading at level. Some read so far below level (as low as a first-grade level, according to some reports[1]) that they require very basic remedial instruction. And while many schools now offer special reading classes at the high school level, teachers of other subjects often find themselves providing some kind of reading instruction.

Spelling and Sounds in English

As the previous section indicates, learning to read is not a simple task, nor is teaching reading. These tasks can be particularly difficult in English because of the language's spelling system. While sounding out words, as in a phonics-based approach to reading, is generally considered effective, it can also lead to problems, because it isn't always easy to predict the sounds of an English word based on its letters. As nearly

[1] See Moran (2000) for a more detailed discussion.

anyone who has ever attempted to learn how to read and write in English can attest, English **orthography** (its writing system) is not easy to learn. Often, it seems that there's no rhyme or reason to English spelling.

To call attention to this reality, George Bernard Shaw once pointed out that English orthography allowed for the spelling "g-h-o-t-i" to represent the word "fish." His reasoning was that the letters "g-h" could represent an "f" sound, as in "rough," while the letter "o" could represent a short "i" sound, as in "women," and the "t-i" spelling could represent an "sh" sounds, as in "notion." This example highlights what we already know—namely that English spelling is not very phonetic; that is, a reader can't predict the exact sounds of a word based on its spelling. Why is English spelling the way it is? Without getting into too much detail, we can boil it down to a few factors:

A. Spoken language varies tremendously over time and space, but written language is fairly constant and resistant to change

Just as the English spoken in the United States is different from the English spoken in Scotland, the English spoken today is different from the English spoken 200 years ago. The fact of the matter is that spoken language changes constantly. This is not the case, however, with written language, and there are some practical reasons for this resistance to change in written language. For one thing, it allows for **mutual intelligibility** across regions. Thus, an English speaking person from Scotland can write a message to an English speaker in the US and be perfectly understood. Because this intelligibility is mutual, the American can just as effectively communicate in writing with the Scot as the Scot can with the American. Another advantage of a constant written language is that it allows for permanency of written documents. If written language were to change as much as spoken language, we might not be able to understand written documents from just a few hundred years ago.

B. English has been influenced greatly by other languages.

As we will see in Chapter 4, English has borrowed a tremendous number of words from other languages. In some cases, we've borrowed them as is, while in other cases we've adapted them somewhat; but in either case, the origin of the words is some other language. When these words are borrowed with their original spellings, spelling problems can occur. An extreme example is the word "hors d'oeuvres." Even a spelling bee champion would probably have trouble with this word because of the French spelling. You can see, then, how the diverse origins of English contribute to its spelling difficulties.

Even with these seeming irregularities and inconsistencies, however, a phonics-based approach to reading remains popular among education professionals. While there is not a perfect correspondence between spelling and sound in English, there is a connection, and using this connection can be a useful part of reading instruction. The main purpose of the rest of this chapter is to familiarize you, at a very conscious level, with the sounds of English.

The Smallest Units of Language: Phonemes

Having prefaced our discussion of phonetics with a discussion of the usefulness of phonetics for teachers and complications associated with English orthography, let's return now to our primary focus—spoken language. Every language has its own inventory of sounds that speakers of that language recognize as being linguistic sounds (as opposed to, say, the sound of a belch). These sounds are called **phonemes**. A phoneme can be defined as a psychologically real unit of linguistic sound. The cumbersome definition is necessary, though you might not fully understand why until Chapter 3 when we explore the psychology realities of speakers with regard to sounds in more detail.

Another way to think about phonemes is to consider that, while many sounds exist in the world, only some of these sounds are used in human language. Furthermore, of all the sounds that exist in human languages, only a fraction of those sounds are used in any one given language. It is only the sounds that are used in a person's language that are linguistically real to a speaker of that language. Believe it or not, some of the sounds of English, sounds that you have been familiar with since birth, are not even recognizable to speakers of other languages. This will become an important issue later in Chapter 3.

Our goals in this chapter, as stated earlier, are to recognize, describe and represent the phonemes of English. We will begin with a discussion of oral anatomy, the organs of the vocal tract. We will then describe the **articulatory features** of each phoneme, meaning we will describe how and where each phoneme is produced in the vocal tract. Finally, we will represent each sound using a phonetic alphabet. In many cases, the symbols we use in our phonetic alphabet will be familiar to you, but in others, the symbols will be new. Don't worry, though, because by the end of the chapter, you will be transcribing back and forth between English orthography and phonetic orthography with ease.

Before proceeding, it would be wise to spend a minute discussing the importance of using a phonetic alphabet. As we have seen, in English orthography, the symbols we use don't always correspond very closely to the sounds they're supposed to represent. The whole point behind a phonetic alphabet is to clear up this confusion. In a phonetic alphabet, there is a single symbol for each sound (phoneme). Also, each phoneme is represented by a single symbol. The clarity created by this bi-directional relationship is essential in the study of phonetics.

The Consonants of English

We'll begin with the **consonants** of English. When we use the word "consonant," however, we mean something different from what you're probably thinking. We're not referring to letters; remember, our focus is on spoken, not written, language. Instead, we're referring to *sounds*. Consonant sounds are produced by obstructing the flow of air as it passes from the lungs through the vocal tract. As you will see, this obstruction occurs in different places and different manners, and we can describe each consonant sound in a unique way by applying these concepts of place and manner.

Describing the Features of Consonants: Place of Articulation

The organs of the vocal tract are shown in Figure 2.1. Notice the orientation of this figure, with the head facing left. This is important, because when phonemes are represented in charts, the charts are always organized according to this orientation.

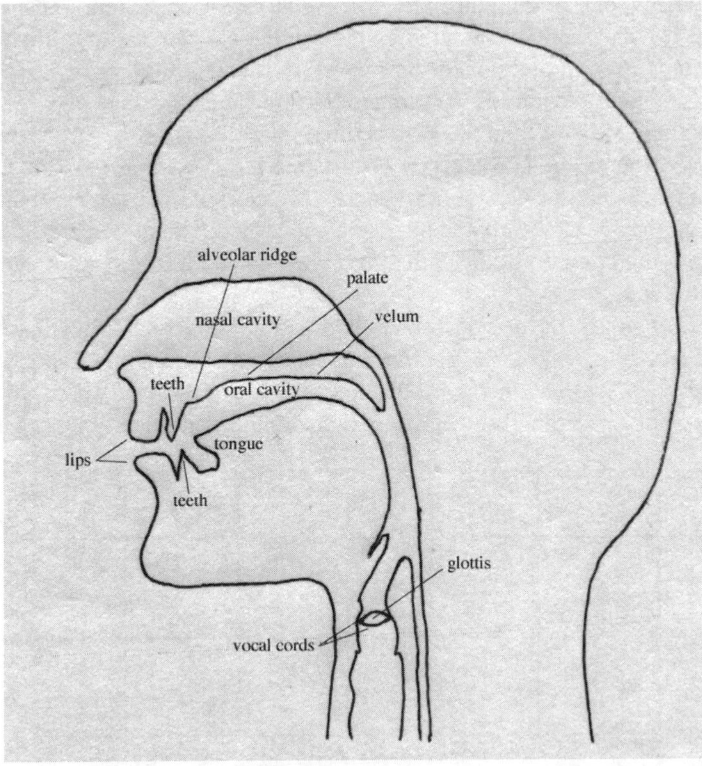

Figure 2.1: The Vocal Tract

When we describe a consonant, one of the features we use is the **place of articulation**. As was noted earlier, consonants are formed by obstructing the flow of air through the vocal tract. We obstruct the flow of air in different places to make different consonants. For example, to form the initial "p" sound in "pill" (represented by the phonetic symbol /p/), we put our lips together to shut off the flow of air before releasing it. Sounds like /p/, that are created by obstructing the flow of air with both lips, are called **bilabial** sounds ("bi-" meaning two, and "labial" meaning lips). Compare the place of articulation of /p/ with the place of articulation of the "f" sound in "fill" (represented by the phonetic symbol /f/). Rather than obstructing the flow of air with both lips, we obstruct it with our lower lip and upper teeth. Sounds like /f/ are called **labiodental** sounds ("labio-" meaning lip, and "dental" meaning teeth).

Before we continue, we need to address the slashes (//) surrounding the symbols used to represent sounds. Whenever we use symbols from our phonetic alphabet, we'll use these slashes. Thus, /p/ represents the phoneme /p/, not the letter "p". When we want to make a reference to the letter "p" from the English alphabet, we'll enclose the symbol in quotation marks (" "). This notation distinction is an important one.

Continuing on our way towards the back of the vocal tract, pronounce the word "thrill" and focus on the initial "th" sound, represented in phonetic orthography by /θ/ (often called "theta"). While you might think of this /θ/ sound as being two sounds because it's represented in English orthography by two letters, in fact it is a single sound. Notice that we produce this sound by putting our tongue between our teeth and obstructing the flow of air with the tongue and teeth. Because of this, sounds like /θ/ are called **interdental** sounds ("inter-" meaning between, and "dental" meaning teeth). Notice that the phonetic symbol used to represent this interdental sound is not one used in English orthography. What you'll see is that new symbols are generally used when English orthography uses multiple symbols for a single sound, as with the "th" sound.

Next, consider the initial "s" sound in the word "sack," represented by the phonetic symbol /s/. To create the /s/ sound, we obstruct the flow of air by placing the tip of our tongue up near the hard, fleshy part of the roof of our mouth directly behind the upper front teeth. This area is called the **alveolar ridge**. Sounds like /s/, then, are called **alveolar** sounds. Now, pronounce the word "sack" and focus on the initial consonant sound. Compare this sound to the initial sound in "shack." Notice how your tongue moves back slightly to make this sound. Instead of being raised to the alveolar ridge, it is raised to the hard palate of your mouth, just behind the alveolar ridge. This initial "sh" sound in "shack" (represented by the symbol /š/ and called "esh"), as well as other sounds produced in the same place, are called **palatal** sounds. Again, notice that the new symbol is used in place of the multiple English symbols "sh."

If you trace your tongue along the roof of your mouth from the alveolar ridge and past the palate, you'll come to a soft, rather than bony, area. While this area is often referred to as the soft palate, its more technical name is the **velum**. We produce some sounds by obstructing the flow of air by touching our tongue to the velum. The sounds, therefore, are called **velar** sounds. An example of a velar sound is the initial /g/ sound in the word "get." Notice, however, that unlike the alveolar and palatal consonants that we looked at before, to make this velar sound, you don't touch the tip of your tongue to the roof of you mouth; instead, you use the heel of your tongue.

Finally, our journey to the back of the vocal tract ends with the **glottis**. This is essentially the beginning of your throat. English has only a single **glottal** phoneme—the initial /h/ sound in the word "hot." Notice how your tongue is not involved in the production of this sound at all (if it were, you'd probably choke yourself). Instead, you obstruct the flow of air by tightening the glottis as the air passes through.

Bilabial	Labio-dental	Inter-Dental	Alveolar	Palatal	Velar	Glottal	Examples
/p/					**/g/**		**pill** **get**
	/f/	**/θ/**	**/s/**	**/š/**		**/h/**	**fill thrill sack shack hot**

Table 2.1: Some English Consonants by Place of Articulation

We can represent all of the sounds we have studied so far, along with the places of articulation used in English, in Table 2.1.

Describing the Features of Consonants: Manner of Articulation

In addition to place of articulation (*where* a sound is produced), when we describe a consonant, we describe its **manner of articulation**, meaning the *way* in which the sound is produced. As you know, consonants are formed by obstructing the flow of air through the vocal tract in particular places. It's also important to note, however, that we can obstruct the flow of air in different *ways* to produce different sounds. As we did in our place of articulation, let's compare the /p/ sound in "pill" and the /f/ sound in "fill." We know that /p/ is bilabial and that /f/ is labiodental, but they also differ in another way. Notice that when you produce the /p/ sound, you completely stop the flow of air and then release it. In the production of the /f/ sound, however, you never completely stop the flow of air; rather, you force air steadily through a narrow opening, created by your lower lip and upper front teeth, in a steady stream. This is a difference in manner of articulation.

To prove the significance of manner of articulation, let's compare two phonemes that are identical in their place of articulation. To produce the /t/ sound in "tack," you raise the tip of your tongue to the alveolar ridge and obstruct the flow of air there. To produce the /s/ sound in "sack," you do the same. Notice, though, that to produce /t/, you must completely stop the flow of air, as you did with /p/. Sounds like /t/ and /p/, that are produced with this complete stoppage are called **stops**. This term speaks for itself. To produce /s/, however, you do not completely stop the flow of air. As we noted before with /f/, you create a narrow opening through which you force a steady steam of air. Sounds like /s/ and /f/ that are produced with this partial obstruction are called **fricatives**. To make sense out of this term, think of the friction that you create when you force air through a narrow opening. It is this friction that gives fricatives their name.

Quick Exercise 2.1

Of the phonemes discussed so far, which are stops and which are fricatives? Pronounce each one and decide.

/p/	/s/
/θ/	/š/
/g/	/t/
/h/	/f/

Not all consonants are stops or fricatives. Consider the initial consonant sound in the word "chip." Although it's spelled with the two English letters "ch," it is, in fact, just a single sound that we represent with the phonetic symbol /č/ and call "C-wedge" (again, notice that we need to use an unfamiliar symbol to represent a sound that English spells with multiple letters). Pronounce this sound and try to determine where it's being produced. You'll probably notice that it's palatal, formed by touching the tip of your tongue to the palate. What sets this sound apart from the other ones we've seen so far, however, is that it's neither a stop nor a fricative, but it combines elements of both. Notice that it begins with a stop, /t/, and ends with a fricative, /š/. Pronounce it slowly and feel your tongue move. Sounds like /č/, which are a combination of a stop and a fricative, are called **affricates**. Appropriately, affricates are placed just below stops and fricatives in consonant charts (see Table 2.2).

All three types of consonants that we have studied so far—stops, fricatives and affricates—can be grouped together in the larger category **obstruents**. Obstruents are characterized by significant obstruction of air. While all consonants are produced through obstruction of air, not all of them involve such significant obstruction. Consider, for example, the initial /m/ sound in the word "mop." Clearly, like /p/, this is a bilabial sound created by putting both lips together. However, while /m/ and /p/ share the same *place* of articulation, note the important difference in their *manner* of articulation. You can prove that /m/ is not a stop by extending the sound. You can hold an /m/ sound for several seconds (until you run out of breath), while you cannot hold /t/ or any other stop consonants. But try holding /m/ while holding your nose. Now it becomes difficult. The reason it's difficult is because the sound /m/ is produced not by *stopping* the flowing the air, but by *redirecting* it through the nose, instead of the mouth. You do, in fact, cut off the flow of air through the mouth by putting your lips together, but you allow the air to escape through the nose, rather than stopping it entirely, as with a stop. Sounds like /m/ that are produced with this manner of articulation are called, appropriately, **nasals**. The other two nasal phonemes in English are the alveolar /n/, as in Nancy, and the velar /ŋ/, called "Eng"), which is generally represented by the "ng" spelling in English. Once again, we have an unfamiliar symbol for a sound that English spelling requires two letters for.

Now let's consider the initial /l/ sound in the word "lip." Feel for the place of articulation, and you'll notice that it's alveolar, with the tip of your tongue touching the alveolar ridge, and the edges of your tongue curled down. Now try to describe its manner of articulation. Clearly, there's no complete stoppage of air, nor is there any friction created. This rules out all the obstruent manners—stop, fricative and affricate. Also, when you hold your nose, the sound is unaffected, so it can't be a nasal, either. In fact, the obstruction of air in the production of the phoneme /l/ is difficult to describe. This elusiveness partially explains the term used to describe sounds such as /l/,which are generally called **liquids**. The other liquid in English is the initial /r/ sound in "rip."

Similarly difficult to describe in terms of their manner of articulation are sounds such as the initial /w/ sound in "west." While you are clearly employing both lips in the production of /w/, which makes it bilabial in terms of its place of articulation, there doesn't seem to be much obstruction of air occurring at all. In fact, sounds like this, which are called **glides** because of the gliding movement of the lips or tongue during articulation, are almost not consonants at all. You'll discover later that they're very similar to vowels. The other glide in English is the initial /y/ sound in "yes."

Nasals, liquids and glides, in contrast to obstruents, are not produced with significant obstruction of air flow. These sounds that are produced with a relatively open air passage are grouped together in a larger class called **sonorants**. Sonorants are placed at the bottom of phoneme charts to indicate their less consonantal quality.

We can now place all of the phonemes we have studied so far on a chart that indicates not only place of articulation, as in table 2.1, but also manner of articulation. This is done in Table 2.2.

place→ ↓manner	Bi-labial	Labio-dental	Inter-Dental	Alveolar	Palatal	Velar	Glottal	Examples
Stops	**/p/**			**/t/**		**/g/**		**pill tack get**
Fricatives		**/f/**	**/θ/**	**/s/**	**/š/**		**/h/**	**fill thin sack show hot**
Affricates					**/č/**			**chip**
Nasals	**/m/**			**/n/**		**/ŋ/**		**mop not sing**
Liquids				**/l/**	**/r/**			**lip rip**
Glides	**/w/**				**/y/**			**west yes**

Table 2.2: Some English Consonants by Place and Manner of Articulation

Describing the Features of Consonants: Voicing

The final feature that we will use to describe consonants is probably the easiest of the three to understand and determine. To illustrate it, let's compare two sounds that are identical in their place and manner of articulation. We'll use the initial /s/ sound in "sue," and the initial /z/ sound in "zoo." To produce both, you raise the tip of your tongue to the alveolar ridge, so they must both be alveolar. Additionally, both are produced by passing air through a narrow opening and creating friction, which makes them both fricatives. Clearly, though, they're different sounds, so something must be different about them. To feel this difference, place a finger on your throat and produce each sound. You'll notice that when you produce the /z/ sound, your throat vibrates, while it doesn't when you produce the /s/ sound. The difference between them, then, is a difference of **voicing**. Voicing refers to whether the vocal cords are vibrating when you produce the sound or not. Sounds like /z/, which are produced with this vibration, are called **voiced** consonants, while sounds like /s/, which are *not* produced with this vibration, are called **voiceless** consonants.

Quick Exercise 2.2

Of the phonemes discussed so far, which are voiced and which are voiceless? Pronounce each one with your hand on your throat and decide.

/p/ /s/ /m/ /č/ /h/

/θ/ /š/ /r/ /y/ /f/

/g/ /t/ /l/ /w/ /z/

An interesting point to notice with regard to the voicing distinction is that in English, most obstruents come in voiced and voiceless pairs. That is, with the exception of /h/, for every obstruent in English, there is another phoneme that is identical in its place and manner of articulation, but different in its voicing. Examples of such pairs are /s/ and /z/ (both alveolar fricatives), and /p/ and /b/ (both bilabial stops).

place→ ↓manner	Bi- labial	Labio- dental	Inter- Dental	Alveolar	Palatal	Velar	Glottal	Examples
Stops [-voice]	**/p/**			**/t/**		**/k/**		**pill tack kill**
Stops [+voice]	**/b/**			**/d/**		**/g/**		**big dot get**
Fricatives [-voice]		**/f/**	**/θ/**	**/s/**	**/š/**		**/h/**	**fill thin sack show hot**
Fricatives [+voice]		**/v/**	**/ð/**	**/z/**	**/ž/**			**vine the zoo measure**
Affricates [-voice]					**/č/**			**chip**
Affricates [+voice]					**/ǰ/**			**judge**
Nasals [+voice]	**/m/**			**/n/**		**/ŋ/**		**mop not sing**
Liquids [+voice]				**/l/**	**/r/**			**lip rip**
Glides [+voice]	**/w/**				**/y/**			**west yes**

Table 2.3 The Consonants of English

All of the consonant phonemes are represented in the chart in Table 2.3. Notice how the chart is organized by place of articulation, manner of articulation and voicing. One of the purposes behind using features to describe each phoneme is to be able to distinguish each one from the rest. We can do this using the three features discussed so far. These features are referred to as **distinctive features** because of their ability to distinguish phonemes from each other.

Quick Exercise 2.3

Several new symbols appear on the chart in Table 2.3. While they haven't been discussed in the text, you should be able to make sense out of them by using their distinctive features and the example words provided. To test your understanding of them, think of two words (don't use any of the example words from the chart) that contain each phoneme. Spell each word using English orthography, and then underline the letters that represent each phoneme.

Symbol	Example Word	Example Word
/ð/ ("Eth")		
/ž/ ("Z-wedge")		
/ǰ/ ("J-wedge")		

The Vowels of English

While we have seen that English has many consonants, 24 in total, they alone are not sufficient for us to speak. In fact, they're useless without vowels. Without vowels, we wouldn't be able to speak. You probably learned that there are five (sometimes six) vowels in English—"a", "e", "i", "o" and "u" (and sometimes "y"). The truth is that there are far more than six vowels in English. Remember, our focus is on sounds (phonemes), not letters, so when we talk about vowels, we mean vowel *sounds*. Vowel sounds are different from consonant sounds in that they are *not* produced by obstructing the flow of air as it passes through the vocal tract. Instead, we create vowels through a combination of tongue position, lip rounding and muscle tension. And, unfortunately, the distinctive features of vowels, while every bit as real as those for consonants, are not always as easy to see, feel or hear. Some are more difficult than others, but hopefully by the end of the next section, you'll understand them all.

Describing English Vowels: Tongue Height

Of the distinctive features of vowels, tongue **height** is one of the easiest to understand, largely because you can actually see it with your eyes. Stand in front of a mirror and say the words "meet" and "mat." You'll notice that your jaw drops significantly when you go from "meet" to "mat." This is because the vowel in "meet," represented by the symbol /i/, is produced with the tongue high in the mouth, while the vowel in "mat," represented by the symbol /æ/, is produced with the tongue low in the mouth. Your jaw drops to accommodate your tongue, which rises and falls depending on the vowels you produce. Appropriately, vowels like /i/ are called **high vowels**, and vowels like /æ/ are called **low vowels**.

Now, throw the word "mate" into the mix. Remaining in front of the mirror, say "meet," "mate," and "mat" consecutively. Notice that after "meet" your jaw drops somewhat to say "mate" and then drops again to say "mat." The reason your jaw drops first to say "mate" and then again to say "mat" is because the vowel in "mate," represented by the symbol /e/, is neither as high as /i/ or as low as /æ/; it's somewhere between the others in terms of height. Vowels such as /e/ are called **mid vowels**.

We can represent the vowels studied up to this point on a chart that indicates their differences in height, as in Table 2.4.

High	/i/ (m**e**et)
Mid	/e/ (m**a**te)
Low	/æ/ (m**a**t)

Table 2.4: Some English Vowels by Height

Describing English Vowels: Frontness

The next distinctive feature of vowels, **frontness**, is far more difficult to see or feel. As a point of reference, let's return to the vowel /i/ and contrast it with another vowel. Say the words "keep" and "coop" and focus on the vowels. "Keep," of course, contains /i/, but "coop" has a different vowel, one that we represent using the phonetic symbol /u/. If you focus very closely on the vowels, you might be able to notice that your tongue is farther forward when you pronounce the /i/ vowel, and a little farther back when you pronounce the /u/ vowel. Vowels like /i/, which are produced in the front of the mouth, are called **front vowels**, while vowels like /u/, which are produced in the back of the mouth, are called **back vowels**.

Now let's return briefly to tongue height. Again, stand in front of a mirror and say the words "coop," "cope" and "cop." Notice that your jaw is high for "coop" but lowers somewhat when you say "cope" and then even more so when you say "cop." This is because the /u/ in "coop," like /i/, is a high vowel, while the /o/ in "cope," like /e/, is a mid vowel, and the /a/ in "cop," like /æ/, is a low vowel. So, we see that the six vowels we've studied so far can be distinguished by their height and frontness.

While the majority of the vowel phonemes of English are either front or back vowels, not all are produced with such extremes of frontness. There are, in fact, vowels that are between front and back vowels in terms of their frontness. These vowels are called, predictably, **central vowels**. Although in number, they are far less plentiful than front and back vowel phonemes, these central vowels occur with an incredibly high rate of frequency, so their importance in English is tremendous. Unfortunately, however, they can cause major problems for non-native speakers of English.

A useful word to illustrate two of the central vowels of English is "above." If you compare the two vowels in this word with the vowels already discussed, you'll notice that they don't match any of them. You'll also notice that while not identical to each other, these two vowels sound very similar. In fact, they are nearly identical in every respect differing only in terms of the stress with which they are spoken. Notice that when you say the word "above," there is more stress on the second syllable. The first one is so unstressed, that it's barely audible. The symbols that we use for these two closely related vowels are /ə/ and /ʌ/, respectively. The common name for /ə/ is "**schwa**," a name that comes up repeatedly in elementary and secondary school literature. We can represent the entire word phonetically as /əbʌv/.

The third central vowel is similar to /ə/ but has an /r/-like quality to it. This is the sound that follows the initial /f/ in the word "fur." We represent this sound with the phonetic symbol /ɚ/. You can think of it as an /r/-colored schwa. It is used in both stressed and unstressed syllables, as in the word "burner," which can be transcribed as /bɚnɚ/.

Table 2.5 combines the two vowels features discussed so far, height and frontness, in its representation of the vowels studied up to this point.

	Front	Central	Back
High	/i/ (m**ee**t)		/u/ (c**o o**p)
Mid	/e/ (s**a**y)	/ɚ/ (f**ur**) /ə/ (**a**bove) /ʌ/ (ab**o**ve)	/o/ (c**o**pe)
Low	/æ/ (s**a**t)		/a/ (c**o**p)

Table 2.5: Some English Vowels by Tongue Height and Frontness

Describing English Vowels: Tenseness

The third distinctive feature of vowels, **tenseness**, is also difficult to pinpoint. Let's return to the vowel /i/ in "meet" and compare it now to the vowel /ɪ/ in "mitt." Your jaw doesn't drop when you go from /i/ to /ɪ/, so there's no significant difference in terms of height, nor is there any significant difference in their frontness. Instead, what distinguishes /i/ from /ɪ/ is the amount of muscle tension in the vocal tract when you produce the two vowels. /i/ is produced with a high degree of tension. Vowels like /i/ are, therefore, called **tense vowels**. /ɪ/, on the other hand is produced with far less tension. Vowels like /ɪ/, therefore, are called **lax vowels**. Notice that /i/ and /ɪ/ are identical in terms of their height and frontness, so the feature tenseness is needed to distinguish them from each other. We can now describe /i/ and /ɪ/ more fully:

/i/ is a high, front, tense vowel
/ɪ/ is a high, front, lax vowel

Just as the tense vowel /i/ has a lax counterpart /ɪ/, so too, do nearly all of the other tense vowels in English. For example, we have both a *tense*, high, back vowel -- /u/ -- and a *lax*, high, back vowel -- /ʊ/. /u/, as you will recall, is the vowel in the word "coop," while /ʊ/ is the vowel in "could." The other tense/lax pairs are listed below with example words:

mid, front, tense /e/: "mate"
mid, front, lax /ɛ/: "met"

mid, back, tense /o/: "coat"
mid, front, lax /ɔ/: "caught"

Table 2.6 combines tenseness with the height and frontness to represent all of the vowels studied up to this point.

[2] note that many dialects of American English, including most California dialects, do not have this vowel; instead, speakers of these dialects substitute the low, back, lax vowel /a/, as in "job".

		Front	Central	Back
High	[+tense]	/i/ (m**ee**t)		/u/ (c**oo**p)
	[-tense]	/ɪ/ (m**i**tt)		/ʊ/ (c**ou**ld)
Mid	[+tense]	/e/ (m**a**te)	/ɚ/ (f**ur**)	/o/ (b**oa**t)
	[-tense]	/ɛ/ (m**e**t)	/ə/ (**a**bove) /ʌ/ (ab**o**ve)	/ɔ/ (c**au**ght)
Low	[+tense]			
	[-tense]	/æ/ (m**a**t)		/a/ (c**o**p)

Table 2.6: Some English Vowels by Height, Frontness and Tenseness

A Final Feature of Vowels: Roundedness

While all the features that we have discussed so far are adequate for distinguishing each vowel phoneme from the rest in English, there is one more feature that is useful to discuss—**roundedness**. The best way to see this feature is with your eyes. Stand in front of a mirror and say the words "feed" and "food" out loud. Notice the shape of your lips after the initial /f/. When you say "feed," your lips are spread, almost in a smiling position. When you say "food," however, your lips form the shape of an "o." This is because the vowel in "food," which is /u/, is a **rounded vowel**, meaning you produce it by rounding your lips. The /i/ in "feed," on the other hand, is an **unrounded vowel**, because you do not produce it with rounded lips. In English, only the high and mid back vowels, /u, ʊ, o, ɔ/, are rounded vowels. All other vowels in English are not rounded. To see this for yourself, stand in front of the mirror again and say all of the words in Table 2.6.

Difficult Vowels to Describe: Diphthongs

You've noticed by now that for every phoneme, both consonant and vowel, we have been able to provide a list of features to describe the sound. There are some vowel phonemes, however, that are very difficult to describe using the features that we've discussed so far. An example of such a sound is the vowel in the word "high." After the initial /h/, there is a vowel sound that seems to start in one place and end in another. Specifically, this vowel begins low and back in your mouth, where /a/ is, and ends high and front in your mouth, where /i/ is. This vowel, represented by the phonetic symbols /ay/, is actually two sounds blended into one (you can think of it as a combination of a vowel plus a glide). Because it is two sounds in one, it is a called a **diphthong**, the "di-" part meaning "two," and the "-phthong" part meaning "sound."

The other diphthongs in English are the vowel sounds in "cow" (represented by the phonetic symbols /aw/) and the vowel sound in "boy" (represented by the phonetic symbols /ɔy/). You'll notice that the three diphthongs are listed *below*, rather than *on*, the complete vowel chart in Table 2.7. This is because it is impossible to place diphthongs in any one spot. After all, they are blends of two sounds, so the only way to place them on the chart would be to give them two spots connected by an arrow. This would be too cumbersome. Instead, we place the diphthongs below the chart, with only the **monophthongs**, single vowel sounds, on the chart.

		Front	Central	Back	
High	[+tense]	/i/ (m**ee**t)		/u/ (c**oo**p)	Rounded vowels
	[-tense]	/ɪ/ (m**i**tt)		/ʊ/ (c**ou**ld)	
Mid	[+tense]	/e/ (m**a**te)	/ɚ/ (f**ur**)	/o/ (b**oa**t)	
	[-tense]	/ɛ/ (m**e**t)	/ə/ (**a**bove)* /ʌ/ (ab**o**ve)*	/ɔ/ (c**au**ght)**	
Low	[+tense]				
	[-tense]	/æ/ (m**a**t)		/a/ (c**o**p)	

* /ə/ and /ʌ/ are essentially the same in terms of their articulatory features, but /ə/ is used in unstressed syllables, while /ʌ/ is in stressed syllables

** some speakers don't have /ɔ/ in their dialect; they use /a/ instead

DIPHTHONGS: vowel + glide

/ay/ night

/ɔy/ boy

/aw/ cow

Table 2.7: The Vowel Phonemes of English (monophthongs and diphthongs)

Quick Exercise 2.3

Familiarize yourself with the vowel phonemes of English (see Table 2.7) by providing a complete description of each of the vowel phonemes below. A complete description for a vowel phoneme will include the phoneme's height, frontness, tenseness and roundedness.

/u/

/æ/

/e/

Some Important Points about Vowels

Vowels as Approximations

An important point to note at this juncture is that there is a tremendous amount of variation from person to person when it comes to vowels. While most native speakers of English tend to pronounce most consonants in a very similar way, they differ significantly in terms of vowel production. So, keep in mind that when we describe vowels in terms of their distinctive features, we can only arrive at *approximations* for these sounds. That is, your high back tense vowel, /u/, is very likely a little higher or a little lower, or a little more tense or a little more lax than many other people's. There's nothing wrong with this; rather, it reflects the tremendous linguistic diversity that exists among speakers of any language.

The Importance of Schwa in English

As we saw earlier, schwa is a very frequently used vowel in English. As you know, schwa is used in unstressed syllables. While other vowels are sometimes used in unstressed syllables, they're generally tense vowels. Native English speakers have a tendency to substitute schwa for lax vowels when stress is taken away from them. A good example to illustrate this phenomenon is the pair of words "substance" and "substantial," as illustrated in Table 2.8. Note the lax vowels in the stressed syllables in each word, which are replaced by schwa when the same syllables lose their stress.

"**sub**stance"	/**sʌb**stəns/
"sub**stan**tial"	/səb**stæn**šəl/

Table 2.8: Schwa in Unstressed Syllables (stressed syllables are bolded)

Because nearly every English word that contains more than one syllable has at least one unstressed syllable, as the words in Table 2.8 do, schwa is used with great regularity. However, schwa doesn't exist in many languages; thus, for many English Language Learners (ELL students), schwa isn't a linguistic sound. Learning to hear it and pronounce it, then, poses great problems for these students. But because of its widespread use in English, learning to hear and pronounce it is also essential if ELL students who want to sound like native speakers of English. Also, because of its centralized position and lack of stress, it can even be hard for native English speakers to identify, even though such speakers produce it with such regularity. As a result, when transcribing words, students often have trouble identifying schwa. Be aware that the difficult-to-identify vowels in unstressed syllables of English words, as opposed to the more easily identified tense vowels, are usually schwas.

Second Language Issues: Phonemic Inventories

Because many of the students reading this text are interested in teaching, it will be useful for us to discuss issues related to second language learning throughout the book. Many classrooms these days are populated by students from different first language (L_1) backgrounds, and one of their most important goals is to become fluent in English, which for them is a second language (L_2). As their teacher, you can make a major difference in their success by understanding their linguistic realities, in both a general and specific way. This understanding comes from an appreciation for the differences and similarities that languages can have, in general, as well as from specific knowledge about English and about your students' L_1. Keep in mind that people learning a second language will unconsciously apply the rules of their first language to their second. It stands to reason, then, that where the rules of the L_1 and L_2 are similar, a second language leanrer will be able to use, or **transfer**, knowledge of his or her L_1 to the L_2. On the other hand, where the rules of the L_1 *differ* from those of the L_2, there will be **interference**, meaning these will be particularly problematic areas.

The first issue to note with regard to interference is that not every language has the same phonemic inventory. Certain English phonemes, like /p/, are fairly common in languages throughout the world. Others, however, such as /θ/, are far less common. Remember that phonemes are psychologically real sounds, so the /θ/ in "thick" is real to a native English speaker, but probably won't be real to speakers of other languages. These people generally can't hear or pronounce phonemes that are unfamiliar to them, so they end up substituting similar phonemes that *are* real to them. You've probably heard native German speakers (among others) pronouncing "thick" as an English speaker would pronounce "sick," with an /s/ at the beginning. What these English language learners are trying to do is substitute a similar sound that *is* psychologically real to them. /s/ differs from /θ/ only slightly in its place of articulation—alveolar vs. interdental; otherwise they are exactly alike. A German speaker beginning to learn English might not even hear /θ/, let alone have the ability to produce it. Differences between the phonemic inventories of languages, then, contribute to accents. For such speakers who want to lose their accent in English, or at least reduce their accent, it's essential to somehow become aware of this phoneme. Hopefully, their teachers can help them.

Summary

In this chapter we studied the phonemes of English. We described the features of the consonant and vowel phonemes of English and learned to represent them using phonetic orthography. We also explored some of the potential difficulties non-native speakers of English might have when trying to learn English as second language.

Exercises

Phonetics Practice: Description of Phonemes

For each consonant sound (phoneme),

a) describe the sound in terms of its voicing, place of articulation and manner of articulation, and
b) write an English word (using English orthography) that contains the sound, underlining the English letters that represent the sound

phoneme	description	English word
ex. /t/	voiceless alveolar stop	tell
1. /l/		
2. /ǰ/		
3. /b/		
4. /w/		
5. /š/		
6. /f/		
7. /g/		
8. /n/		

For each vowel sound (phoneme),

a) describe the sound in terms of its height, frontness, tenseness and roundedness, and
b) write an English word (using English orthography) that contains the sound, underlining the English letters that represent the sound

phoneme	description	English word
ex. /ɛ/	mid, front, lax, unrounded vowel,	enter
1. /i/		
2. /ʊ/		
3. /æ/		
4. /e/		
5. /ɔ/		
6. /u/		

Phonetics Practice: Phoneme Analogies

[Adapted from Bar Lev (1999)]

For each set, determine the relationship between the first two sounds (phonemes) and apply that relationship to fill in the blank. One has been done for you as an example.

example: /k/ : /g/ = /p/ : ___/b/___

[/k/ and /g/ are both velar stops, differing only in terms of their voicing, so we need to determine which phoneme is identical to /p/ in terms of place and manner of articulation, but different in terms of its voicing]

example: /i/ : /u/ = /e/ : ___/o/___

[/i/ and /u/ are both high and tense, differing only in terms of their frontness, so we need to determine which phoneme is identical to /e/ in terms of height and tenseness, but different in terms of its frontness]

1. /o/ : /ɔ/ = /e/ : ________	2. /æ/ : /a/ = /ɪ/ : ________
3. /u/ : /o/ = /i/ : ________	4. /š/ : /s/ = /r/ : ________
5. /p/ : /t/ = /b/ : ________	6. /ŋ/ : /g/ = /m/ : ________
7. /z/ : /s/ = /g/ : ________	8. /č/ : /š/ = /ǰ/ : ________
9. /m/ : /n/ = /p/ : ________	10. /t/ : /d/ = /f/ : ________

Transcription Exercises

Celebrity Names

Using the transcription provided, spell out each name using regular English orthography.

1. /ǰɛri saynfɛld/
2. /piwi hɚmən/
3. /prɪns čarlz/
4. /jæki čæn/
5. /ranəld məkdanəld/
6. /oprə wɪnfri/
7. /lətrɛl spriwɛl/
8. /pʊdən hɛd wɪlsən/
9. /arnəld šwartsənegɚ/
10. /dɛnəs ðʌ mɛnəs/
11. /bɛri sændɚz/
12. /mantgʌmri bɚnz/
13. /sədam husen/
14. /dɛnzɛl wašɪŋtən/
15. /yuǰin rabənsən/
16. /ði artəst fɔrmɚli non æz prɪns/

Lines from Songs

Transcribe each of the following lines using the phonetic symbols in this chapter. Treat each word as if it were in isolation (that is, transcribe each word individually)

1. "I can't get no satisfaction"

2. "As a matter of fact I like beer"

3. "I'm just a sucker with no self esteem"

4. "Fly me to the moon and let me play among the stars"

5. "My baby takes the morning train"

6. "And she's buying a stairway to heaven"

7. "Can we forget about the things I said when I was drunk?"

8. "Lump lingered last in line for brains and the one she got was kinda rotten and insane"

9. "Conjunction junction what's your function?"

10. "You've got to change your evil ways, baby"

11. "Well, you can do side bends or sit ups, but please don't lose that butt"

12. "Should I stay or should I go now?"

Transcription Jokes

Sometimes humor can be difficult to decode in phonetic writing. Write the following phonetically transcribed joke in regular English orthography.

Joke #1:

/ nidɪŋ tu ɪnkris ɪts rɛvənuz ʌ manəstɛri goz ɪntu ðʌ fɪš ænd čɪps bɪznəs ænd bikʌmz notəd fɔr ɪts kwəzin. let wʌn nayt ʌ trævələ˞ ræps an ðʌ dɔr ænd ʌ mæn ɪn ʌ rob spɔrtɪŋ ʌ fʌni hɛrkʌt opənz ɪt. əpan siyɪŋ hɪm ðʌ trævələ˞ æsks

ar yu ðʌ fɪš frayə˞

ænd ðʌ robd mæn hu opənd ðʌ dɔr riplayz

no aym ðʌ čɪp mʌŋk /

___

___

___

___

___

___

___

___

___

___

___

___

___

Joke #2:

/ ðʌ tako bɛl čəwawa ʌ dobɚmən ænd ʌ bʊldɔg ar ɪn ʌ dɔgi bar hævɪŋ ʌ kul wʌn wɛn ʌ gʊd lʊkɪŋ fimel kali kʌmz ʌp tu ðɛm ænd sɛz :

huwɛvɚ kæn se lɪvɚ ænd čiz ɪn ʌ sɛntəns kæn tek mi hom.

so ðʌ dobɚmən sɛz : ay lʌv lɪvɚ ænd čiz.

ðʌ kaliz rispans ɪz : ðæts nat gʊd ənʌf.

so ðʌ bʊldɔg sɛz : ay het lɪvɚ ænd čiz.

tu ðɪs ðʌ kali sɛz : ðæts nat kriyetəv.

faynəli ðʌ tako bɛl čəwawa sɛz : livɚ əlon.....čiz mayn. /

____

____

____

____

____

____

____

____

____

____

____

____

____

____

____

____

Joke #3:
/ ʌ lɪŋgwɪstəks prəfɛsɚ wʌz lɛkčɚɪŋ wʌn de əbawt nɛgətəvz ænd pazətəvz.
ɪn sʌm læŋgwəǰəz hi sɛd tu nɛgətəvz fɔrm ʌ pazətəv bʌt ɪn ʌðɚ læŋgwəǰəz ðɪs ɪz nat ðʌ kes.
hawɛvɚ hi sɛd ɪn no læŋgwəǰəz du tu pazətəvz mek ʌ nɛgətəv.
ʌ studənt ɪn ðʌ bæk ʌv ðʌ rum ðɛn mʌtɚd ʌndɚ hɪz brɛθ yæ rayt /

Strange but True Transcriptions

Even in phonetic orthography, some things seem unbelievable. Write the following phonetically transcribed true stories in regular English orthography.

/ ʌ pɛr ʌv mɪšəgən rabɚz ɛntɚd ʌ rɛkɚd šap nɚvəsli wɛvɪŋ rivalvɚz. ðʌ fɚst wʌn šawtəd

nobədi muv

wɛn hɪz partnɚ muvd tu opən ðʌ kæš rɛǰəstɚ ðʌ startəld fɚst bændət šat hɪm./

/ dɛnəs nutən wʌz an trayəl ɪn ʌ dɪstrəkt kɔrt fɔr ðʌ armd rabɚi ʌv ʌ kənvinyəns stɔr wɛn hi fayɚd hɪz lɔyɚ. hi wʌz duwɪŋ ʌ fɛrli gʊd ǰab ʌv dəfɛndɪŋ hɪmsɛlf əntɪl ðʌ stɔr mænəǰɚ tɛstəfayd ðæt nutən wʌz ðʌ rabɚ. nutən ǰʌmpt ʌp əkyuzd ðʌ wʊmən ʌv layɪŋ ænd ðɛn sɛd

ay šʊd hæv blon yɔr ɛfɪŋ hɛd ɔf

ðʌ dəfɛndənt ðɛn kwɪkli ædəd

ɪf ay hæd bɪn ðʌ wʌn ðæt wʌz ðɛr

ðʌ ǰɚi tʊk lɛs ðæn twɛnti mɪnəts tu kənvɪkt nutən. /

The Connection between English Spelling and Sounds

As we have discussed, the connection between spelling and sounds in English is not as close as many people would like it to be. This lack of correspondence can make reading and writing in English difficult. Below are some exercises designed to help you see some of the issues that can cause problems for people learning to read and write English. You should also consider this more transcription practice.

A. Some spellings can represent different sounds in different words

Transcribe each of the following words:

though	bough	cough
tough	through	

For each word, determine the set of sounds that the spelling "ough" represents:

(th)ough /   /   (b)ough /   /   (c)ough /   /   (t)ough /   /   (thr)ough /   /

B. Some sounds can be represented by multiple spellings in different words

Transcribe each of the following words:

author	solar	hurt
stir	her	heard
feature		

For each word, determine the vowel sound that is represented by the underlined letters, and represent that vowel phoneme with a phonetic symbol:

auth<u>or</u> /   /   sol<u>ar</u> /   /   h<u>ur</u>t /   /

st<u>ir</u> /   /   h<u>er</u> /   /   h<u>ear</u>d /   /

featu<u>re</u> /   /

How many different spellings are there for this one vowel sound? ____________

Add to this the fact the one of the greatest basketball players of all-time is "Larry Byrd," and a character in *Alice in Wonderland* is the "Cheshire Cat," and you can really see the potential confusion.

<continued on the next page>

C. A single English letter can represent multiple sounds in a given word

Transcribe the following words:

tax	music

For each word, count the number of English letters in the word:

tax	music

For each word, determine the actual number of sounds in the word:

tax	music

For each word, determine the English letter that represents multiple sounds:

tax	music

D. A single sound can be represented by multiple English letters in a given word

Transcribe the following words:

check	thing	shoe

For each word, count the number of English letters in the word:

check	thing	shoe

For each word, determine the actual number of sounds in the word:

check	thing	shoe

For each word, determine the English letter combinations that represent a single sound:

check	thing	shoe

3

Phonology: The Sound System of English

In Chapter Two we studied the phonemes of English. We identified these phonemes and described their articulatory features. When we did this, though, we treated each sound in isolation. In reality, of course, linguistic sounds are generally not used in isolation. Instead, we string sounds together to produce comprehensible speech. When sounds are used together they often affect each other in ways that we are not consciously aware of. We will see, however, that there is nothing random about this interaction; instead, it is very systematic. **Phonology** is the study of these sound systems. In this chapter our goals will be as follows:

- to understand the key concepts of phonology
- to familiarize ourselves with some rules of American English phonology
- to learn the process of phonological analysis

Levels of Representation

Perhaps the single most important concept in phonology is that of **levels of representation**. What this means simply is that what we think of as a single sound can actually be two different sounds at two different levels, one a deep, unconscious level, and the other a surface level. The best way to understand this concept is to illustrate it.

Begin by saying the words the "cop" /kap/ and "keep" /kip/ aloud. At one level, in our minds, the initial sound in each word is the same, namely the phoneme /k/. If you pay careful attention to the way you produce the initial sound in each word, however, you'll notice that the place of articulation is slightly different. Specifically, the /k/ in "keep" is produced slightly farther forward than the /k/ in "cop." That is, their place of articulation is different. They sound the same to you because unconsciously, deep in your mind, they *are* the same. This deep level is called the **underlying level** because it cannot be observed (heard) by anyone. As soon as we produce a sound that is deep in our minds, it is out on the **surface level** and can be observed (heard). We see then that we can analyze the sound /k/ in these two words at two levels—they are the same at the underlying level but different at the surface level; hence, they have different representations at different levels.

Another example is provided by the words "pit" /pɪt/ and "spit" /spɪt/. Again, you probably feel that the /p/ sound is the same in each, which indicates that at the underlying level, they are the same. A closer inspection, however, reveals a much more complicated picture. Say each of these words while dangling a piece of paper in front of your mouth (keep your head tilted back slightly). Notice that the piece of paper moves when you say "pit" but not when you say "spit." This is because the /p/ in "pit" is accompanied by a puff of air but the /p/ in "spit" has no puff of air. Although you think, deep in your mind, that the two /p/ sounds are the same, in fact they are two distinct sounds at the surface level, as is proven by the fact that one of the /p/ sounds moves the paper while the other one does not.

Phonemes and Allophones

Now that we've illustrated what is perhaps the most difficult concept presented in this book, we need to introduce some new terminology and notations. Let's return for a moment to the contrast between the underlying and surface levels. Recall that we defined a phoneme as a psychologically real unit of linguistic sound. This means that your brain identifies phonemes as being real and distinct from each other. Phonemes are what you unconsciously understand at the underlying level. The reason you think that the /p/ sounds in the words "pit" and spit" are the same is because each word contains the phoneme /p/. What we saw, however, was that at the surface this phoneme is sometimes accompanied by a puff air and sometimes is not. The surface level representations are not really linguistic realities for us, as is evidenced by the fact that you thought they were the same until you stuck a piece of paper in front of your mouth. Instead, they are variations of the reality, the phoneme, that we produce when we speak. These surface level variations are called **allophones** of a phoneme.

So what we've seen is that the phoneme /p/ has two allophones in English, one of which has a puff of air, and one of which does not. Likewise, the phoneme /k/ has two allophones in English, one of which is produced in the velar region, and one of which is produced slightly farther forward towards the palatal region. In order to analyze the system that governs how these phonemes are used, we must somehow represent their two allophones in a way that is distinct from the way we represent the phonemes; in addition, this system of notation has to show a difference between the allophones. To accomplish this goal, we will use square brackets, [ ], to represent surface level allophones, instead of the slashes, / /, that we use to represent underlying phonemes. Graphically, then, we can illustrate the different levels of representation of the phonemes /p/ and /k/ as follows:

phoneme (underlying) — allophones (surface)

/p/ → [p] ("regular" /p/)
/p/ → $[p^h]$ (aspirated /p/)

[p] and $[p^h]$ are allophones of the phoneme /p/

The superscripted [h] symbol indicates **aspiration**, the puff of air that made the paper move.

phoneme (underlying) — allophones (surface)

/k/ → [k] ("regular" /k/)
/k/ → [ǩ] (palatalized /k/)

[k] and [ǩ] are allophones of the phoneme /k/

The wedge above the [k] indicates **palatalization**, a movement of the place of articulation of a sound towards the palate. This symbol, called a diacritic, should be familiar to you. Recall that many of the palatal consonants on our consonant chart are also represented with a wedge over the symbol. This should help you connect the concept of palatalization with the wedge diacritic.

The Systematicity of Phonology

Having made the distinction between allophones and phonemes, the next question to address must be "what leads us to produce different allophones at different times?" Why, for example, did we aspirate the /p/ in "pit" but not the /p/ in "spit?" Was it random? The answer is an emphatic "no!" Recall that language is very systematic, and the phonology of a language is no exception to this systematicity. To prove this to yourself, say "pit" with a piece of paper in front of your mouth ten times and you'll see that the paper moves *every* time. Then do the same with "spit" and you'll see that the paper *never* moves. This proves that, at least in these two words, there is some systematic rule that governs how we use the phoneme /p/.

The fact of the matter is that *every* time you want to use the phoneme /p/, regardless of the specific words, there are certain rules, such as the aspiration rule, that might apply to the production of /p/ at the surface level. You unconsciously and automatically apply rules depending on the **environment** in which you use the phoneme. The environment of a sound is basically made up of two main factors:

1) The *position* of the phoneme within a word

- word initial (at the beginning of a word)
- word internal (somewhere in the middle of a word)
- word final (at the end of a word)

2) The phoneme's *surrounding sounds*

- the preceding sound (the sound that precedes it, usually immediately)
- the following sound (the sound that follows it, usually immediately)

Phonological analysis involves determining the rules that govern how phonemes are produced at the surface level by investigating the environment in which each allophone is produced. For example, if you analyze the [p] and [pʰ] allophones of the phoneme /p/ with regard to the factors above, you'll notice that the aspirated allophone is used word initially, while the unaspirated one is used internally. It seems that whether we aspirate /p/ or not depends on where in a word we want to use it. In contrast, both the [k] and [k̆] allophones of /k/ are used word initially, so we need to look elsewhere to describe the difference in their environments. If we do this, we will see that [k] is followed immediately by [a], while [k̆] is followed immediately by [i]. Therefore, we can hypothesize that whether we palatalize /k/ or not depends on the sound that we follow it with. These are the kinds of general observations that we need to make. Of course, to test our hypothesis we will need to look at much more data (and we will), but for now, this should suffice to illustrate the concept of environment.

Quick Exercise 3.1

For each phoneme in the word below, describe its environment in terms of position in the word and surrounding sounds. See points 1 and 2 above for models.

"risk" [rɪsk]

[r]

[ɪ]

[s]

[k]

Determining the Relationship Between Sounds

Another very important, and closely related, aspect of phonological analysis is determining the relationship between sounds. That is, are the sounds in question two separate phonemes in that language, or are they allophones of the same phonemes? To answer this question, we need to return to the idea of a phoneme being a psychologically real unit of linguistic sound. If two sounds are separate phonemes in a given language, native speakers of that language will recognize them as being different; on the other hand, if two sounds are allophones of a single phoneme, native speakers will recognize them as being the same sound, because at the underlying level, they are.

Contrastive Sounds

In some cases, sounds are **contrastive**. This means that a native speaker of the language in which the sounds are used recognizes them as being two distinct (different) sounds. The way to prove that two sounds are contrastive is to find a **minimal pair** with respect to the two sounds in question. Minimal pairs are pairs of words with *different meanings* that have *exactly the same sounds* in the same order except for a *single difference* in sounds. In data set (1), using the sounds [k] and [g] in English, we see minimal pairs that illustrate a contrastive relationship between the two sounds. These are minimal pairs that are distinguished by the sounds [k] and [g].

(1)	[kʌl] cull	[pɛk] peck	[bɪ́kɚ] bicker
	[gʌl] gull	[pɛg] peg	[bɪ́gɚ] bigger

Each of these pairs of words is a minimal pair with respect to [k] and [g]. That is, for each pair, there is only one difference in the sounds of the words, and that difference is [k] vs. [g]. Notice how everything else is the same between the pairs, and exchanging [k] for [g] creates a *contrast* in meaning (hence the term contrastive). Notice also that the only way to create a minimal pair with respect to two sounds is to put them in the *exact same environment* in terms of position within a word and surrounding sounds. Specifically, both sounds appear in all three positions within a word, both sounds are preceded by, from left to right in the data, nothing (∅),[ɛ] and [ɪ], and both sounds are followed by [ʌ], nothing (∅) and [ɚ]. When two sounds are in the exact same environment, we say that they are in **overlapping distribution**. In this data, [k] and [g] are in overlapping distribution.

Important points:

- Minimal pairs prove contrast between two sounds; contrastive sounds are necessarily different phonemes.
- Minimal pairs are created by putting two sounds in the same environment (overlapping distribution).

Quick Exercise 3.2

In the following data set, circle the two words that comprise the minimal pair that prove that [s] and [t] are contrastive.

[tɪk] tick	[stɪk] stick	[sak] sock	[stak] stock	[mæst] mast
[mæsk] mask	[sɪk] sick	[tæsk] task	[sɪt] sit	[kɪs] kiss

Non-Contrastive Sounds

While some sounds, like [k] and [g] are contrastive, others are **non-contrastive**. This means that native speakers do *not* recognize them as being two distinct sounds; instead, they are perceived as being the same sound, even though they are, on the surface level, different in some way. We will use the example of the sounds [k] ("regular" /k/) and [ǩ] (palatalized /k/), described previously, and data set (2).

(2)	[ǩip] keep	[ǩɪl] kill	[ǩæp] cap	[ǩep] cape	[ǩɛpt] kept
	[kʌp] cup	[kol] coal	[kap] cop	[kup] coop	[kʊd] could

Notice that there are no minimal pairs with respect to sounds [k] and [ǩ]. Because it is not possible to find any minimal pairs with respect to these two sounds, we can conclude that they must be non-contrastive; that is, they cannot create a contrast in meaning when one is substituted for the other.

Also, because we were unable to find them in the exact same environment, a necessary condition for finding a minimal pair, we can conclude that they are in **complementary distribution.** This means that where one of the sounds is used (its environment), the other never is, and vice-versa. To determine what aspect of their environments is different, we need to look at the two aspects described earlier—position of the sound within a word and surrounding sounds. When we do this, we see that in terms of position within words, [k] and [ǩ] appear in the same place. That is, they both appear word-initially. This is overlapping, not complementary. Therefore, we need to look elsewhere. If we look instead at surrounding sounds, we will see that [ǩ] *always* appears before front vowels (in this data, [i], [ɪ], [æ], [e] and [ɛ]) and never appears before central or back vowels. In sharp contrast, [k] *never* appears before front vowels, but *always* appears before central and back vowels ([ʌ], [o], [a], [u], [ʊ]). Because there is no overlap between their environments with respect to the following sound, we determine that they are in complementary distribution based on the following sound. This deeper investigation helped us specify the general observation we made previously that the surrounding sounds determine which allophone of /k/ a native speaker of English will use.

Important points:

- When two sounds are non-contrastive, we can't create a minimal pair with respect to the two sounds; non-contrastive sounds are necessarily allophones of the same phoneme.
- If two sounds cannot be put in overlapping distribution to create a minimal pair, they're in complementary distribution.

Recall that we described **allophonic variation** (the different surface level forms that a phoneme can take) as being very systematic. We don't randomly palatalize /k/, for example; instead, we do it in a very systematic way. When determining the environment in which this palatalization occurs, we looked at some data and listed a number of sounds that follow [k̑]. If, as we are proposing, phonology is systematic, there must be something about these following sounds that is common. In fact, as we noted earlier, they all do share a distinctive feature, namely being front vowels. This suggests systematicity in a way that a mismatched group of sounds which do not all share some feature would not. Sets of sounds like ones that follow [k̑] in English are called **natural classes**. Natural classes are sets of sounds that share one or more features. In this case, with [i], [ɪ], [æ], [e] and [ɛ], we have the natural class of front vowels.

Quick Exercise 3.3
Complete each natural class by adding the necessary phoneme.

/m, n,   /   /p, t,   /   /v, z, ž   /   /u, ʊ, o, ɔ,   /   /i, ɪ, u,   /

Environment and Contrast

At this point we need to make sure we see the connections between the concepts we've discussed so far. Specifically, we need to see how environment and contrast are related. Recall that the way to prove contrast between two sounds is to create a minimal pair with respect to them. We did this, for example, with [kʌl] ("cull") and [gʌl] ("gull"). The two words are identical in their sounds except for the difference between [k] and [g]. What signals a different meaning to a speaker of English is the change from [k] to [g] and vice-versa. We know, then, that they are contrastive in English. Notice that the only way we could create this minimal pair was to use both sounds in the exact same environment—word initially, preceded by ∅ and followed by [ʌ]. So, to create a minimal pair to prove contrast, we must be able to use the sounds in overlapping distribution. Conversely, sounds that are in complementary distribution and can *not* be used in the same environment, cannot possibly be used to create a minimal pair because creating a minimal pair necessarily involves using two sounds in overlapping distribution. Take the case of [k̑] and [k]. Because one can *only* be used before front vowels and the other *never* can, we can't possibly use them in the same environment to create a minimal pair; this means we can't prove contrast between these two sounds, because we can't keep all the other sounds in the word the same.

Phonological Rules

Having explored the basics of phonology, we now need to look at some specifics to illustrate the concepts more clearly and to familiarize ourselves with formal phonological analysis. As we have discussed, allophonic variation is 100% systematic. That is, when a given phoneme has multiple surface level allophones, the allophone we produce is determined by a rule that we know, though unconsciously. In some cases, as we will see, although native speakers of a language have no trouble following their language's phonological rules, these rules can be extremely complex. As we've discussed, being a speaker of a language does not qualify a person to talk about that language, and one of the most important goals of an introductory linguistics course is to help you bring your unconscious understanding of English to the surface. Phonological analysis is one in which students can make their unconscious understanding of their language more conscious. In addition to this general goal, the specific goal of a phonological analysis to is describe phonological rules by analyzing a set of data. This process involves all of the skills and knowledge discussed so far in this chapter.

The first and most basic step in an analysis is to determine the relationship between the sounds being focused on in the analysis. If you determine that the sounds are contrastive, then you know they must be different phonemes. Recall that finding a minimal pair is the key to making this determination. If this is the case, then there is no rule to predict when the two sounds will occur because they are not allophones of a single phoneme. If, however, you determine that the two sounds are not different phonemes, your task will be to describe a rule that governs the allophonic variation. This will necessitate determining the differences between the environments of the sounds. In other words, you must determine what is complementary about their distribution.

Because it is often difficult to analyze our native language objectively, we will illustrate this process by using non-English language data. No knowledge of the language is required to complete the analysis. All you need is knowledge of distinctive features and an understanding of the thought process involved. Our task is to analyze the two sounds [n] and [m] in Egaugnal using data set (3) (assume for this analysis that Egaugnal and English share the same phonemic inventory).

(3)	[kamwa] soccer	[lumbe] women	[pompi] victory	[limmu] exciting
	[rana] penalty	[winzi] kick	[zondu] score	[bunku] final

We begin by attempting to prove contrast by looking for a minimal pair. While both sounds are used word internally, we see from the data that [m] is followed by [w], [b], [p] and [m], while [n] is followed by [a], [z], [d] and [k]. Because there is no overlap in terms of the immediately following sounds, we cannot find a minimal pair with respect to [m] and [n], and we can conclude that [m] and [n] are non-contrastive and in complementary distribution in Egaugnal. This means they must be allophones of the same phoneme. Now we need to write a rule that explains this allophonic variation. To simplify the process somewhat, we'll assume for the time being that, of the two surface forms, one is more basic (the one that's used primarily). This basic form is the one that exists at the underlying level. This is what we'll use to refer to the phoneme. Let's assume for the moment that the phoneme is /n/; our task is to explain how and when /n/ becomes [m]. One option is the following:

/n/ becomes [m] before [w]
/n/ becomes [m] before [b]
/n/ becomes [m] before [p]
/n/ becomes [m] before [m]

This seems to be accurate, but we want to try to write a single rule, if possible, that is also accurate. When explaining allophonic variation, it's best to be as economical as possible. This requires the analyst to **generalize** by looking for natural classes. Recall that a natural class is a set of sounds of a language that share at least one common feature. A quick look at our consonant chart reveals that all of the sounds that follow [m] are bilabial consonants. Therefore, these sounds constitute the natural class of bilabial consonants. Instead of writing four separate rules for each specific environment, we can state this rule by using the natural class:

/n/ becomes [m] before bilabial consonants

Now, instead of having four separate rules, we have written one general rule which encompasses all four of the specific ones. This is what is meant by generalizing.

Determining the Basic Form of a Phoneme

In our analysis of Egaugnal, we assumed that /n/ was the basic form of the phoneme, and we wrote our rule to explain how /n/ became [m]. This was not just an arbitrary choice. In determining which allophone is the basic form, we need to determine which allophone appears in the most different environments (not necessarily the most words in the data). In this data, [m] appears in only one environment—before bilabial consonants. [n], on the other hand, appears in many different environments—before vowels and a variety of very different consonants. Clearly there is no natural class that can be identified with regard to [n]'s environment. Because [n] appears in so many different environments, it is the basic form. We can represent this phoneme as follows:

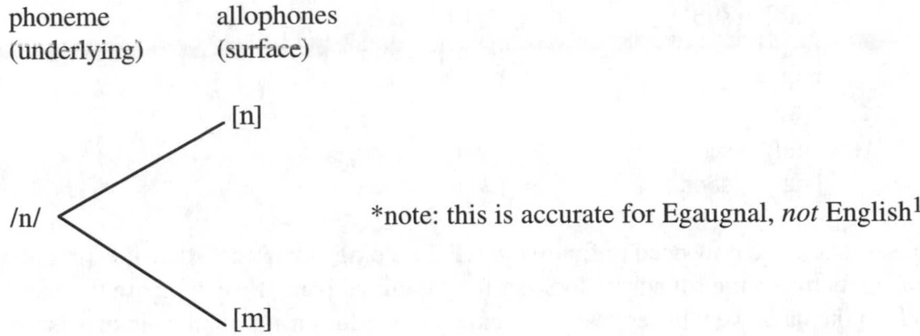

If we were to hypothesize that /m/ was the basic form of the phoneme, we would have to write a longer rule, namely the following:

/m/ becomes [n] before vowels, alveolar fricatives, labio-dental fricatives and velar stops

Compare this long rule to the very concise one we described earlier. The previous rule is much more economical because it utilizes a single natural class.

Rule Types

At this point you may be asking yourself why phonological rules exist. Do we need them or do they simply add a useless layer of complexity to language? This is not an easy question to answer completely, but in some cases we will see that phonological rules do seem to serve a useful purpose. Take, for example, the rule we described a moment ago for the phoneme /n/ in Egaugnal. Through the application of this rule, speakers of Egaugnal change the alveolar nasal phoneme /n/ to a bilabial nasal allophone [m] when it precedes a bilabial consonant. The result of this rule is that certain words are easier to pronounce because a speaker's vocal articulators (tongue, lips, etc.) don't have to move as far to produce one sound after another. Instead of having to go from an alveolar straight to a bilabial, a speaker, after applying this rule, can simply produce two bilabials consecutively. This is more efficient. Rules of this type, which lead to easier articulation, are called **rules of assimilation**, because a sound becomes more like a surrounding sound. We will look at other examples of rules of assimilation shortly.

Modeling Phonological Analysis with Four Rules of English

To help you learn some important rules of English phonology and to help you see the process of analysis modeled in more detail, we will look at four specific rules of English -- two vowel rules and two consonant rules.

Vowel Nasalization in English

We will begin by analyzing the surface level data for English in data set (4). Note that the tilde (~) above certain vowel symbols indicates a nasalized vowel. Nasalized vowels are produced by redirecting the flow of air through the nasal cavity. Our goal will be to investigate the relationship between nasalized and non-nasalized vowel in English.

To illustrate to yourself that these transcriptions are accurate at the surface level, try pronouncing each of the words twice, once normally, and once while holding your nose. For example, say "bid" normally and then with your nose pinched closed, and you'll notice little, if any, difference between the vowel sounds.

---

1 Egaugnal is not a real language. The data has been created to illustrate concepts.

Try this with "bin," however, and you'll notice a big difference. It sounds very odd with your nose closed. This is because you are trying to redirect the flow of air through your nose when you say the vowel in "bin," but with your nose closed, the air can't escape. The same is true with all of the words that have a nasalized vowel. Try it and see.

(4)						
[bɪd]	bid	[sʌb]	sub	[kab]	cob
[bɪ̃n]	bin	[sʌ̃m]	sum	[kãm]	com
[fed]	fade	[sid]	seed	[sæg]	sag
[fẽn]	feign	[sĩn]	seen	[sæ̃ŋ]	sang
[sayd]	side	[sud]	sued	[wet]	wait
[sãyn]	sign	[sũn]	soon	[wẽn]	wane

Having made this observation, we now need to figure out what's going on. Recall that the first step is to determine the relationship between the sounds by looking for a minimal pair. If we compare the nasalized and non-nasalized vowels in the data, we will see that in no case can we find a minimal pair that is created by nasalization. Such a minimal pair of words would be identical in every regard except for the nasalization of a vowel. [bɪd] and [bɪ̃n], for example, do not constitute a minimal pair because they differ not only in the nasalization of the vowel, but also in the final consonant. Because we can't find a minimal pair with respect to [ɪ] and [ɪ̃] , we can't prove contrast and instead look to see what is complementary about their distribution. They both appear word internally, but what jumps out is the fact that the nasal vowel [ɪ̃] is followed by [n], a nasal consonant, while the non-nasal vowel [ɪ] is followed by [d], a non-nasal consonant. We can then write a rule stating that [ɪ] becomes nasalized before [n]. This rule is formalized below:

Nasalization rule #1: /ɪ/ becomes [ɪ̃] before [n]

Continuing down the first column of data, the analysis for [e] and [ay] is exactly the same (see "fade" vs. "feign" and "side" vs. "sign"). We can now formalize two more rules:

Nasalization rule #2: /e/ becomes [ẽ] before [n]
Nasalization rule #3: /ay/ becomes [ãy] before [n]

The data in the second column, specifically "seed" vs. "seen" and "sued" vs. "soon," reveal the same situation with regard to [i] and [u], leading us to formalize two additional rules:

Nasalization rule #4: /i/ becomes [ĩ] before [n]
Nasalization rule #5: /u/ becomes [ũ] before [n]

So far we have five distinct rules, which is rather cumbersome. If possible, we'd like to collapse these rules into one. The way to do this is to generalize our rule to a natural class of sounds affected by this nasalization rule. Looking at the distinctive features of these five sounds, the only similarity they share is that they're all vowels. Because we're looking for something systematic, we have every reason to expect that these vowels are functioning as a natural class, although an incomplete one. By generalizing we can indicate the systematicity of the rule while simplifying it into the rule below:

Nasalization rule #6: vowels become nasalized before [n]

As a rule of assimilation, this makes sense. It does not, however, complete the analysis. We still have not dealt with the data using [æ] and [ʌ]. What we see, though slightly different from what we've already observed, is not too surprising. Specifically, we see nasalization of [æ] before [ŋ] (see "sag" vs. "sang") and nasalization of [ʌ] before [m] (see "sub" vs. "sum), leading to the following additional rules:

Nasalization rule #7: /æ/ becomes [æ̃] before [ŋ]
Nasalization rule #8: /ʌ/ becomes [ʌ̃] before [m]

Once again, we're looking for something systematic, so we need to try to see a connection between our previous rule, #6, and the two new ones. Now generalizing to a natural class in terms of the environment of the vowels, the affected phonemes, will be useful. We see that the sounds creating the nasalization are [m], [n] and [ŋ] , all of which share the features nasal and consonant. We can now combine all of our rules into one:

Final nasalization rule: vowels become nasalized before nasal consonants

Quick Exercise 3.4

Circle the words in the list below that would be pronounced with a nasalized vowel on the surface by a native speaker of English.

/sit/	seat	/sin/	scene	/sʌn/	sun	/sæt/	sat
/rɛd/	red	/rɛn/	wren	/rɛk/	wreck	/rim/	ream

Vowel Lengthening in English

Now consider the surface level data for English in data set (5). Note that a colon (:) after a vowel indicates a lengthened, or extended, vowel. Lengthened vowels are produced over a longer period of time than unlengthened vowels. Our goal is to investigate the relationship between lengthened and unlengthened vowels in English.

(5)					
[wet]	wait	[bʌk]	buck	[rayt]	right
[we:d]	wade	[bʌ:g]	bug	[ray:d]	ride
[rɪp]	rip	[rop]	rope	[rut]	root
[rɪ:b]	rib	[ro:b]	robe	[ru:d]	rude
[pis]	peace	[lif]	leaf	[bæč]	batch
[pi:z]	peas	[li:v]	leave	[bæ:ǰ]	badge

By now you are probably already viewing the data with a more trained eye. If so, you probably noticed no minimal pairs with respect to any vowels and their lengthened forms. Then, while looking for something complementary about the distribution of lengthened and unlengthened vowels, you might also have noticed that /ɪ/ and /o/ are lengthened before [b] (see "rip" vs. "rib" and "rope" vs. "robe"). This leads to a few initial rules:

Lengthening rule #1: /ɪ/ becomes [ɪ:] before [b]
Lengthening rule #2: /o/ becomes [o:] before [b]

Continuing, we see that both [ay] and [e] can also be lengthened, specifically before [d] (see "right" vs. "ride" and "wait" vs. "wade"). We can then add two more rules:

Lengthening rule #3: /ay/ becomes [ay:] before [d]
Lengthening rule #4: /e/ becomes [e:] before [d]

Once again, in our effort to economize our rules and to look for systematicity, we can try to generalize to natural classes. Beginning with the phonemes affected, namely /ɪ/, /o/, /ay/ and /e/, the only feature that they all share is that of being vowels. Because their specific vowel features are so varied, we will assume that whatever the system that lengthens each of these vowels also lengthens all vowels. This leads us to the first generalized rule:

Lengthening rule #5: vowels become lengthened before [b] and [d]

A quick glance at the data, however, indicates that this rule is incomplete because we see vowels also being lengthened before other consonants, for example [æ] before [ǰ] (see "badge" vs. "batch") and [i] before

[v] (see "leave" vs. "leaf"). To complete our rule, we need to identify a natural class in terms of the environment of the lengthened vowels. The sounds that we have seen after lengthened vowels so far are [b], [d], [ǰ] and [v], all of which are voiced consonants. We can now complete our rule as follows:

Final lengthening rule: vowels become lengthened before voiced consonants

Quick Exercise 3.5

Circle the words in the list below that would be pronounced with a lengthened vowel on the surface by a native speaker of English.

/sit/	seat	/sid/	seed	/sʌk/	suck	/sæt/	sat	/sin/	scene
/rɛd/	red	/wɛb/	web	/rɛk/	wreck	/rɪg/	rig	/tem/	tame

Which of these words would also be pronounced with a nasalized vowel on the surface by a native speaker of English?

Aspiration in English

Data set (6) focuses on a rule that you are already somewhat familiar with—aspiration in English. However, this analysis will provide a much more complete picture. The goal will be to compare aspirated and unaspirated consonants. Recall that aspirated consonants are ones that are accompanied by a puff of air. For words with multiple syllables, the stressed syllable has been bolded in the spelling.

(6)	[tʰu]	too	[pʰat]	pot	[kʰop]	cope
	[stu]	stew	[spat]	spot	[skop]	scope
	[ritʰɔrt]	re**tort**	[ripʰit]	re**peat**	[rikʰʌvɚ]	re**cov**er
	[ræftɚ]	**raf**ter	[ripɚ]	**rea**per	[strikɚ]	**strea**ker

As with our vowel data, when we look for minimal pairs, we find none. Pairs like "too" and "stew" as well as "cope" and "scope" might look like minimal pairs at first, but each pair differs in *two* ways. First, where "stew" and "scope" have an initial /s/, neither "too" nor "cope" does. Second, while "stew" and "scope" have unaspirated stops before the vowel, "too" and "cope" have aspirated stops. These *two* differences mean they are *not* minimal pairs. Our task now is to discover what is complementary about the aspirated an unaspirated sounds.

We'll begin with what's familiar and focus on [p] and [pʰ]. The first pair of words in the second column, "pot" and "spot," suggest that [pʰ] always occurs word initially, but the next word, "repeat," indicates that it also occurs word internally, as does [p] in the word "reaper." Clearly, then, position within a word is not going to tell us everything we need to know about the environment of aspiration. Neither, though, will the surrounding sounds, as we see from the data that both [p] and [pʰ] are preceded by [i] and followed by [a]. What this tells us is that we need a new aspect of environment to explain the complementary distribution of [p] and [pʰ]. This new aspect of environment is **syllable stress.**

To determine how the environments of [p] and [pʰ] differ, we need to look at syllable stress. Because the first two words in the column have only a single syllable, stress is not an issue in these words. Each of these monosyllabic words can be said to consist of a single syllable with stress. We will focus instead on the two words for which stress is an issue, "repeat" and "reaper." Notice the position of variety of /p/ relative to the stressed syllable. In "repeat" the allophone used is [pʰ] and it occurs at the beginning of the stressed syllable in the word. In "reaper," however, the allophone [p] occurs at the beginning of the unstressed syllable in the word. Each word is repeated below with its transcription and syllable boundaries. Boldface indicates stress.

[ri / **pʰit**] re / **peat**
[**ri** / pɚ] **rea** / per

We are now prepared to describe a rule:

Aspiration rule #1: /p/ becomes [pʰ] at the beginning of stressed syllables (stressed syllable initially)

Now we need to return to the other aspirated consonants. Beginning with [t] and [tʰ], we see the same situation that we saw with [p] and [pʰ]; namely, while both sounds occur word internally and are preceded by [i] and followed by [u], their position relative to the stressed syllable is different. Again, we can represent this graphically:

[ri / **tʰɔrt**] re / **tort**
[**raf** / tɚ] **raf** / ter

This leads us to our second rule:

Aspiration rule #2: /t/ becomes [tʰ] stressed syllable initially

As before, we want to start looking for natural classes. [pʰ] and [tʰ] share two main features of consonants—they are both voiceless and they are both stops. Our hypothesis at this point, then, should be that *all* voiceless stops (meaning the natural class of voiceless stops) are aspirated stressed syllable initially. To test this hypothesis, we need to look no further than the third column of data using [k] and [kʰ]. As the other voiceless consonant in English, /k/ should behave the same way /p/ and /t/ do if our theory is accurate. The data proves us right, as the following representations indicate:

[ri / **kʰʌ** / vɚ] re / **co** / ver
[**stri** / kɚ] **strea** / ker

We can state our next rule as follows:

Aspiration rule #3: /k/ becomes [kʰ] stressed syllable initially

Now we have enough data to describe what we've observed here with one concise rule by generalizing to the natural class to which /p/, /t/ and /k/ belong:

Final aspiration rule: voiceless stops are aspirated stressed syllable initially

Quick Exercise 3.6

Circle the words in the list below that would be pronounced with an aspirated consonant on the surface by a native speaker of English. Accent marks in polysyllabic words indicate stressed vowels. Assume that all syllables in monosyllabic words are stressed.

/sit/	seat	/sid/	seed	/tʌk/	tuck	/kæt/	cat	/əkáwnt/	account
/dɛd/	dead	/pɛg/	peg	/rɛk/	wreck	/bɪg/	big	/əpréz/	appraise

Flapping in American English

Data set (7) illustrates the most complicated rule we have seen so far—the flapping rule in American English. An alveolar flap, represented by the symbol [D], is very similar to a [d] in that it is articulated by touching the tip of the tongue to the alveolar ridge and stopping the flow of air through the vocal tract. It differs from a [d], however, in that it is articulated faster. Our goal will be to compare the alveolar flap with the full alveolar stops in American English.

The only minimal pair that this data reveals is the pair [bɪt] ("bit") and [bɪd] ("bid"). What this tells us, however, is that /t/ and /d/ are contrastive and, therefore, different phonemes of English, and this is nothing new to us. We're concerned now with discovering how [D] works in American English, so only a minimal pair with respect to [D] and some other sound would be relevant. However, we find no such pairs in the data. This tells us to look for something complementary in the distribution of [D] and the full alveolar stops, [d] and [t].

(7)

[čit]	cheat	[bɪt]	bit	[spat]	spot
[čiDɚ]	**cheat**er	[bɪDɚ]	**bit**ter	[spaDi]	**spot**ty
[æt]	at	[bɪd]	bid	[kʌt]	cut
[æDətud]	**at**titude	[bɪDɚ]	**bi**dder	[kʌDɚ]	**cu**tter
[mɪsti]	**mis**ty	[čæptɚ]	**chap**ter	[wʌndɚ]	**won**der

We can begin by comparing [D] and [t] in the data. [D] is only used word internally, but because [t] also appears word internally, we know they overlap in this regard. If we turn to the surrounding sounds, we run into the same problem of overlap. For example, both [D] and [t] are preceded by [æ] (see "at" and "attitude"), and both are followed by [ɚ] (see "bitter" and "chapter") and [i] (see "spotty" and "misty"). Again, this overlap is not what we're looking for.

To find the complementary distribution of [D] and [t], we need to look not just at the preceding *or* following sound, but to look at *both* of them together. A perusal of the data indicates that every time [D] is used, there are vowels on both sides. We can say, then, that [D] is used inter-vocalically (between vowels). Contrast this with the data for [t]. While [t] appears after vowels (see "at") and before vowels (see "blister"), it never appears between two vowels. This leads us to describe the following rule:

Rule #1: /t/ becomes [D] (flapped) inter-vocalically

Now we need to consider [d], and when we do, we will see that the exact same analysis applies to the distribution of [D] vs. [d]. We already know that [D] is only used inter-vocalically; however, [d], like [t], cannot be used inter-vocalically. The data shows it being used after vowels (see "bid") and before vowels (see "wonder") but never between them. Our next rule, then, will be very much like our first:

Rule #2: /d/ becomes [D] (flapped) inter-vocalically

As before, we want to illustrate the systematicity of our rules and make them more concise by generalizing to a natural class for the phonemes affected. The phonemes affected by this rule of flapping are /t/ and /d/, both of which share the features alveolar and stop. Our next rule, therefore, will reference a natural class:

Rule #3: alveolar stops are flapped inter-vocalically

We might be tempted to stop here because, based on this set of data, our rule is accurate. That is, it accounts for all the data in our current set. Normally, this is where you would stop in an analysis; but because our goal here is not just to model the process of phonological analysis, but also to describe English rules as completely and accurately as possible, we need to consider additional data. In light of what we see in data set (8), we'll need to modify our rule slightly:

(8) [ət^{h}æk] a**ttack** [bæDɚ] **ba**tter [ədɔr] a**dore** [æDɚ] **a**dder

Here we see that alveolar stops are *not* always flapped inter-vocalically. In "attack" we see an alveolar stop (/t/) being aspirated inter-vocalically, and in "adore" we see one (/d/) not being affected at all by the inter-vocalic environment. This doesn't mean we have to scrap our previous rule; instead, it means we need to add to it to make it complete enough to account for the additional data. To do this, as we did with the aspiration rule, we need to turn to syllable stress. Notice the position of [D] relative to the stressed vowel in each word in which it appears. In each case, [D] precedes an *unstressed* vowel (see "batter" and "adder"). In contrast, when a sound *other* than [D] is used inter-vocalically, it precedes a *stressed* vowel. If we add this aspect of environment to our rule, we will be able to account for the distribution of [D], [t] and [d] in all of the data:

Final rule: alveolar stops are flapped inter-vocalically when the following vowel is unstressed

Notice how incredibly complicated this rule seems. It's important to understand that these rules can be very complex and that this complexity can pose problems for non-native speakers of English. While this rule is normal and natural to a native speaker (of *American* English, specifically), who can follow it without even thinking about it, it is completely foreign to speakers of many other languages. These English language learners must try to consciously learn a very complicated rule, which is no small task, especially if they don't have a knowledgeable teacher to help them.

Quick Exercise 3.7

Circle the words in the list below that would be pronounced with an alveolar flap on the surface by a native speaker of American English. Accent marks in polysyllabic words indicate stressed vowels. Assume that all syllables in monosyllabic words are stressed.

/sítɪŋ/	seating	/sídlɪŋ/	seedling	/tʌk/	tuck	/kǽti/	catty
/əkáwntənt/	accountant	/dɛdli/	deadly	/rɛ́kəǰ/	wreckage	/bígəst/	biggest

Phonological Analysis Resource

The kind of analysis that we have modeled here can be very difficult for students because it's so unfamiliar. However, understanding the concepts behind it, as well as the overall goals and individual steps involved can greatly facilitate the process. This section is designed to be a resource for you as you become more familiar with phonological analysis.

Before beginning, a note regarding the relevance of phonological analysis is in order. Some students of linguistics have a difficult time committing to learning the process because they don't see the value in it. However, upon closer inspection, the relevance becomes more clear. To begin with, in some cases, the analysis will lead you to a description of a rule that you might some day find yourself teaching. The preceding four rules of English represent such possibilities. If your language of instruction is English, then the relevance of an analysis of English data should be clear. Being forced to go through the process of analyzing the data, rather than being fed a "fact" of English phonology, will, hopefully, make the rules clearer to you.

In other cases, however, especially if the data is not English, the relevance might not be so clear. Try to keep in mind, however, that this kind of analysis, like the others modeled in this book, encourages a way of thinking that is essential for anyone who will be dealing with linguistic issues professionally. It does this partly just by reinforcing the fundamental concepts—in this case levels of representation and allophonic variation. Additionally, however, it requires the analyst to pay attention to issues that would otherwise go completely unnoticed; that is, it makes a person more keenly aware of his or her linguistic surroundings. Every educator will be faced at one time or another with a situation in which a student encounters linguistic difficulties that, given the complexity of human language, are not transparent to the untrained observer. On the other hand, a person who has learned to think deeply about and analyze language, stands a much better chance of assessing the problem and perhaps offering a solution. Keep in mind that your linguistics education is not just about learning facts; it is also very much about learning how to think in new ways. In fact, this latter goal is the primary one.

Goals of the Analysis

The overall goal of learning phonological analysis is to train our minds. That said, we need to focus now on the more immediate goal of any given analysis. It is important to always be aware of the big picture—know why you're performing an analysis before you get into the nuts and bolts of analyzing data.

The goals of any given phonological analysis are:

1. to determine the relationship between two or more sounds in a language

and

2. if the sounds are non-contrastive (allophones of the same phoneme), to describe a rule that governs the allophonic variation (when each allophone is used)

Note that a contrastive relationship doesn't allow for much further study. If two sounds are contrastive (different phonemes), there is nothing systematic to look for because there is no phonological relationship between the sounds.

Steps of the Analysis

Because there is a fair amount of detail involved in an analysis of phonological data, it can be helpful to break down the steps in order to make a seemingly overwhelming task much more manageable. Below are two steps that you should follow as you look at the data. It is very important to follow these steps *in this order*, as they will help you mirror the goals stated above during the process of analysis.

1. Do you see any minimal pairs with respect to the sounds you are asked to compare? If so, STOP right here.

If you see a minimal pair, namely two transcriptions that are identical except for one difference, and the two meanings that the transcriptions represent are different, then the two sounds that create that minimal pair are *contrastive*. These sounds are in *overlapping distribution*. When two sounds create a minimal pair, they are *two separate phonemes*.

example: [sɪp] "sip" [dɪp] "dip" ([s] and [d] are contrastive)

You have accomplished your goal of determining the relationship between the sounds, and because this relationship is a contrastive one, there is no more work to be done.

2. If the answer to #1 is "no," then you know you want to look for *complementary distribution*. In a case of complementary distribution, the sounds are *allophones of the same phoneme*.

Now you have to describe a phonological rule by determining what factor(s) condition the allophonic variation. That is, what aspect of environment determines which allophone appears? Is it:

- the position of the sound within the word?
- the immediately surrounding sounds?
- the stress of the syllables?

This is the most challenging part of phonological analysis. To become proficient at such a challenging task, there's no substitute for practice. There are several data sets at the end of the chapter that can be used to practice this kind of analysis. You might also want to go back to the analyses of English rules in this chapter to see these steps at work.

English Spelling Revisited

In the previous chapter, we saw that English spelling is not phonetic. This means we can't predict, based on the spelling of word, how it is pronounced, nor can we predict, based on the pronunciation of a word, how it is spelled. While this may, at first glance, seem to be an unfortunate state of affairs, consider for a minute what a truly phonetic spelling system would be like. Such a system would need a symbol for each and every surface level sound in the language. Thus, instead of having one "p" symbol, we would need at least two—one for [p] and one for [pʰ]. The same would be true for every phoneme with multiple allophones. For example, for our vowels we identified three different allophones—a lengthened allophone, a nasalized allophone and a "regular" allophone. Take the roughly 16 vowel phonemes that most English speakers have and multiply it by three for each allophone and you have 48 surface level vowel sounds. Based on this observation, a phonetic spelling system for English would require at least 48 different symbols just for the vowels alone. Add to this number all the allophones of the 24 English consonants and the number of letters in the alphabet swells to rather cumbersome proportions.

In addition to being unmanageable, a phonetic spelling system would not agree with our psychological realities. For example, while [p] and [pʰ] are, in fact, two different surface level sounds, native speakers of English can't hear the difference between them. As far as we're concerned, they're the same sound, so if we had two letters for these two sounds, how would we know which letter to use? It actually makes sense for English to have a single symbol for both of these sounds, because they are allophones of the same phoneme. So, while English spelling is not phonetic, it is, at least to a certain extent, *phonemic*, meaning a single spelling letter is used to represent a single sound phoneme in many cases.

While this phonemic system makes sense, it can present problems for children when they are first starting to learn how to read and write. Children who are taught literacy through a phonics based approach are encouraged to focus intently on the sounds they hear. This focus is necessarily on the surface level because it is the surface level, not the underlying level, that can be heard. Unfortunately, this focus on the surface level can lead to spelling mistakes. For example, the phoneme /t/ can be pronounced as [t] or [D] at the surface level, and this is a difference that native English speakers can hear if they concentrate on it. Often children hear the voicing in the alveolar flap and associate it with the phoneme /d/, the result being that words like "pretty" and "little" are spelled "prede" and "lidel." Over time, of course, they will learn to spell phonemically, but initially systematic errors of this nature will be common.

English Phonotactics

Up to this point, we have been discussing the concept of a syllable without really having studied it very carefully. This is possible because it's a fairly intuitive concept for most people, and our goal was to use the concept to illustrate other features of language. Now, however, we need to focus more closely on syllables because they are an important aspect of the phonological system of any given language. Specifically, we will study the parts of a syllable and the limitations that languages place on the structures that syllables can take. This is known as the study of **phonotactics**.

The Syllable

A **syllable** is something that most people have an intuitive feel for yet it's very difficult to define. One possible definition of a syllable is a phonological unit consisting of one or more phonemes. The single mandatory part of a syllable is its vowel. Because the vowel is the core of the syllable, it is known as the syllable's **nucleus**. Some syllables, such as the syllable that comprises the monosyllabic word "oh," consist of just the nucleus.

nucleus only: /o/ "oh"

Other syllables contain optional elements before and/or after the nucleus. These optional elements are consonants. When one or more consonants precede the nucleus, they are called the **onset** of the syllable. An example of a syllable with an onset, as well as a nucleus, is the syllable that comprises the word "show."

onset + nucleus: /šo/ "show"

When one or more consonants follow the nucleus, the syllable is said to have a **coda**. The syllable that comprises the word "inn" consists of a nucleus and a coda.

nucleus + coda: /ɪn/ "inn"

This combination of a nucleus and a coda is called the **rhyme** of a syllable. This term should be familiar to you. If you were to try to rhyme words with "inn," you would have to find words with the exact same nucleus + coda combination. This is why this combination is known as the rhyme. Table 3.1 contains words that do and do not rhyme with "inn." Notice that all the words that do rhyme with "inn" have the exact same sounds in the nucleus and coda. The words that do not rhyme with "inn," however, differ in terms of the nucleus, the coda or both; that is, they do not have the exact same rhyme as "inn."

Words that rhyme with /ɪn/ "inn"	Words that do not rhyme with /ɪn/ "inn"
/sɪn/ "sin"	/sʌn/ "son"
/tɪn/ "tin"	/sɪp/ "sip"
/wɪn/ "win"	/sev/ "save"

Table 3.1: Rhyming

Notice that all of the words in Table 3.1 contain all three elements of a syllable—an onset, a nucleus and a coda. We can represent the structure of a syllable graphically, as in Figure 3.1.

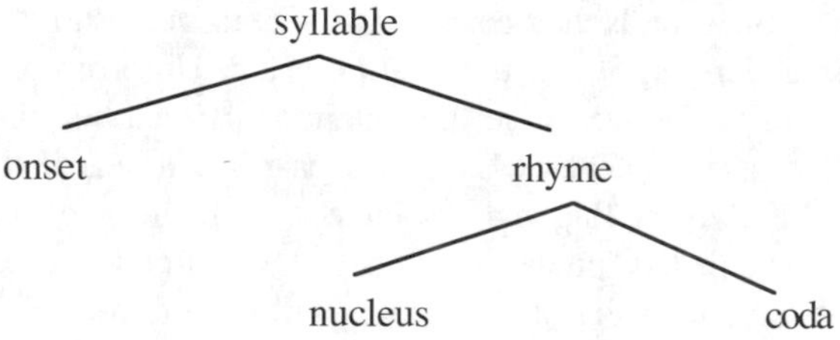

Figure 3.1: Syllable parts

Phonotactic Constraints on Syllable Structure

So far, we've seen three different syllable structures for English words. We can represent these structures according to the consonants and vowels they contain, as in Table 3.2.

Structure	Example monosyllabic word
V	/ʌ/ "a"
CV	/no/ "no"
VC	/ɪn/ "in"
CVC	/tɪn/ "tin"

Table 3.2: Some English Syllable Structures

While these four structures represent every possible combination of the three possible syllable elements (onset, nucleus and coda), they do *not* represent every possible syllable structure in English. Notice that in each of the structures in Table 3.2 there is either no consonant in the onset and coda or there is a single one. In addition to structures like these, English allows structures that contain multiple consonants together in the onset and/or coda of a syllable. These consonants occurring together are known as **consonant clusters**. The syllable structures that a language does and does not allow are known as a language's **phonotactic constraints**. For example, the four structures illustrated in Table 3.2, while allowable in English, might *not* all be allowable in a different language. English has fairly loose phonotactic constraints, allowing for complex consonant clusters. Table 3.3 illustrates consonant clusters in both the onset and coda of syllables.

While these consonant clusters are easy for a native English speaker to pronounce and seem perfectly normal and natural to such a speaker, they can be very difficult for speakers of other languages. This is because not all languages allow consonant clusters in a syllable. For a speaker of one of these languages, such clusters are not a linguistic reality and can only be learned with great effort. Even then, they can be problematic for many non-native speakers of English, especially if they come from languages that have more restrictive phonotactic constraints than English. The result is an accent, sometimes a very strong one, and possibly even comprehension problems. Again, we see how differences between languages can lead to second language learning difficulties. Recall from Chapter 2 that where a language learner's L1 and L2 differ, there will be interference, meaning the learner will have problems in those areas.

Structure	Example monosyllabic word
CCV	/stu/ "stew"
VCC	/ænt/ "ant"
CCVCC	/stɪnt/ "stint"

Table 3.3: Consonant Clusters in English Syllables

Quick Exercise 3.8

Table 3.3 lists just a few of the possible syllable structures in English. To explore the many possibilities of English syllables more completely, think of a one-syllable word that fits each of the structures below. To be safe, you might want to first write the word in regular English orthography and then transcribe it using the phonetic alphabet. Your focus should be *sounds*, not letters. Consider diphthong *single* vowel sounds.

V	CV	CCV
VC	CVC	CCVC
VCC	CVCC	CCVCC
VCCC	CVCCC	CCVCCC
CCCV	CCCVC	CCCVCC
CCCVCCC	CVCCCC	

To illustrate the concept of interference with regard to phonotactic constraints, we will use data from Japanese. Unlike English, Japanese does not allow a wide range of syllable structures. The vast majority of all syllables in Japanese are CV syllables. Japanese, like all languages, also allows V syllables (with a nucleus only), and it also allows very limited CVC structures—only when the consonant in the coda is a nasal. Primarily, however, syllables are CV in Japanese. One obvious result of this is the difficulty Japanese speakers have with pronouncing syllables like those in Table 3.3. Additionally, however, when Japanese borrows words from English, it must adapt those words to fit the phonotactic constraints of Japanese. Table 3.4 illustrates the adaptation of expressions borrowed from English to Japanese.

We see from these examples that Japanese must change the structure of every syllable in these expressions to CV in order to make them conform to the phonotactic constraints of Japanese. This is what makes them recognizable to Japanese speakers.

"McDonald's"

	CVC CV CVCCC
in English	/mɪk da nəldz/
	CV CV CV CV CV CV
in Japanese	/ma ku dɔ na ru do/

"word processor"

	CVC CCV CV CV
in English	/wɚd pra sɛ sɚ/
	CV CV CV CV CV CV
in Japanese	/wa do pu ro sɛ sa/

Table 3.4: English and Japanese Phonotactics

Problems associated with phonotactic constraints can also be seen at another, more specific, level. Take, for example, the difficulty that Spanish speakers have with English words like "ski." Table 3.5 shows the English pronunciation and syllable structure, along with that of a Spanish speaker.

"ski"

	CCV
by a native English speaker	/s k i /
	VC CV
by a native Spanish speaker	/e s k i /

Table 3.5: English and Spanish Phonotactics

Based on the Japanese data in Table 3.4, we might hypothesize that Spanish does not allow consonant clusters on the onset of a syllable. Further data, however, such as that in Table 3.6, does not support this hypothesis. We see that, in fact, Spanish does allow onset clusters.

	CCV CVC CV
"pregunta" (question)	/ p r e g u n t a /
	CCV C
"tres" (three)	/ t r e s /

Table 3.6: Onset Clusters in Spanish

Because onset clusters are clearly allowable in Spanish, the problem must lie at a different level. More specifically, while Spanish *does* allow onset clusters, it does *not* allow certain specific combinations of clusters. In the case of "ski," we can hypothesize that an /sk/ cluster is not allowed in the onset of a Spanish syllable. Further data, such as that in Table 3.7, supports our hypothesis and allows us to make a generalization that /sk/ clusters are never allowable in Spanish.

"school"		"scope"	
	C C V C		C C V C
by a native English speaker	/s k u l /	by a native English speaker	/s k o p /
	V C C V C		V C C V C
by a native Spanish speaker	/e s k u l /	by a native Spanish speaker	/e s k o p /

Table 3.7: More English and Spanish Phonotactics

Because /sk/ clusters are not a psychological reality for a Spanish speaker, he or she will insert the vowel /e/ to add another syllable and break up the /sk/ cluster. In the Spanish speaker's pronunciation in Table 3.5, the /s/ becomes the coda of the first syllable and the /k/ becomes the lone consonant in the onset of the second.

Data Analysis 3.1

Analyze the following data in light of the point illustrated in Tables 3.5 and 3.7 about /sk/ clusters in Spanish. What generalization can you make about Spanish? Hint: think about natural classes.

"stop"		"speak"	
	C CV C		C CV C
by a native English speaker	/s t a p /	by a native English speaker	/s p i k /
	VC CV C		V C CV C
by a native Spanish speaker	/e s t a p /	by a native Spanish speaker	/e s p i k /

These problems, of course, are not uni-directional. The psychological reality of a native English speaker is limited to the allowable syllable structures of English, unless such speakers are bilingual. Just as the Spanish speaker will have trouble with the /sk/ onset cluster in "ski," so, too, will an English speaker have difficulty with structures that are foreign to them. An excellent example is an English speaker's inability to correctly pronounce the common Vietnamese name "Nguyen." As the transcriptions in Table 3.8 indicate, this name has, as the initial sound in its coda, a velar nasal. While English does have a velar nasal in its phonemic inventory, the phonotactics of English do not allow for this velar nasal in the onset of a syllable. Therefore, English speakers have trouble pronouncing this name.

"Nguyen"	
	C C V C
by a Vietnamese speaker	/ ŋ w ɛ n /
	C C V C V C C V C V C C V C
by an English speaker	/ g w ɛ n / or / ə n g u y ə n / or / w ɛ n /

Table 3.8: English and Vietnamese Phonotactics

Somehow, the English speaker must try to make this name fit the phonotactic constraints of English. In the first adaptation, the English speaker substitutes the voiced velar stop for the velar nasal to produce the allowable /gw/ onset cluster. In the second, the English speaker tries to produce an /n/ and a /g/ consecutively, thinking mistakenly that these two sounds should be used based on the spelling; but because an /ng/ onset cluster is not allowable in English, a vowel is inserted before the cluster to break it up. In the third adaptation, the cluster is reduced to a single consonant, /w/, which is allowable as an onset in English. The unallowable onset consonant, /ŋ/, is eliminated altogether, one way or another.

A final point we can make before moving on is that any new word that we create in English must conform to the phonotactic constraints of English. Comedians and children often make up new words, and when they do this, they unconsciously create words that fit the phonotactics of their language. It would never occur to them to create words that did not fit the phonotactics of their language because unfamiliar syllables structures simply don't make sense to them.

Quick Exercise 3.9

Below is a list of made-up words represented at the phonemic level. Determine which of them could be new words in English based on their syllable structure, and circle these words. For words that could not be English words, highlight the part of the syllable that does not conform to English phonotactics.

/ktip/ /tfɛnt/ /klɪsk/ /zlɪft/ /stɚkt/ /flepn/ /prunt/

Syllable Stress in English

As we saw in our study of phonetics, when English words have more than one syllable (polysyllabic words), there is almost always one syllable that has primary stress. To sound like a native speaker of English, a person must know which syllable to stress in a polysyllabic word. How easy is it, however, to predict where the primary stress is? Consider the words in Table 3.9, each of which has four syllables.

Clearly, knowing which syllable to stress is no easy task. This is because syllable stress in English is variable and largely unpredictable. Native speakers who have heard these words before intuitively know where the stress should be placed, but an English language learner does not.

Word		Stressed syllable
/ **rɛ** plə ket əd/	replicated	1st
/ ə **sæ** sə net /	assassinate	2nd
/ æ də **lɛ** sənt /	adolescent	3rd
/ su pɚ əm **poz** /	superimpose	4th

Table 3.9: Variable Syllable Stress in English (bold syllables are stressed)

Does this mean, then, that there are no rules that one can learn about English syllable stress? As the data in Table 3.10 indicates, there are some trends that can be noted.

Word Pairs	Example Sentences
contest (N)	The contests at McDonalds were rigged.
con**test** (V)	The league contested the boy's age.
produce (N)	Produce has a relatively short shelf life, even in a refrigerator.
pro**duce** (V)	The collision produced a nasty welt just above his eye.
progress (N)	Progress is easily measured in terms of wins and losses.
pro**gress** (V)	The team progressed steadily over the course of the season.
conduct (N)	The child's conduct was atrocious.
con**duct** (V)	He conducted himself in a shameful manner.

Table 3.10: Contrastive Stress In English

Each of these words which has two grammatical functions—they can be both a noun and a verb. What distinguishes the noun from the verb is differing syllable stress. And the pattern is clear—in the noun the first syllable is stressed, while in the verb the second syllable is stressed. What this tells us, then, is that while English syllable stress is largely unpredictable, it is not completely unpredictable. In fact, there are some rules that can be taught, this being one such rule.

Quick Exercise 3.9
Provide three more pairs of words, like those in Table 3.10, that illustrate contrastive stress with noun and verb functions.

The data in Table 3.10 also tells us that stress can be contrastive in English. By contrastive, we mean that changing the stress of the syllables in a word can change its meaning, in this case from a noun to a verb or vice-versa. This contrastive potential of syllable stress in English can also be seen in compound expressions, such as White House and blackbird. Table 3.11 illustrates the difference between these expressions as compounds and as distinct words in a multi-word expression. The compounds refer to specific entities, the president's home and a type of bird, respectively, while the non-compounds simply refer to generic nouns with color adjectives describing them.

compounds	non-compounds
White House	white **house**
blackbird	black **bird**

Table 3.11: Compounds and Stress in English (bold syllables are stressed)

Summary

In this chapter we have examined how linguistic sounds work in a complex system. We have seen that there are complex rules that govern how we use sounds in a language. These phonological rules lead us to produce different versions (allophones) of the same phoneme depending on the environment in which we use the phoneme. These differences led us to a theory of levels of representation. We also examined English syllable structure and stress in English. Like all languages, English has rules (phonotactic constraints) that govern the possible structures a syllable can take. We also saw how stress can be used in a contrastive way in English.

Exercises

Minimal Pair Practice

One of the skills necessary for performing phonological analysis is the ability to recognize minimal pairs in data. Using the words below, create as many minimal pairs as you can. There are at least 11 minimal pairs. Keep in mind that some words might be part of more than one pair. For each pair, list the two sounds that create the contrast and also the feature(s) that distinguish the sounds. An example has been done for you.

1. / bot /	boat	9. / frid /	freed
2. / plet /	plate	10. / plad /	plod
3. / grid /	greed	11. / krap /	crop
4. / fred /	frayed	12. / bɪrd /	beard
5. / drap /	drop	13. / grin /	green
6. / grɪn /	grin	14. / rot /	wrote
7. / bon /	bone	15. / plat /	plot
8. / bɪrz /	beers	16. / wɪrd /	weird

minimal pairs	contrasting sounds	description of difference
/bot/ - /bon/	/t/ - /n/	manner of articulation, voicing

Contrastive and Non-Contrastive Sounds

As we have discussed, in any given language, some pairs of sounds are contrastive, meaning a native speaker recognizes them as being different, while others are non-contrastive, meaning a native speaker of the language does not recognize them as being different. The following exercise will help you understand the difference between these two relationships.

Proving contrast

The only way to prove that two sounds are contrastive is to find a minimal pair with respect to the sounds in question. Below you have been given pairs of sounds in English. Use each pair to create a minimal pair of words in English. Some will be easier than others, but you will be successful in each case if you try hard enough. The first one has been done for you as an example.

Sounds	**Minimal pair**	**Sounds**	**Minimal pair**
/p/ /t/	/pap/ pop /tap/ top	/d/ /s/	
/p/ /b/		/m/ /n/	
/k/ /g/		/w/ /y/	
/s/ /š/		/f/ /s/	
/č/ /š/		/θ/ /f/	
/i/ /ɪ/		/e/ /o/	
/u/ /a/		/ʊ/ /ɪ/	

Assuming you were successful in each case, you just proved what our English consonant and vowel charts suggest—namely that each of the sounds represented on the charts is a phoneme. To create the minimal pairs, you placed each sound in exactly the same environment (100% overlap), and used the two sounds to create a contrast in meaning. The contrast is due to the fact that a native speaker of English perceives the two sounds to be different sounds.

Proving a lack of contrastive

Now try to make a minimal pair with respect to the following pair of sounds.

[k] and [k̄]

The reason you can't do it is because, to a native speaker of English, these sounds are the same sound (they are allophones of the same phoneme). Another way to look at it is this: because the sounds are in complementary distribution, you couldn't put them in the exact same environment. To create a minimal pair, two sounds must be placed in the exact same environment (overlapping distribution) in two different words.

Practice with Natural Classes

For each of the sets of sounds, determine if a complete natural class is represented. If so, state the description of that natural class. The first one has been done for you.

1. /m, n, ŋ/ : this is the natural class of nasal consonants

2. /p, t, k, v/ : ____________________

3. /v, ð, z, ž/ : ____________________

4. /k, g, ŋ/ : ____________________

5. /š, ž, č, ǰ, r, y/ : ____________________

6. /p, b, m, w/ : ____________________

7. /p, t, k, f, θ, s, š, h, č/ : ____________________

8. /u, ʊ, o, ɔ/ : ____________________

9. /i, e, u, o, ɚ/ : ____________________

10. /æ, a/ : ____________________

11. /ɪ, u, ʊ/ : ____________________

12. /i, ɪ, e, ɛ, æ/ : ____________________

Determining Distribution

Determining the distribution of sounds—overlapping or complementary—is an important part of phonological analysis. Use the following foreign language data to determine the distribution of the pairs of sounds provided below. Remember that because this is not English data, the relationships and distributions of the sounds could be different from those in English. Your responses should be based on the data. For each word, you have been given a surface level transcription and an English translation.

Egaugnal (southeastern dialect)

[ɛšalapye]	election	[šɔkyɔl]	fraud	[ǰɛzɪne]	chad
[rɔlɔbɛn]	to hang	[kazɛku]	to vote	[kazɛki]	to count
[ǰɛžʊne]	to cheat	[θɔgyɔl]	to whine	[ɛšalabye]	butterfly
[šɔgyɔl]	ballot	[kæzɛki]	to confuse	[rɔlɔpɛn]	handicap
[ǰɔlo]	lawsuit	[sɛžɔse]	court	[sɪšʊno]	judge

For each pair below, determine a) if they are in overlapping or complementary distribution, b) if they are in overlapping distribution, the minimal pair that you found, and c) if they are in complementary distribution, the aspect of environment in which they are complementary. The first one has been done for you as an example.

<table>
<tr><td>[s] and [š]
a) complementary
b) N/A (not applicable because they are in complementary distribution)
c) surrounding sounds, specifically, the frontness of the following vowel</td><td></td></tr>
<tr><td>[p] and [b]
a)
b)
c)</td><td>[r] and [l]
a)
b)
c)</td></tr>
<tr><td>[u] and [i]
a)
b)
c)</td><td>[o] and [ɔ]
a)
b)
c)</td></tr>
</table>

<continued>

(The data and example have been repeated for your reference)

Egaugnal (southeastern dialect)

[ɛšalapye]	election	[šɔkyɔl]	fraud	[ǰɛzɪne]	chad
[rɔlɔbɛn]	to hang	[kazɛku]	to vote	[kazɛki]	to count
[ǰɛžʊne]	to cheat	[θɔgyɔl]	to whine	[ɛšalabye]	butterfly
[šɔgyɔl]	ballot	[kæzɛki]	to confuse	[rɔlɔpɛn]	handicap
[ǰɔlo]	lawsuit	[sɛžɔse]	court	[sɪšʊno]	judge

For each pair below, determine a) if they are in overlapping or complementary distribution, b) if they are in overlapping distribution, the minimal pair that you found, and c) if they are in complementary distribution, the aspect of environment in which they are complementary. The first one has been done for you as an example.

[s] and **[š]** a) complementary b) N/A (not applicable because they are in complementary distribution) c) surrounding sounds, specifically, the frontness of the following vowel	
[y] and **[ǰ]** a) b) c)	**[z]** and **[ž]** a) b) c)
[k] and **[g]** a) b) c)	**[š]** and **[θ]** a) b) c)
[e] and **[ɛ]** a) b) c)	**[æ]** and **[a]** a) b) c)

English Phonology Practice

Using your knowledge of the four English phonological rules discussed in class and in the text book (aspiration, flapping, lengthening, nasalization), transcribe the following English words at *both* the underlying level (phonemic) and the surface level (allophonic). Bolded syllables are stressed. For each response, you will need to write *two transcriptions*—one at the underlying level (before any rules are applied), and one at the surface level (after applying any rules that are appropriate). Use the first one as an example. To be consistent, always apply vowel rules before consonant rules.

paddock /pædək/ [pʰæ:Dək] (Note that the /p/ is aspirated because it's stressed syllable initial, while the intervocalic /d/ is flapped because of the following unstressed vowel; also, the first vowel is lengthened because it is followed by the voiced /d/ at the underlying level.)

1. **pa**ddock [pʰæDək] (surface) /pædək/ (underlying)		11. **ca**tty (surface) (underlying)
2. **sim**ply (surface) (underlying)		12. fa**tal**ity (surface) (underlying)
3. **attun**ed (surface) (underlying)		13. **spea**ker (surface) (underlying)
4. **ta**tter (surface) (underlying)		14. **tu**tor (surface) (underlying)
5. **accom**plish (surface) (underlying)		15. **plum**ber (surface) (underlying)
6. **spli**tter (surface) (underlying)		16. **tac**tics (surface) (underlying)
7. **skate**board (surface) (underlying)		17. out**ra**geous (surface) (underlying)
8. **ki**tty (surface) (underlying)		18. spi**ttoon** (surface) (underlying)
9. **ski**ttish (surface) (underlying)		19. re**tai**ner (surface) (underlying)
10. fan**tas**tic (surface) (underlying)		20. me**tal**lic (surface) (underlying)

English Phonology Problems

[ay] and [ʌy] Diphthongs

[Adapted from Department of Linguistics (1994), p. 115]

Some eastern dialects of American English contain the diphthongs [ay] and [ʌy] in their phonetic inventory. Use the following data from one of these dialects of English to determine if these sounds are allophones of the same phoneme or separate phonemes in that dialect. Follow the steps of analysis outlined below to arrive at your conclusion.

1. [bʌyt]	bite	9. [fʌyt]	fight
2. [taym]	time	10. [tay]	tie
3. [bay]	buy	11. [tʌyp]	type
4. [rayd]	ride	12. [rʌys]	rice
5. [naynθ]	ninth	13. [rayz]	rise
6. [fayəl]	file	14. [fayɚ]	fire
7. [rʌyt]	write	15. [lʌyf]	life
8. [bʌyk]	bike	16. [bayd]	bide

Are there any minimal pairs with respect to [ay] and [ʌy] ?

Describe the environment in which each sound appears.

Are the sounds in complementary or overlapping distribution?

Are the sounds allophones of the same phoneme, or are they of different phonemes?

If they are allophones of the same phoneme, what determines which allophone is used, and which allophone is the basic form (the one we should name the phoneme after)?

Based on your analysis of the data, which of the following pronunciations is/are phonologically possible in this dialect of English?

[kraym] [mʌyl] [wayl] [brayb] [kwayt] [səblaym]

[m] [n] [m̪] and [n̪]

Many dialects of American English contain the sounds [m], [n] [m̪] (a labiodental nasal) and [n̪] (an inter-dental nasal) in their phonetic inventory. Use the following data from English to determine if these sounds are allophones of the same phoneme or separate phonemes. Follow the steps of analysis outlined below to arrive at your conclusion.

1. [tim]	team	10. [æm̪fəθiyətɚ]	amphitheater
2. [tɛn̪θ]	tenth	11. [æntənɪm]	antonym
3. [sɪn̪θɛtɪk]	synthetic	12. [æm̪fɪbiyən]	amphibian
4. [æn̪θəm]	anthem	13. [tɛn]	ten
5. [nayn̪θ]	ninth	14. [æmpəl]	ample
6. [tin]	teen	15. [ɛm̪fætɪk]	emphatic
7. [mɛnd]	mend	16. [lɪm̪f]	lymph
8. [nayn]	nine	17. [maym]	mime
9. [tɛns]	tense	18. [tændəm]	tandem

Are there any minimal pairs with respect to any combination of [m] [n] [m̪] and [n̪] ?

Describe the environment in which each sound appears.

Are the following pairs of sounds in complementary or overlapping distribution?
Are these pairs allophones of the same phoneme, or are they of different phonemes?

[m] and [n][1]

[n] and [n̪][1]

[m] and [m̪][1]

Based on your analysis of the data, which of the following pronunciations is/are phonologically possible in this dialect of English?

[fɪlm̪] [n̪u] [pænt] [mʌn̪θs] [ænθræks] [tɛmpt]

[sɛvən̪θ] [kʌmftɚbəl]

[t] and [D] (alveolar flap) **and [ʔ]** (glottal stop) **in American English**

This data may be a little difficult for you, partly because of what you already know about English phonology. A helpful hint, though, is not to think **too** much about what you already know, and instead focus primarily on the data before you. (Note that accents indicate stressed syllables.)

[spɪt]	spit	[ríʔən]	written	[míʔənz]	mittens	[stɪk]	stick
[líðəl]	little	[píʔəns]	pittance	[bǽðəl]	battle	[lɪt]	lit
[gáʔən]	gotten	[kɚt]	curt	[fæðɚ]	fatter	[fǽʔən]	fatten
[pístəl]	pistol	[gat]	got	[kɚ́ʔən]	curtain	[bæt]	bat

1. Are there any minimal pairs in this data? If so, what are they, and what do they tell you?

2. Based on this data, describe the relationship between each pair of sounds. For each pair, decide a) if the sounds are contrastive or non-contrastive, b) if the sounds are in complementary or overlapping distribution, and c) if the sounds are allophones of the same phoneme, or different phonemes.

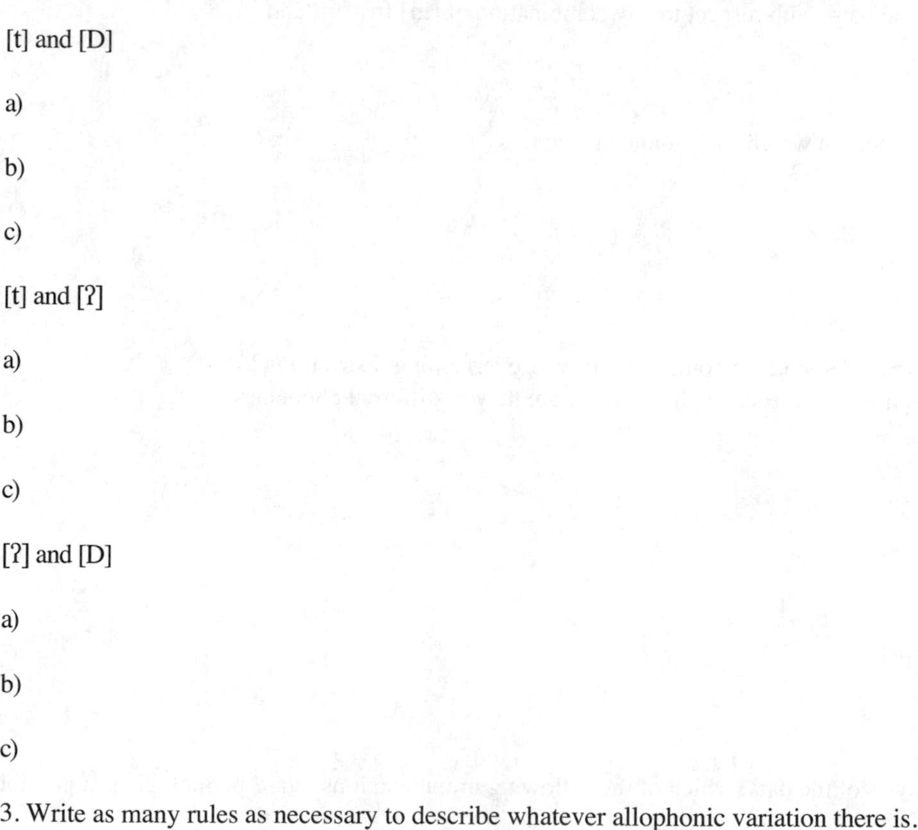

[t] and [D]

a)

b)

c)

[t] and [ʔ]

a)

b)

c)

[ʔ] and [D]

a)

b)

c)

3. Write as many rules as necessary to describe whatever allophonic variation there is.

4. <u>Based on this data</u>, which of the following pronunciations is/are phonologically possible in American English?

[ráʔən] [smíDən] [sɚ́tən] [léʔəl] [plǽsDɚ] [líDɚ]

Spanish Phonology Problems

Many dialects of Spanish have both [s] and [z] in their inventory of sounds. Use the data below to determine if these two sounds are allophones of the same phoneme or different phonemes.

[izla]	island	[rasko]	I scratch
[riezgo]	risk	[resto]	remainder
[eski]	ski	[fuersa]	force
[sinko]	five	[vamos]	we go
[dezde]	since	[mizmo]	same
[espalda]	back	[fiskal]	fiscal
[hablas]	you speak	[sabes]	you know

Are there any minimal pairs with respect to [s] and [z]?

Describe the environment in which each sound appears.

Are the sounds in complementary or overlapping distribution?

Are the sounds allophones of the same phoneme, or are they of different phonemes?

If they are allophones of the same phoneme, what determines which allophone is used, and which allophone is the basic form (the one we should name the phoneme after)?

Based on your analysis of the data, which of the following pronunciations is/are phonologically possible in this dialect of Spanish?

[azul] [pezkado] [servesa] [graznar] [nariz] [rason]

Spanish (continued)

[Adapted from Cowan & Rakušan (1998), pp. 32–33]

Using the following data from Spanish, along with the English translations, compare the following two sounds: [g] and [ɣ] (Note that [ɣ] is a voiced velar fricative.)

1. [seɣún]	according to	6. [grieɣo]	Greek
2. [maŋgo]	mango	7. [galán]	gallant
3. [neɣar]	to refuse	8. [gustar]	to please
4. [aɣo]	I make/do	9. [miɣa]	crumb
5. [agresivo]	aggressive	10. [agrio]	bitter

Are there any minimal pairs with respect to [g] and [ɣ]?

Describe the environment in which each sound appears.

Are the sounds in complementary or overlapping distribution?

Are the sounds allophones of the same phoneme, or are they of different phonemes?

If they are allophones of the same phoneme, what determines which allophone is used, and which allophone is the basic form (the one we should name the phoneme after)?

Based on your analysis of the data, which of the following pronunciations is/are phonologically possible in this dialect of Spanish?

[negasion] [regalar] [maɣo] [ɣwapo] [gato] [soga]

Additional Phonology Problems

Italian

[Adapted from Department of Linguistics (1994), p. 111 and Cowan & Rakušan (1998), p. 66]

Using the following data from Italian, along with the English translations, answer the questions that follow. You will be asked to focus on [n] and [ŋ].

1. [tinta]	dye	7. [tiŋgo]	I dye
2. [mandate]	you (pl) send	8. [teŋgo]	I keep
3. [dansa]	dance	9. [fuŋgo]	mushroom
4. [nero]	black	10. [byaŋka]	white
5. [ǰɛnte]	people	11. [aŋke]	also
6. [parlano]	they speak	12. [faŋgo]	mud

1. Are there any minimal pairs in this data? If so, what are the pairs and what can we conclude based on these pairs?

2. Determine the phonetic environments in which the sounds [n] and [ŋ] appear. Are there any natural classes that appear in these environments?

3. Based on the answer to #2, determine whether [n] and [ŋ] are in complementary or overlapping distribution. How did you determine this?

4. Are the sounds allophones of the same phoneme, or are they of different phonemes?

5. If they are allophones of the same phoneme, state the rule(s) that determine which allophone is used.

6. How does the relationship between [n] and [ŋ] in Italian compare with their relationship in English, and what problems would this pose for Italians trying to learn English and English speakers trying to learn Italian?

Based on your analysis of the data, which of the following pronunciations is/are phonologically possible in Italian?

[tɛnda] [sapone] [portovaŋo] [trovano] [buoŋo]

Korean

[Adapted from the Department of Linguistics (1994), p. 114 and Kaplan (1995), p. 63]

Korean has both [s] and [š] in its phonetic inventory. Use the following data from Korean, along with the English translations, to determine if these sounds are allophones of the same phoneme or separate phonemes. If they are allophones of the same phoneme, determine which is the basic form of the phoneme and describe the environment in which the other form appears. That is, write a rule to describe what is happening.

1. [ši]	poem	11. [sal]	flesh
2. [mišin]	superstition	12. [časal]	suicide
3. [šinmum]	newspaper	13. [kasu]	singer
4. [tʰaksaŋšikye]	table check	14. [sanmun]	prose
5. [šilsu]	mistake	15. [kasəl]	hypothesis
6. [ošip]	fifty	16. [čəŋsonyən]	adolescents
7. [čašin]	self	17. [miso]	smile
8. [paŋšik]	method	18. [susek]	search
9. [kanšik]	snack	19. [tapsa]	exploration
10. [šikɛ]	clock	20. [soǰaŋ]	director

1. Are there any minimal pairs in this data? If so, what are the pairs and what can we conclude based on these pairs?

2. Determine the phonetic environments in which the sounds [s] and [š] appear. Are there any natural classes that appear in these environments?

3. Based on the answer to #2, determine whether [s] and [š] are in complementary or overlapping distribution. How did you determine this?

4. Are the sounds allophones of the same phoneme, or are they of different phonemes?

5. If they are allophones of the same phoneme, state the rule(s) that determine which allophone is used.

6. How does the relationship between [s] and [š] in Korean compare with their relationship in English, and what problems would this pose for Koreans trying to learn English and English speakers trying to learn Korean?

Based on your analysis of the data, which of the following pronunciations is/are phonologically possible in Korean?

[kaši] [so] [sipsan] [sɛk] [šinho] [masi]

Egaugnal

Using the following data from Egaugnal, along with English tranlsations, answer the questions that follow. You will be asked to focus on the sounds [f] and [v].

1. [šifta]	sign	6. [koviki]	joke
2. [davla]	message	7. [luvdami]	insane
3. [pavi]	ugly	8. [valafpo]	travesty
4. [pofki]	embarrass	9. [wakinuv]	controversy
5. [mifsi]	laugh	10. [pifčov]	inform

1. Are there any minimal pairs in this data? If so, what are the pairs and what can we conclude based on these pairs?

2. Determine the phonetic environments in which the sounds [f] and [v] appear. Are there any natural classes that appear in these environments?

3. Based on the answer to #3, determine whether [f] and [v] are in complementary or overlapping distribution. How did you determine this?

4. Are the sounds allophones of the same phoneme, or are they of different phonemes?

5. If they are allophones of the same phoneme, state the rule(s) that determine which allophone is used.

6. How does the relationship between [f] and [v] in Egaugnal compare with their relationship in English, and what problems would this pose for Egaugnalians trying to learn English and English speakers trying to learn Egaugnal?

Based on your analysis of the data, which of the following pronunciations is/are phonologically possible in Egaugnal?

[vivda] [fofo] [dɛfto] [mivi] [wɛfsa] [lovgo]

Sindhi (a language spoken in southern Asia)

[Adapted from the Department of Linguistics (1994), p. 111]

[pənu]	leaf	[tɚu]	bottom	[dɚu]	door
[vəju]	opportunity	[k^həto]	sour	[ǰəǰu]	judge
[seki]	suspicious	[bəju]	run	[p^hənu]	snake hood

Compare the sounds [p] and [p^h] in Sindhi.

Are they in overlapping or complementary distribution?

Are they contrastive or non-contrastive?

Are the allophones of the same phoneme or are they different phonemes?

How does this differ from their relationship in English?

Would this difference create more problems for an English speaker trying to learn Sindhi, or a Sindhi speaker trying to learn English? Explain your answer.

Practice with Phonotactics

[Adapted from Hudson (2000), p. 237]

As you know, English allows a wide range of syllable structures. This does not mean, however, that anything goes as far as syllable structure in English is concerned. The following exercise should help you see the limits of syllable structure in English.

Determine the possible syllable onsets in English by combining a *phoneme* (not a letter) in the vertical column at the left of the table with a phoneme from the horizontal row along the top of the table. For each possible onset, write a number in the appropriate box and provide an English word (don't use names) that illustrates the onset. The first three have been done for you.

	any vowel	p	b	f	v	t	d	s	k	g	h	š	č	ǰ	l	r	m	n	y	w
p	1														2	3				
b																				
f																				
v																				
θ																				
ð																				
t																				
d																				
s																				
z																				
š																				
ž																				
č																				
ǰ																				
k																				
g																				
h																				
l																				
r																				
m																				
n																				
ŋ																				
y																				
w																				

1. pick /pɪk/ 2. please /pliz/ 3. pray /pre/

4. ____ 5. ____ 6. ____

7. ____ 8. ____ 9. ____

10. ____ 11. ____ 12. ____

13.______ 14.______ 15.______

16.______ 17.______ 18.______

19.______ 20.______ 21.______

22.______ 23.______ 23.______

25.______ 26.______ 27.______

28.______ 29.______ 30.______

31.______ 32.______ 33.______

34.______ 35.______ 36.______

37.______ 38.______ 39.______

40.______ 41.______ 42.______

43.______ 44.______ 45.______

46.______ 47.______ 48.______

49.______ 50.______ 51.______

52.______ 53.______ 54.______

55.______ 56.______ 57.______

58.______ 59.______ 60.______

Note that the combinations of consonants + any vowel illustrate single consonant onsets (the vowel is, of course, the nucleus, and is therefore *not* part of the onset). Every other combination, however, illustrates an onset cluster of consonants. This exercise does not address the possible English onset clusters of three consonants that you saw in Quick Exercise 3.8.

The grid has 480 combinations of onsets. Of these 480 combinations of onsets, how many does English allow? ________ What is the percentage of allowable onsets? ____________

What kinds of sounds are most often the first consonant of an onset cluster in English?

What kinds of sounds are most often the second consonant of an onset cluster in English?

Contrastive Analysis

Analyze the onset of the first syllable of each of the following foreign language words and decide if its structure is allowable in English. The words have been written phonetically.

Language	*Word*	*Meaning*	*OK?*		*Language*	*Word*	*Meaning*	*OK?*
French	[žɛ]	I (pronoun)			Russian	[nyɛt]	no	
Swahili	[ŋombe]	cow			Lango	[lyɛt]	hot	
Russian	[zdaniyə]	building			German	[knöçəl]	knuckle	

4

Morphology: English Word Structure and Formation

Morphology is the study of word formation. The term "morphology" comes from the Greek word *morphe*, meaning "form," which should give you an idea as to what morphology is all about. Our goals in this chapter will be the following:

- to divide words into categories based on their form and function
- to analyze English words by breaking them down according to their units of meaning
- to study the most common types of word formation in English

Word Classes

A useful place to begin a discussion of words is a study of **word classes**. Such classes are also known as **lexical categories** or, more commonly, **parts of speech**. Many people, regardless of whether they've had training in linguistics, are at least somewhat familiar with terms such as "noun" and "verb." These are labels that linguists have attached to groups of words that belong together based on their "behavior." Exactly what we mean by this will become apparent soon.

Classification is a process used in many areas of scientific study to explain or account for various phenomena. In biology, for example, living beings are classified according to a variety of features. Humans and dogs are both classified as mammals because they share certain characteristics, such as giving birth to live young and being warm-blooded, among others. The process used by biologists to classify living beings is very similar to that used by linguists to classify words. Specifically, it is a descriptive process that is based on actual observation. Remember that a linguist's job is to explain actual linguistic phenomena, not to govern how language should be used. Therefore, what we need to do is make observations of real language and divide words into classes based on their actual characteristics. What we'll see is that the traditional definitions that many of us grew up with are, to a certain extent, inadequate.

Classification Criteria

While there are a variety of criteria that could be used in a classification of words, in this chapter we will focus on two—**function** and **form**. For now, we will limit our discussion of the function of a word to its meaning. Therefore, we will consider a word's function to be the type of meaning it represents. For example, some words are used to represent physical objects, while others are used to represent qualities or characteristics of those physical objects. The simple functional definitions presented in this chapter are the ones that most people are familiar with, so it makes sense to begin with them. We'll soon see, however, that they're not very scientific.

Form definitions, on the other hand, are both more scientific and more helpful in distinguishing classes of words from each other. During the course of our study of morphology, we will see that a single word can take on multiple forms. We'll use patterns of formation to describe or define word classes.

Major Classes

We will begin with the word classes that are considered **major classes** before continuing with **minor classes**. Major classes have more members than minor classes and continue to accept new members as a language grows and evolves. For this reason they are also sometimes called **open classes**. Think of a slang word that you learned recently and you can be almost certain that it belongs to one of the major, or open, classes.

Nouns

One of the categories most familiar to the average person is the class linguists have called **noun**. Traditionally, nouns are defined functionally as words that represent people, places and things. While this can be a good place to start in determining whether a word is a noun or not, it alone has certain limitations. To begin with, deciding what *is* and is *not* a "thing" is problematic due to the vague nature of the word "thing." While it's clear that an object like a book is a thing, it's not so clear whether emotions like "love" and "hate" can be considered things. How about the word "emotion" itself? Is it a thing? The difficulty in answering questions like these leads us to look further in our effort to classify nouns.

More useful and scientific is an observation that can be made with regard to the form possibilities of nouns. Below in Table 4.1 are two different forms of words that are part of the noun category.

Form A	Form B
teacher	teachers
school	schools
book	books
emotion	emotions
goose	geese

Table 4.1: Noun Forms

For each word, there is a singular form, in the column marked "Form A," and a plural form, in the column marked "Form B." This leads us to the observation that nouns are words that can take a plural form. Plurality means more than one. While this observation might seem plainly obvious and barely worth mentioning, we'll see that it is actually very useful in distinguishing nouns from other types of words.

So, one way we can define nouns is to say that they are words that can be marked **number**; that is, they can be singular in number or can be made plural in number by adding something to them. Another term for this change in form is **inflection**. When a word is *inflected*, as nouns are for number, its form changes slightly without creating a new word. For example, each of the words in column B in Table 4.1 is a slightly different form of the same word just to its left in column A. Returning to our point, this form definition is much more scientific than our earlier functional definition. Is it, however, adequate? Try to make the noun "advice" fit this definition, as we have in (1) and you'll be unsuccessful. Recall that the asterisk before a sentence indicates ungrammaticality.

(1) * Liz received several <u>advices</u> from her therapist after her most recent divorce.

While many nouns, such as those in Table 4.1, can be inflected for number, others, such as "advice" cannot. This invokes a concept, namely **subcategorization**, that we'll cover in more detail in a later chapter. What we mean by subcategorization is that for every category of words that we identify, we can further classify the members of that category into smaller categories based on other characteristics of their behavior. Two subcategories of nouns are **countable nouns**, those that can be pluralized, and **uncountable nouns**, those that cannot be pluralized (alternative terms for these subcategories are count and non-count nouns). All of the nouns in Table 4.1 are countable nouns, but "advice" is not. That's why example (1) is ungrammatical.

The inability of "advice" to be made plural also tells us that we are going to need another criterion, in addition to form and function, to provide a truly adequate definition of the class of nouns. This is true for all classes and will be covered in a later chapter.

An additional point that needs to be made is that not all countable nouns are inflected for number in the same way. While most of the words in Table 4.1 can be made plural by adding an "-s", others, like "goose," cannot. Such words are known as **irregular** words because they don't follow the same pattern of inflection as most words in their category. Many irregular nouns in English are made plural by changing the vowel, as with "goose" vs. "geese;" others are made plural with unique endings, such as "child" vs. "children;" and still others can be made plural without changing their form at all, as with "deer" vs. "deer". Irregulars contribute to the difficulties that people have when trying to learn a second language.

Finally, we need to consider one additional form that nouns can take. Contrast the forms of the noun "oil" in (2) and (3):

(2) The <u>oil</u> in the can has an unpleasant odor.
(3) The <u>oil's</u> odor was unpleasant.

While "oil" is, for the most part, uncountable, we see that it can be inflected for some meaning other than number. Clearly, this meaning is one of possession, in that the odor is part of, or belongs to, the oil. Rather than simply saying nouns can be inflected for possession, it would be wise to invoke the more general term **case**. Case refers to the relationship between a noun and some other element in a sentence. The important relationship in this sentence is that of possession between the noun "oil" and another noun "odor." We can now add to our description of nouns by saying that they are words that can be inflected for case, specifically the possessive case.

Data Analysis 4.1

Sometimes, the distinction between countable and uncountable nouns is not perfectly clear. Decide which of the following nouns are definitely countable, definitely uncountable, or potentially both. For those that are potentially both, does the meaning seem to change when the noun is used as a countable noun compared to when it's used as an uncountable noun?

oil	pen
beer	finger
excitement	paper

Verbs

Also familiar to many people is the class known as **verbs**. Traditionally, verbs are defined as words that show actions or states (as in states of being, not states of the union). Again, the traditional functional definition is both unscientific and inadequate. The verb "to hope," for example, represents neither an action nor a state, though it does describe something that people "do." As we did with nouns, we need to make observations about the forms that verbs can take. We'll do this by observing the data in Table 4.2.

Form A	Form B	Form C	Form D
walk	walked	walks	walking
look	looked	looks	looking
hope	hoped	hopes	hoping

Table 4.2: Some English verb inflections

Comparing the forms in column A with those in column B, we see that the difference in meaning is one of time frame. Specifically, the forms in the A column are used to talk about "actions or states" in the *present* time, while those in the B column are used to talk about actions or states in the *past* time. Examples are provided below in (4) and (5).

(4) <u>present</u>: This year, we <u>walk</u> ten miles to school every day.
(5) <u>past</u>: Last year, we <u>walked</u> twenty miles to school every day.

The time frames are generally referred to as **verb tenses**, though as we'll see later, the concept of a tense is more complicated. So, we can begin to provide a more scientific definition of verbs by noting that they are words that can be inflected for tense. Again, this might seem obvious, but try to make a noun like "teacher" fit this definition, as we have in (6), and you'll see that the definition is, in fact, very useful for distinguishing nouns from verbs.

(6) * I teachered the students last term.

As with nouns, there are irregularities with verbs. While most verbs follow a regular pattern of inflecting for tense, namely adding "-ed", some are made past tense by changing a vowel ("write" vs. "wrote"); some are made past tense by changing a consonant ("make" vs. "made"); some are made past tense by making a unique change ("buy" vs. "bought"); and others still are made past tense without any change at all ("put" vs. "put"). Again, try to appreciate the complexity of the language. Learning the regular system is difficult enough, but add the irregularities, and the task becomes daunting indeed.

Continuing with our analysis of the data in Table 4.2, how can we describe the difference between the forms in column A and those in column C? Are they different in terms of their tense? Compare (4) above to the slightly different (7) below.

(7) This year, he walks ten miles to school every day.

Clearly, both verbs are present tense. In fact, there really isn't any meaning difference between the two words at all. Instead, the difference is purely grammatical; namely it's an issue of **subject-verb agreement**. In English, a verb must agree with its **subject** (who or what is "doing" the verb) in terms of that subject's **person** and **number**. We're already familiar with number—singular vs. plural. The concept of person, however, is probably new to many of you and is a little less obvious. Person has to do with perspective. When I am talking about myself, I am speaking in the 1st person ("I walk to school"). When I am talking to you, I am speaking in the 2nd person ("You walk to school"). When I am talking about anyone else not associated with you or me, I am speaking in the 3rd person ("He walks to school").

You are probably most familiar with the concept of person in the context of a foreign language classroom. Anyone who has taken a Spanish class, for example, has seen charts like the one in Table 4.3.

	singular	plural
1st person	(yo) hablo *I speak*	(nosotros) hablamos *we speak*
2nd person	(tu) hablas *you speak*	(vosotros) hablais *you speak*
3rd person	(el) habla *he speaks*	(ellos) hablan *they speak*

Table 4.3: Present Tense Spanish Verb Conjugations—the verb "hablar" (to speak)

This is a verb conjugation chart that shows the forms that the verb "hablar" must take for every different combination of person and number of the subject; that is, it must agree with it's subject in terms of person and number. The same is true of English, though to a much lesser extent, as the chart in Table 4.4 illustrates.

	singular	plural
1st person	(I) speak	(we) speak
2nd person	(you) speak	(you) speak
3rd person	(he) speaks *	(they) speak

Table 4.4: Present Tense English Verb Conjugations—the verb "to speak"

Note that in English, there are only two forms of regular verbs in the present tense—one that agrees with 3rd person singular subjects (the one marked with an asterisk {*}), and one that agrees with all other subjects. So, we can now add to our definition of verbs by saying that they are words that can be inflected for person and number, as well as tense.

If only it were that simple. While tense, person and number help us explain the differences among the verbs in columns A, B and C in Table 4.2, it does not account for the difference between column D and all the others. These verbs by themselves do not indicate a particular tense, nor do they indicate the person or number of the subject. Examples (8) through (11) illustrate this. Notice that the form of the verb "walking" remains the same regardless of the time of the action and the person and number of the verb's subject.

(8) present: He is walking to school.
(9) past: He was walking to school
(10) 3rd person singular: He is walking to school.
(11) 2nd person plural: You (all) are walking to school.

The "-ing" added to the verb tells us something more complicated than tense, person or number. It tells us the **aspect** of the verb. Aspect is best defined as time within time or internal time. Within each time frame (past, present and future) we can refer to actions or states in slightly different ways. Though (8) and (12) are both in the present time frame, the timing of the action mentioned is different. You can probably feel the meaning of the aspect in (8) as one of an action in progress, as opposed to the action in (12) which is less immediate, but more regular. The aspect of the verb "to walk" in (8) through (11) is called **progressive**, while that of (12) is called **simple**.

(12) He walks to school.

So now we can add further to our definition of verbs by saying that they can be inflected for aspect, as well as tense, person and number.

Data Analysis 4.2

A. The form of the verb "to walk" is the same in (8) and (9), but the time of the verb in (8) is present while that in (9) is past. How do we indicate the difference in time?

B. The form of the verb "to walk" is the same in (10) and (11), but the subject of the verb in (10) is 3rd person singular while that in (11) is 2nd person plural. Is there any subject-verb agreement in these sentences?

Adjectives

Another relatively familiar category is **adjectives**. Traditionally, adjectives are described functionally as words that modify or describe nouns. This is actually a fairly useful definition, though like all of the functional definitions we've seen so far, it's fairly unscientific. Consider the underlined words in (13).

(13) He's a mean man and she's a nasty woman, which makes them two unpleasant people.

Each of the underlined words modifies a noun; that is, each word tells us something about some quality or characteristic of a noun. "Mean" tells us something about the man, "nasty" tells us something about the woman, and "unpleasant" tells us something about the people. One of the problems with this functional definition, however, is that it fails to distinguish between adjectives and other words that also modify nouns in some way. For example, "a" modifies "man" and "woman," and "two" modifies "people," but, as we'll see later, they behave in ways that are very different from adjectives. This means we need to look for a form definition for adjectives.

(14) He's a <u>meaner</u> person than she is, but she's a <u>nastier</u> person than he is.
(15) However, Leroy Brown is the <u>meanest</u> and <u>nastiest</u> person around.

In each of the examples above, the adjectives are used in a form different from those in (13), and these new forms signal a slightly different "meaning." In (14) and (15), there is an element of comparison. In (14), two entities, "he" and "she," are being compared in terms of how nasty and mean they are. This form, characterized by an "-er" ending, is called a **comparative** form. In (15), Leroy Brown is being compared to more than one other entity; in fact, he is being compared to a large group of people. The form required here, when more than two entities are being compared, is called a **superlative** and is characterized by the ending "-est." Try this with the other two modifying words in (13), "a" and "two", and you'll see that this is a characteristic specific only to adjectives.

As we saw with nouns, however, sometimes form definitions don't apply to every word in a category. For example, while "mean" and "nasty" can be used in a comparative and superlative form, "unpleasant", as illustrated in (16), can *not*. This indicates the need for another component to our word class definitions, a need we will address in Chapter 6.

(16) *While Leroy Brown is <u>unpleasanter</u> than most, he's not the <u>unpleasantest</u> man of all.

With this evidence before us, we are now prepared to describe the form characteristics of adjectives. We can say that adjectives are words that can be inflected for comparison, though we acknowledge that *not all* adjectives fit this form definition.

Data Analysis 4.3

Imagine that an ELL student has asked you to explain a rule that will help him or her know when it's possible to inflect adjectives for comparison and when it's not possible. Use the following data sets to describe a rule. After each data set, describe a rule or modification based on that set.

Data Set #1:

<u>acceptable</u>	<u>unacceptable</u>
mean, meaner, meanest	unpleasant, unpleasanter, unpleasantest
smart, smarter, smartest	foolish, foolisher, foolishest
sad, sadder, saddest	intelligent, intelligenter, intelligentest

Initial Rule:

Data Set #2:

<u>acceptable</u>	<u>unacceptable</u>
silly, sillier, silliest	careful, carefuller, carefullest
nasty, nastier, nastiest	complete, completer, completest

Modification #1 to the Rule:

Data Set #3:

<u>acceptable</u>	<u>unacceptable</u>
little, littler, littlest	terrible, terribler, terriblest
simple, simpler, simplest	horrible, horribler, horriblest
able, abler, ablest	conceivable, conceivabler, conceivablest

Modification #2 to the Rule:

Data Set #4:

acceptable	unacceptable
good, better, best	good, gooder, goodest
bad, worse, worst	bad, badder, baddest
	fun, funner, funnest

Modification #3 to the Rule:

Final Rule:

Adverbs

The last of the major classes is the class known as **adverbs**. Unfortunately, this category is difficult to define because its members are so diverse. This diversity has led some linguists to refer to it as the garbage category. It seems when we don't know how else to classify a word, we throw it in the garbage category. With this in mind, we'll do our best to define adverbs.

As soon as we begin to discuss the function of adverbs, the label "garbage category" becomes clear. Consider the underlined adverbs in (17):

(17) Unfortunately, some motorists drive very quickly, which creates extremely dangerous freeways.

What is the function of each adverb? Clearly, they are all performing a modifying function, but is the function of each one the same? Table 4.5 matches each adverb with the element in the sentence it modifies. Based on their functions, we can subcategorize adverbs, as indicated by the subcategory names at the right of the chart.

adverb	modified element	adverb type (subcategory)
unfortunately	"some motorists drive very quickly" (a sentence)	sentence adverb
very	"quickly" (another adverb)	intensifier
quickly	"drive" (a verb)	manner adverb
extremely	"dangerous" (an adjective)	intensifier

Table 4.5: English Adverb Functions

The names of the subcategories help explain their function. Sentence adverbs say something about an entire sentence; for example, what is unfortunate in (17)? The answer must be that some motorists drive very quickly, which is a *sentence*. What do "very" and "extremely" do in (17)? The answer is that they *intensify* the meaning of the words that follow them. And what does "quickly" tell us in (17)? It tells us the *manner* in which people drive.

So, having gone through this analysis, what exactly can we say the function of an adverb is? Well, according to our data, adverbs can have one of four different functions. Specifically, adverbs can:

- modify sentences
- modify other adverbs
- modify verbs
- modify adjectives

Our inability to nail down a concise functional description of adverbs reminds us of why they are often called the garbage category.

When we turn our attention to a description of the form of adverbs, we will find that we have even less success than with their function. While it's true that many adverbs end in "-ly," as many of us learned in grade school, clearly not all do. "Very" is just one of many adverbs that do not end in "-ly." Also, not all words ending in "-ly" are adverbs. The adjectives "friendly" and "lovely" are proof of this. Perhaps the most useful thing we can say about the form of adverbs is that, unlike the other major classes, they cannot be inflected for any "meaning." This is actually fairly useful because it helps us distinguish them from the other major categories, all of which, as we have just seen, can be inflected for some meaning.

Quick Exercise 4.1

According to the paragraph above, "friendly" and "lovely" are adjectives. Prove that this is accurate by creating sentences in which you use each word in a way that conform to the form definition of an adjective.

"friendly" sentence:

"lovely" sentence:

Minor Classes

Minor classes, as was mentioned earlier, are classes with fewer members and are generally not open to new members. Very rarely do new words belonging to a minor class make their way into the language. Hence, these classes are also known as closed classes. We will save most of our discussion of closed classes for Chapter 6. For now, we will discuss only the one closed class that we can describe in terms of the forms it can take.

Pronouns

Traditionally, **pronouns** are defined as words that take the place of, or substitute for, nouns. Recall that nouns are traditionally described functionally as words that represent persons, places and things. So, pronouns, if they substitute for nouns, must also represent persons, places and things. Examples (18), (19) and (20) seem to support this description.

(18) *Advertisers* can be creative. They must be clever to sell products.
(19) *California* makes great cheese. It makes better cheese than Wisconsin.
(20) *Cheese* tastes great. Unfortunately, it is loaded with saturated fat.

In each example, the underlined pronoun is substituting for the italicized noun that precedes it. Also, notice that the nouns they substitute for represent, respectively, persons, a place and a thing. For now, then, we'll stick with the functional definition of a pronoun as a word that substitutes for a noun. Later on, however, we'll look at more data that will cause us to rethink this definition.

As with the other classes we've looked at, we want to look for a form definition of pronouns that will be more scientific than the functional definition. Because of the similarity between nouns and pronouns in terms of function, we might expect to see similarities in terms of their form. In fact, this is the case; and we do mean "case." Consider the forms of the underlined pronoun in (21):

(21) He loves her deeply, but she despises him because of his foul odor.

Recall that we defined "case" as the relationship between a noun and some other element in the sentence. Let's now extend that definition to pronouns, as well as nouns, and determine what relationships are indicated by the different forms of the pronouns in (21). The final form, "his," should remind us of the possessive noun form that we saw earlier (as in "oil's"). Here, the important relationship is one of possession between the pronoun and the noun "odor."

The "meaning" of the other forms, however, is new to us because in this way, nouns and pronouns behave slightly differently. Here, the important relationship is not between the pronouns and some noun, but between the pronouns and a verb. Note that with the male (masculine) pronoun, when we use the form "he," we are using it as the **subject** of the verb "loves." To use familiar terms, think of a subject of a verb as being who or what "did" or "does" the verb (in Chapter 6, we'll be more scientific in our definition of subject). Conversely, when we use the form "him," we are using it as the **object** of the verb "stand." Again, using familiar terms, think of an object of a verb as being who or what received or receives the action of the verb (this, too, will be defined more scientifically in Chapter 6). The exact same analysis can be applied to the use of the female (feminine) pronoun. The only difference is that "her" is the object of "loves" and the subject of "stand." The general concept, however, is the same. We can conclude this discussion, then, by saying that pronouns, like nouns, can be inflected for case. The difference is that pronouns can be inflected more extensively for case (subject, object and possessive) than nouns (one form for both subject and object and a second for possessive). We can use this observation, as demonstrated in the contrast between (21) and (22), to distinguish pronouns from nouns.

(22) The <u>man</u> loves the <u>woman</u> deeply, but the <u>woman</u> despises the <u>man</u> because of the <u>man's</u> foul odor.

Note that the forms of "man" and "woman" do not change when the case changes from the subject to the object of a verb.

Quick Exercise 4.2

There's no regular pattern of inflection for pronouns. Complete the following chart to prove it, using three personal pronouns in English, a masculine one (used for males), a feminine one (used for females) and a neuter one (used for "things" without gender).

	Masculine (John)	Feminine (Jane)	Neuter (information)
Subject			
Object			
possessive			

The Structure of Words

The Morpheme

Now that we're familiar with the major classes of words, we can turn our attention to the way these words are structured. When it comes to the structure of words, most people without linguistic training are likely to view them as being made up of letters or sounds. While this may be technically true for written and spoken words, respectively, it's not particularly helpful. We can also think of words as being made up of **morphemes**, and we'll soon see that full understanding of a word's meaning requires us to analyze its morphemes.

Morphemes can be thought of as the minimal units of meaning in language. Be careful not to confuse morphemes with phonemes, which we described earlier as being units of sound. A phoneme, by itself, does not convey meaning; it must be combined with other phonemes. A morpheme, however, by itself has "meaning." We use quotation marks around the word "meaning" because, as we will soon see, the kind of meaning a morpheme has can vary tremendously.

The concept of a morpheme can be fairly intuitive. Consider the words and their morphemes in Table 4.6. Hopefully, you'll intuitively *feel* the units of meaning indicated.

# of morphemes	Example Words			
one	act	worth	with	
two	act + ive	worth + y		re + ject
three	act + ive + ate	un + worth + y		re + ject + ed
four	de + act + ive + ate	un + worth + i + ness		

Table 4.6: Some English Words and their Morphemes

Don't worry that, in some cases, the sounds and spellings of a morpheme change (for example, in "unworthiness," the letter "i" was a "y" in the root "worthy"). Remember, what's important is the unit of meaning, not the sounds or spellings used to represent those meanings.

Quick Exercise 4.3

For each of the words below, determine the number of morphemes it has. Then answer the question below.

friend	friends	friend's	lucky	silly
unlucky	the	cigar	carefully	

Does the number of morphemes always equal the number of syllables?

Classification of Morphemes

Let's return for a moment to the comment earlier that different morphemes can have very different meanings. Consider, for example, the "meanings" of the morphemes "act," "-y," "with" and "un-" in Table 4.6. They represent a wide range of "meanings." In addition to this, we'll see that different morphemes also have very different "behaviors," specifically in terms of how they combine with other morphemes. Because of this diversity in meaning and behavior, it would be wise to classify morphemes by making several useful distinctions.

Free Morphemes vs. Bound Morphemes

Perhaps the easiest distinction to make is that between **free morphemes** and **bound morphemes**. As the terms suggest, free morphemes can be used alone, while bound ones must be attached to some other morpheme or morphemes. Working with the word "worthiness" from Table 4.6, we can classify one of the morphemes ("worth") as free and the other two ("-i-" and "-ness") as bound. "Worth" can be used alone as a word, while the other two cannot.

Quick Exercise 4.4

For each of the morphemes below (taken from Table 4.6), determine whether it is free or bound.

act	de	ive	y	worth	with
un	ness	re	ject	ed	ate

Lexical Morphemes vs. Grammatical Morphemes

Another useful, though less clearly defined, distinction is that between **lexical morphemes** and **grammatical morphemes**. Lexical morphemes are ones that have a "real world" sort of meaning. By this, we mean that a person can actually picture an object, action or characteristic. For this same reason, they are often called content morphemes. Lexical morphemes have meanings that correspond to the functions of the major word classes—nouns, verbs, adjectives and adverbs. Using the word "worthiness" again, we can classify "worth," with its noun meaning, as lexical, and both "-i-" and "-ness" as grammatical. A useful way to think about this distinction is to think about how you could define the "meaning" of a morpheme. If you can define it with a synonym (a word with a very similar meaning), it's probably a lexical morpheme. "Worth," for example, can be defined, at least partially, by the use of the synonym "value." Try doing this with "-i-" and "-ness" and you'll have serious trouble. Also try doing this with the grammatical morpheme "with" and you'll likewise have difficulty.

Quick Exercise 4.4

For each of the morphemes below (taken from Table 4.6), determine whether it is lexical or grammatical.

act	de	ive	y	worth	with
un	ness	re	ject	ed	ate

Root Morphemes vs. Affix Morphemes

The next important distinction is between **root morphemes** and **affix morphemes**. Root morphemes, similar to the roots of a tree, are morphemes around which larger words are built. Just as a tree begins at its roots, so, too, does a word made up of multiple morphemes. Affixes, on the other hand, are additional morphemes that are added to roots to create multi- or poly-morphemic words. Think of affixes as being branches of the tree. Once again, the word "worthiness" helps us illustrate the distinction. The root of the word, the morpheme with the bulk of the word's meaning, is "worth." Added to the root are the affixes "-i-" and "-ness."

At this point, you may be noticing certain trends. Specifically, roots tend to be both lexical and free, while affixes appear to be grammatical and bound. While it's true that affixes will always be grammatical and bound, there are some exceptions to the trend for roots to be free. The word from Table 4.6 that best illustrates this is "rejected." A careful analysis of this word reveals three morphemes, none of which are free; however, the word must be built around one single morpheme. Which one could it be? The only morpheme with a real world, or major class, meaning is "-ject," which cannot stand alone. To arrive at some meaning of this morpheme, which we must do in order to justify calling it a morpheme, we need to think of additional words (generate more data) that use the morpheme, such as "subject," "inject" and "project." When we do this, we see that all of the words have a common meaning—that of placing something some way, either backwards (reject), in an inward direction (inject) or forward (project). Through this analysis, we can justify calling "-ject" a **bound root** morpheme. Its meaning is, roughly, "to place".

Another important point to be made with regard to affixes is their position relative to the root to which they are attached. Using the word "reverted," we see that in some cases, as with "re-," they are attached before the root. Such affixes are called **prefixes**. In other cases, they are attached after the root, as is the case with the past tense affix "-ed." Affixes like these are called **suffixes**.

Quick Exercise: 4.5

In each of the words below, determine which morpheme is the root morpheme and decide whether that root is free or bound.

reduce	unhappily
prediction	proactively
mindful	reverted

Inflectional Affixes vs. Derivational Affixes

The final distinction that needs to be made with regard to affixes is that between **inflectional affixes** and **derivational affixes**. In short, inflectional affixes do not create new words when they attach to existing words; instead, they simply change the form of that word slightly. Examples of inflectional affixes are the morphemes we discussed when we defined word classes in terms of the different forms they could take. The past tense suffix "-ed," for example, attaches to verbs to change the tense of those verbs, but not to create a new word. This is why we described verbs as being *inflected* for tense. The number of inflectional affixes in English is very limited. They are listed in Table 4.7, and you'll see that they include all of the inflections for major classes covered earlier in this chapter. Note that they are all suffixes in English.

Inflectional morpheme	Example
plural ***-s, -es*** (noun)	Latrell hates all coach-***es***.
possessive ***-'s, s'*** (noun)	Latrell-***'s*** contract is huge.
comparative ***-er*** (adj.)	Latrell is mean-***er*** than PJ.
superlative ***-est*** (adj.)	Latrell is the mean-***est*** of all the players.
3rd person singular ***-s*** (verb)	Latrell like-***s*** to choke coaches.
past tense ***-ed, irregular forms, ∅*** (verb)	Latrell threaten-***ed*** to kill PJ.
past participle ***-ed, -en, ∅*** (verb)	Latrell hasn't spok-***en*** to PJ in months.
present participle ***-ing*** (verb)	Latrell is count-***ing*** his money right now.

**Note that, although you're given the spellings of these morphemes, the spellings are *not* the morphemes. They are only used to represent the morphemes. The morphemes can, and do, exist without these spellings being present. This is what is meant by the symbol ∅. An example would be "The two deer ran into the woods;" the word "deer" is plural in this sentence, but there's no spelling or sound to represent the plural morpheme.

Table 4.7: The Inflectional Morphemes of English

Derivational affixes, on the other hand, do create new words. They do this in one of two ways, depending on the morpheme. Some derivational morphemes significantly change the meaning of a word they attach to, while others don't change the meaning significantly, but do change its word class (i.e. the way the word is used in a sentence). Table 4.8 provides some examples of derivational affixes. Note that, unlike inflectional affixes, derivational affixes can be both prefixes and suffixes in English.

Function	Morpheme	Example Word
change meaning	un-	un + happy
change meaning	re-	re + write
change a noun into a verb	-ize	trauma(t) + ize
change a noun into an adjective	-y	health + y
change an adjective into an adverb	-ly	foolish + ly

Table 4.8: Some Derivational Morphemes of English

The number of derivational affixes in English is far greater than the number of inflectional affixes. To list them all here would require far too much space. Note that the "meaning" of derivational morphemes varies tremendously from one to another. In some cases, as with the morpheme "un-," the "meaning" can be expressed fairly simply through the use of synonyms, in this case "not." In other cases, however, as with morphemes like "-ize" and "-ment," the "meaning" is more of a function; that is, "-ize" changes words to verbs, and "-ment" changes words to nouns. Notice that in order to "define" these morphemes, we need to use grammatical terms.

Quick Exercise 4.6

Each of the words below contains two morphemes, a root and a derivational affix. Decide if the derivational affix changes the meaning or class of the root.

rewrite	hopeless
unclear	creation
unhappy	helpful

Do you notice a general trend with regard to the behavior of derivational prefixes vs. suffixes?

Figure 4.1 graphically depicts all the distinctions discussed in this section.

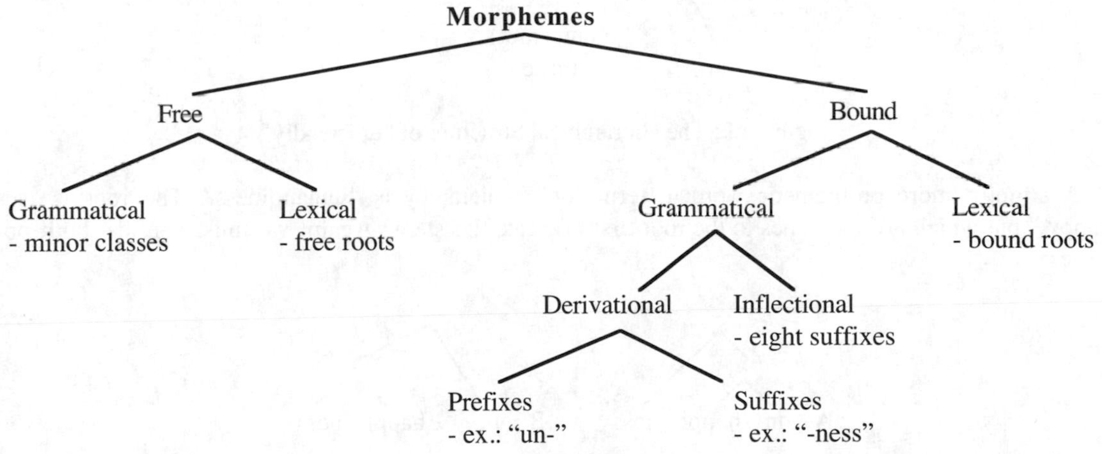

Figure 4.1: Morpheme Types

The Hierarchical Structure of Words

Now that we've covered the basics of word classes and morphemes, we are prepared to dive into our investigation of the internal structure of words. Because we, as English speakers, are programmed to think in a **linear** way (a straight line, for example, from left to right) when it comes to words, we are inclined to view poly-morphemic words as a group of morphemes strung together from left to right. If we return to the concept of a root morpheme, however, we'll see that this is not accurate. In the adjective "unfriendly," for example, "friend" is clearly the root, the morpheme with the bulk of the meaning. Thus, the word begins with the morpheme that is actually the second one in terms of the linear structure.

From this example alone, we can see that a linear analysis will not be particularly helpful in determining the structure of words. Instead, we need to look at the **hierarchical structure** of words. Hierarchical structure refers to levels and is independent of linear structure. Returning to the adjective "unfriendly," we can say that hierarchically, the word begins with (is built around) the root morpheme "friend," a noun. This is the initial morpheme at the bottom level of the hierarchy. Again, the tree root analogy proves useful in understanding the concept.

Next, we have to determine which of the affixes, "un-" or "-ly," attaches to the root at the next level of the hierarchy. The two possibilities are presented in A and B:

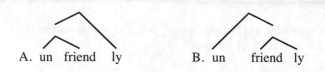

Hierarchy A presents a problem in that the proposed **stem**, meaning the intermediate structure, is "unfriend," which isn't a word. Hierarchy B, on the other hand, proposes "friendly," which *is* a word (an adjective), as the stem. At the next level in hierarchy B, the prefix "un-" is attached to create an **antonym** (a word with a opposite meaning) of the adjective stem. Thus we see that the hierarchical structure of the word, formally represented in Figure 4.2, is very different from the linear structure. Specifically, the morpheme that is first linearly is actually last hierarchically.

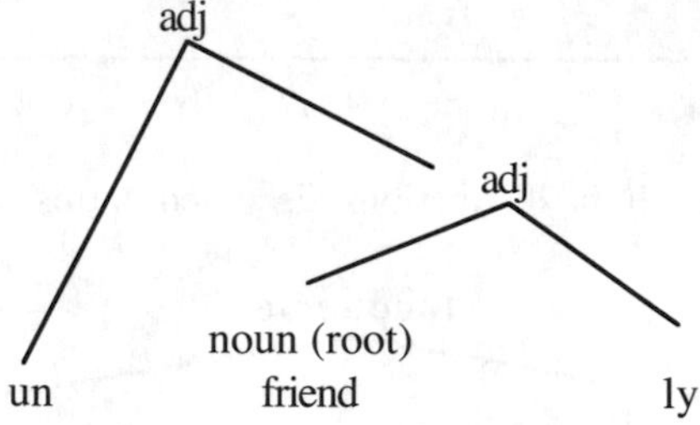

Figure 4.2: The Hierarchical Structure of "unfriendly"

A slightly more problematic word in terms of its hierarchy is "unhappiness." The root is clearly "happy," but which affix attaches to the root first to create the stem? Again, we must consider both possibilities:

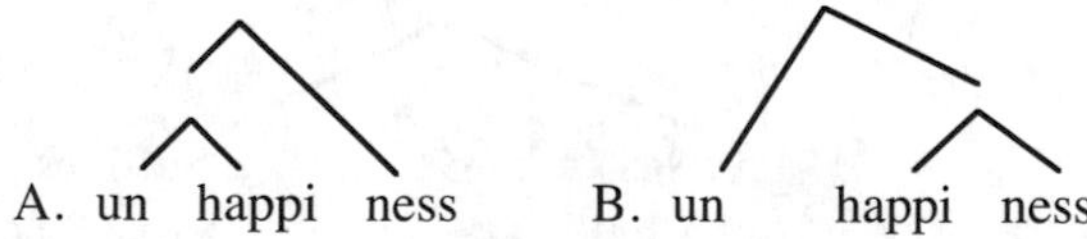

In this case, unlike the previous example, the choice is not immediately clear because both "unhappy" and "happiness" are words. What we need to do in this case is analyze all the morphemes in question to see how they "behave." If we look at additional data, such as that presented in Table 4.9, we'll see that "un-" attaches to either verb *or* adjective roots and stems, while "-ness" attaches only to adjective roots and stems.

word	root/stem type	word	root/stem type
un + pleasant	adjective	serious + ness	adjective
un + certain	adjective	sad + ness	adjective
un + do	verb		
un + wrap	verb		

Table 4.9: Behavior of "un-" and "-ness"

Based on this observation, we can only conclude that "unhappy" is the stem, because "un-" couldn't possibly attach to the noun stem "happiness," but it could attach to the adjective "happy." The hierarchical structure of "unhappiness," therefore, is the one represented in Figure 4.3.

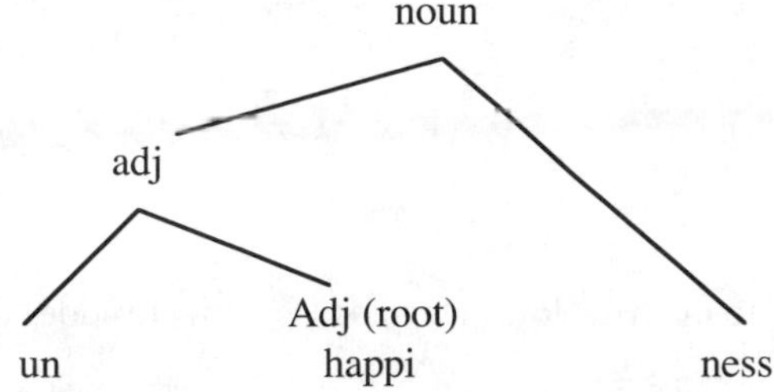

Figure 4.3: The Hierarchical Structure of "unhappiness"

Quick Exercise 4.7

Draw tree diagrams like those just illustrated for each of the following words.

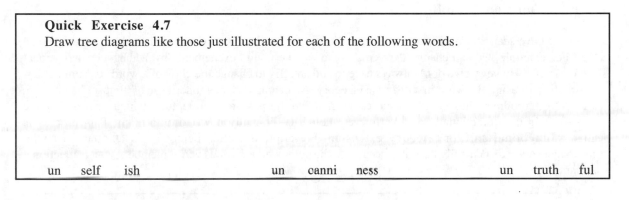

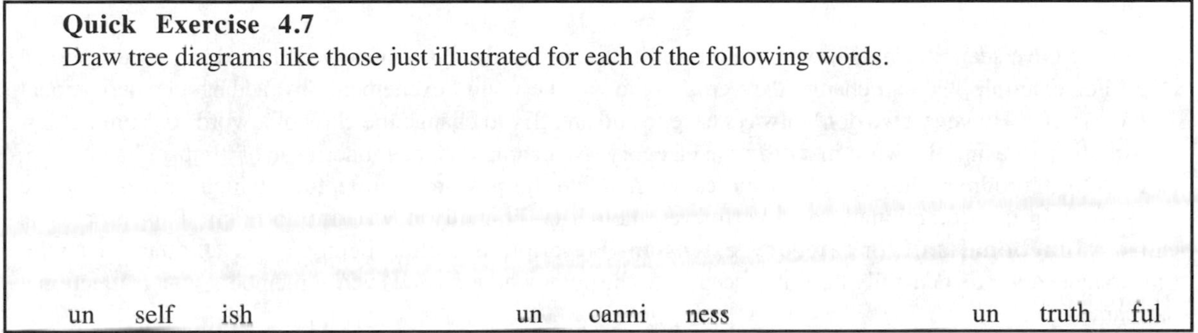

un self ish
un canni ness
un truth ful

Word Creation in English

In this section, we will look at some of the ways we create words in English. We will see that learning new words does not always require learning something completely new. Instead, in many cases, we build on what we already know. While reading about these processes in English, keep in mind that not all languages do things in the same way. What is perfectly normal and logical to a native English speaker might be completely bizarre and incomprehensible to speakers of other languages.

Affixing

As the preceding section suggests, **affixing**, or **derivation**, is an amazingly useful tool for creating new words in English. If a person knows X number of morphemes, he or she actually knows X + Y words if he or she understands how to use affixing. By mixing and matching affixes with roots, a speaker can add new words to his or her vocabulary. This is especially true if the affixes are **productive affixes**. Productive affixes are ones that are used in many words. "Un-," for example, is very productive. You can probably think of dozens of words with "un-" in just a few minutes. And you learned these words by knowing their roots and the prefix "un-." Essentially, you doubled that part of your vocabulary when you learned just one additional morpheme.

Quick Exercise 4.8

Mixing and matching the morphemes below, create as many English words as you can. Use ONLY the morphemes provided.

act, create, -ion, -ive, -ly

Now add the morpheme "relate" to the list. How many additional words does the one additional morpheme allow you to create?

Functional Shift

As we have seen, in English we have the ability to change the class of a word by adding a derivational affix. For example, we can change the verb "excite" to the noun "excitement" by adding the derivational suffix "-ment." However, we don't always have to add an affix to change the class of a word. In some cases, we simply start using the word in a different category. An example is the modern use of "impact" as a verb, as in "Over-enrollment has *impacted* the campus." Note the past tense inflection, which proves that the word is being used functionally as a verb, even though traditionally it was only a noun. This process is called a **functional shift** or **category extension**. Prescriptivists often bemoan this tendency, but with time extended words generally become accepted to the point where no one even remembers which functional use came first.

Quick Exercise 4.9

Each of the words below can be both a noun and a verb. Which use do you think came first? What's the basis for your determination?

transition

proposition

reference

hope

help

Semantic Shift

Similar to a functional shift, in which the grammatical function of a word changes, is a **semantic shift**, in which the meaning of a word changes somewhat. Take, for example, the words "hawk" and "dove." At one time, these words had only a literal meaning; that is, they were used to refer to birds. Now, however, they have taken on a figurative meaning and can be used to refer to people in government and, specifically, the military. Military personnel who are generally in favor of armed, aggressive action are called "hawks," while those favoring peaceful diplomatic resolutions to conflict are called "doves." These new figurative meanings are related to the original literal ones in that hawks are birds of prey that kill for food, while doves are not.

Quick Exercise 4.10

Think of three pairs of words that are related by a semantic shift.

1.

2.

3.

Compounding

In our earlier analysis of poly-morphemic words (words with more than one morpheme), we found that every word had an easily identifiable root. When we analyze a word like "bookstore," however, we see that this is not always the case. In such words, called **compounds**, two free root morphemes are combined to form a single word. English uses this process of compounding fairly extensively. Additional examples of compounds include "basketball" and "backstop."

Quick Exercise 4.11

Mix and match the following free morphemes to create as many compounds as you can.

mate soccer room basket key ball board house

Blending

Words like "motel" and "smog" are similar to compounds in that they are words formed by the combination of two other words. They are different from compounds, however, in that only parts of the words are used. "Motel," for example, is a **blend** of "motor" and "hotel," using the first part of one word and the last part of the other. Similarly, "smog" is a blend of "smoke" and "fog." Interestingly, after they have been used for a while, most blends are not easily recognized as blends by speakers of English. Instead, they are accepted as single morphemes.

Quick Exercise 4.12

New blends are being created all the time, often as new products are invented. These new products don't fit the terms in existence at the time of their invention, so new words are created for them. For each product description, try to determine the blend that was created for it.

Women's clothing that is a cross between a skirt and a pair of shorts:

Eating utensil that is a cross between a spoon and a fork:

Borrowing

As we noted in Chapter 2, English has borrowed many words from other languages. In fact, this **borrowing** has been so prolific that roughly 85% of English words that were used a thousand years ago have disappeared, many of them replaced by borrowed words[1]. Clearly, English is not shy about borrowing words. Examples of fairly recently borrowed words are "karate" and "macho." They were at one time only words in Japanese and Spanish, respectively, but now we consider them English words as well.

Quick Exercise 4.13

Many borrowed words refer to foods. For each of the languages below, think of a food word that English has borrowed.

Japanese:

French:

Spanish:

Italian:

Acronyming

Some new words are created by taking the initials of multi-word phrases and pronouncing them as a single word. A common example in English is the word "scuba," which stands for "self-contained underwater breathing apparatus." Words like scuba are called **acronyms**. It's important to distinguish acronyms, which are pronounced as words, from abbreviations, like FBI (for Federal Bureau of Investigation), in which the initials are pronounced individually. As with blends, over time, speakers of English accept acronyms to the point where they consider them single morphemes. While many English speakers are aware that "scuba" is an acronym, most are probably not aware that "laser" is an acronym as well. It comes from the phrase "light amplified by stimulated emission of radiation." Note that acronyms do not always include the initial letter of every word in the phrase. In the case of "laser," the "b" in "by" and the "o" in "of" are omitted.

Quick Exercise 4.14

Acronyms become so accepted as "regular" words that over time we don't remember their origins. What do the following acronyms represent?

radar

posh[2]

Root Creation

While all of the preceding types of word creation involve building on existing words, in some cases we create entirely new words from names, especially brand names. Examples of such **root creations** are "kleenex" and "band-aid." They were at one time **proper nouns** but have come to be used as **common nouns**. Proper nouns are basically names; that is, they have a unique referent. If you refer to your friend Albert, there is only one of him in the world. Common nouns, on the other hand, are non-names, meaning they do *not* have a unique referent. If, for example, you use the word friend, it could refer to many people. Often, these created common roots that were once proper nouns become such a part of our vocabulary that we're not even aware of their origin and can't remember the generic term for the meaning. This, of course, represents the ultimate marketing achievement.

---

[1] See Whitehall (1983), p. ix, for a more detailed discussion.

[2] There is some disagreement as to whether "posh" is truly an acronym with roots in a longer expression.

Quick Exercise 4.15

Sometimes, roots created from brand names become such a part of our lexicon that we don't know how to describe their meaning using common terms. What's the generic expression for each of the created roots below?

Kleenex:

Band-aid:

Q-tip:

Scotch tape:

Quick Exercise 4.16

While we neatly described words as being created through one particular process, the reality of the situation is that words are sometimes created through a combination of multiple processes. Determine which processes were combined to create each of the following words.

Bandaid:

Xerox (v):

Yuppie:

Transition (v):

Summary

In this chapter we classified words according to their form and function. Then we studied the internal structure of words, focusing on morphemes, which we defined as minimal units of meaning. We looked at various types of morphemes and how they came together in a hierarchical way to form poly-morphemic words. Finally, we studied some of the ways new words are created in English.

Exercises

Word Class Exercise

Put each of the words at the bottom of the page in the class or classes in which they belong. For each choice, provide some kind of data (use form data whenever possible) that supports your choice. The best data are sentences in which you use inflected forms of words, though this might not always be possible. Note that in some cases, words can belong to multiple classes; just be sure to provide enough data to justify all of your decisions. An example has been done for you.

nouns	data
intern	The former president has a thing for interns. (plural)

verbs	data

adjectives	data

adverbs	data

pronouns	data

intern, glass, goofy, he, resign, incessantly, strangle, disk, computer, impeach, president, kiss,

quick, flash, create, divorce, voraciously, silly, she, class, exercise, crazy, complain, they,

challenge, intend, error, paper, write, hot, me, coin, emotion, acquire

Derivational Morpheme Exercise (three pages)

Below are tables of derivational morphemes organized by the class of words that each morpheme is used with (for morphemes that change the meaning of a root or stem) or used to create (for morphemes that change the class of a root or stem). Using the example word(s) provided, along with additional data that you generate, determine the meaning and/or function of each morpheme. The term "meaning" is usually used for morphemes that change the meaning of roots and stems without changing the word class, and the term "function" is usually used for morphemes that change the class of a word. A few have been done for you as examples. In each case, think about the meaning and/or class of the root or stem without the affix, and then compare it to the word(s) with the affix attached.

Adjective Derivational Affixes (affixes that derive adjectives):

prefixes	meaning/function	example words
in-		intolerant
un-		unhappy
pro-	"for" or "in favor of"	pro-war
anti-		anti-war
omni-		omnipotent
super-		supersonic
ultra-		ultrasensitive

suffixes	meaning/function	example words
-like		childlike
-ant		resistant
-ful		helpful
-able/ -ible		understandable/ convertible
-ive		active
-ous		humorous
-ory	verb → adjective (having the quality of some verb)	obligatory
-less		speechless
-like		life-like

Noun Derivational Affixes (affixes that derive nouns):

prefixes	meaning/function	example words
non-		nonfactor
neo-	"new"	neoclassicism
suffixes	meaning/function	example words
-ant		assistant
-er	verb → noun (one who does some verb)	writer

suffixes	meaning/function	example words
-age		shortage leakage
-ist		sexist
-ture		departure
-ment		excitement
-ness		happiness
-ship		leadership
-tion		contraction
-ity		scarcity
-ism		sexism realism
-al		arrival
-ance		acceptance

Verb Derivational Affixes (affixes that derive verbs):

prefixes	meaning/function	example words
de-		deconstruct
en-		endanger
re-		rewrite
un-		undo
dis-		disassociate
be-		befriend

suffixes	function	example words
-en		harden lengthen
-ize	adjective → verb (to give something the quality of some adjective)	sensationalize rubberize
-ify		glorify
-ate		oxygenate

Adverb Derivational Affixes (affixes that derive adverbs):

suffixes	function	example words
-ly		happily
-wise		lengthwise

Morpheme Practice

For each of the following English words, identify all of its morphemes and provide a full description for each morpheme. The first one has been done for you as an example.

conversion -vert: bound, lexical root
con-: bound, grammatical, derivational prefix
-sion: bound, grammatical, derivational suffix

1. governments

2. senselessly

3. thickeners

4. unspeakable

5. repeatedly

6. thoughtfully

7. paraphrasing

8. contradictions

9. protracted

10. dishonorable

Morphology Trees Exercise

One way to illustrate how the derivational morphemes on your list work is to draw trees indicating the hierarchical structure of the word. To do this, start by identifying the root morpheme, and then add each affix, identifying the word class of each subsequent stem. Use your knowledge of the meaning/function of each affix to help determine the structure. Below is an example:

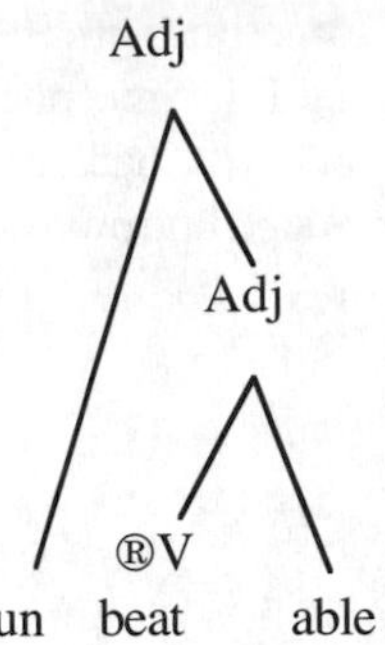

Using the model above, draw trees for the words below. Mark the root morpheme with an "R" (R) and attach all other morphemes in the correct hierarchical order. Mark the word class of each word that is created with each morpheme addition. Use the space above each word to do your work. (Note: assume all roots to be *free* roots.)

1. revaccinations
2. inability
3. reenactments
4. disestablishment
5. recapitalization
6. unreasonableness
7. dehumidifier
8. encampments
9. uncharacteristically

Bound Roots in English

Although the majority of root morphemes in English are free, there are many bound root morphemes as well. The source of these bound morphemes is generally another language, often Latin. Knowing the meaning of these Latin roots, along with affixes, can help you understand the meaning of words you've never seen before (that is, it can help you increase your vocabulary, as well as that of your students).

Combine each of the bound roots below with as many of the given prefixes as you can. Then provide a definition of each word based on the meaning of the morphemes. Keep in mind that sometimes, the actual meaning of a word does not *exactly* correspond to the combination of the meaning of its morphemes. Therefore, if your guessed definition doesn't exactly match your dictionary's (or the one you had in your head already), that doesn't mean the world has gone awry; it only indicates that we adapt borrowed morphemes somewhat to fit our uses.

bound roots	origin and meaning
"-voke"	from the Latin "vocare" meaning "to call"
"-vert"	from the Latin "vertere" meaning "to turn"

prefixes	origin and meaning
"con-"	from the Latin "com-" meaning "together" or "with"
"re-"	from the Latin "re-" meaning "back"
"in-"	from the Latin "in-" meaning "in"
"di-"	from the Latin "dis-" meaning "apart"
"sub-"	from the Latin "sub-" meaning "below"
"pro-"	from the Latin "pro-" meaning "front"
"e-"	from the Latin "ex-" meaning "out"

English words	Meaning

English Word Creation Practice

Classify each of the words beneath the table according to the process used to create the word.

Coumpounding
Borrowing
Blending
Acronyming

piano, waterbed, telecast, NOW, keychain, sunburn, zip (as in zip code), chunnel, robot, UNESCO, waste-basket, PIN, linguini, gasahol, handbook, infotainment, doorknob, pretzel

5

Morphophonology: Where Morphology Meets Phonology

Now that we've covered both phonology and morphology, we're prepared to look at the interaction of these two areas. Just as phonemes are not generally used in isolation, neither are morphemes. We'll see that when morphemes are used together, they often affect the way the neighboring morphemes sound. As with phonology, this interaction is very systematic. Because the study of such systems includes aspects of both morphology and phonology, it is often referred to as **morphophonology**. Our goals in this chapter will be the following:

- to understand the key concepts of morphophonology
- to learn the process of morphophonological analysis
- to familiarize ourselves with some rules of American English morphophonology

Key Concepts and Terms

Morphophonology, as the term suggests, is a combination of morphology (word structure) and phonology (sound systems). When morphemes are combined into multi-morphemic words, the sounds that represent the morphemes can change. Thus, the phonetic representation of a morpheme, its surface level form, can vary from one word to the next. Similarly, when two mono-morphemic words (one morpheme each) are spoken consecutively, the sounds that represent the two words can also change. If you understand phonology, morphophonology should be fairly easy for you. If you're still having trouble with phonology, make sure you solidify your understanding of it, or your understanding of morphophonology will suffer.

Relating some of the terms of morphophonology to phonology should help your understanding. As in phonology, in which we discovered that for each underlying phoneme there might be several different surface level allophones, we will see in morphophonology that an underlying **morpheme** can have multiple surface level **allomorphs**. That is, what we think of as a single unit (a single morpheme) can actually have more than one pronunciation (multiple allomorphs). This is what was meant by the "changes in phonetic representation" referred to above. We can use the following analogy, then, to begin our discussion of morphophonology:

phoneme : allophone = morpheme : allomorph

Morphophonological Analysis

The basic idea in this kind of analysis is to isolate the morpheme being investigated, determine how many different phonetic forms (allophones) it takes, and write a morphophonological rule that states what conditions the allomorphic variation. In this section, we will investigate two morphemes of English, one a root morpheme, and one an affix.

Root Allomorphy

In some cases, root morphemes have multiple allomorphs. This phenomenon is often called **root allomorphy**. We can observe root allomorphy by comparing a root morpheme both as it is pronounced alone and when used with affixes. The following data using the morpheme "hymn" (meaning a song of praise, usually religious) will help us illustrate an analysis of root allomorphy (note that accent marks indicate stressed vowels):

[hɪm]	hymn	[hɪ́mnədi]	hymnody	[ədi]	{suffix}	[əl]	{suffix}
[hɪ́mnəl]	hymnal	[hɪmnáləǰi]	hymnology	[aləǰi]	{suffix}		

Because we need to isolate the morpheme before we can analyze it, the first step is to separate all multi-morphemic words into their individual morphemes. If we compare the multi-morphemic words containing the morpheme "hymn" to the form of each of the suffixes that are attached to the root to form the multi-morphemic word, we can easily draw morpheme boundaries like the following:

[hɪmn/ədi] hymnody [hɪmn/aləǰi] hymnology [hɪmn/əl] hymnal

In these words, the morpheme "hymn" is composed of the following sounds: [hɪmn]. Notice, however, that in the first word in the data, which is the morpheme "hymn" without any affixes attached, the morpheme is composed of the sounds: [hɪm]. Because the morpheme has two phonetic realizations, we say that it has two allomorphs, and we represent them as follows (with the morpheme on the left and the allomorphs on the right):

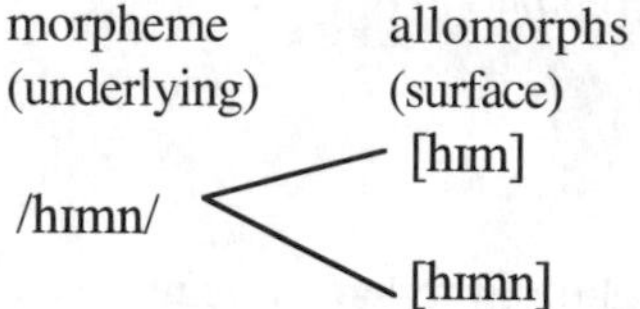

As we do with phonemes in a phonological analysis, we want to determine the basic form of the morpheme in a morphophonological analysis. We see here that /hɪmn/ is being presented as the basic form (note the slanted lines to indicate an underlying form). As in phonology, this is not an arbitrary choice. We need to consider which allomorph appears in the most environments. In some cases, this will be obvious. In others, however, the answer is not so obvious. In this data, for example, it appears that each allomorph appears in a single environment, [hɪm] with no sounds following, and [hɪmn] with a sound following. In cases such as this one, in which there is not an obvious choice, we need to consider each possibility. The two possibilities are presented below.

A) /hɪm/ → [hɪmn] when a sound follows (specifically a vowel)
B) /hɪmn/ → [hɪm] when no sound follows

If option (A) is correct, then there is some rule that leads native English speakers to insert an [n] at the end of the morpheme when there's a following sound. This, however, does not make much sense. This is because **rules of insertion** are used to separate two phonetically similar sounds, thus making them easier to distinguish (we'll see more of this type soon), but the /m/ of /hɪm/ and the vowels that follow it in the words that have the [hɪmn] allomorph, are not at all similar. Thus, there would be no need to separate them.

Option (B), on the other hand, makes much more sense. If it is correct, then there is some rule that leads native English speakers to delete the /n/ following /m/ when no sound follows it. Such **rules of deletion** make it easier to pronounce a word, often by reducing difficult clusters of consonants, as is the case in this data. Recall from Chapter 3 that certain clusters of consonants are not allowable according to the rules of English phonotactics. Specifically, in this case, English phonotactics do not allow [mn] clusters in the coda of a syllable (try to think of words that have this cluster of consonants in a coda and you'll see), so we unconsciously delete the second consonant in the cluster to make the word "hymn" fit the phonotactic constraints of English. Notice, however, that while we alter the pronunciation of the root when it is used alone, we do not alter its spelling. Root allomorphy like this often accounts for seemingly odd spellings such as silent consonant letters at the ends of roots.

Generally, though not always, the data you are asked to work with will provide you with clearer choices regarding the basic form of a morpheme. However, because we use mostly real language data, and real languages are immensely complex, some analyses are not as "clean" as others. Just be sure to consider every possibility, and try to make sense out of each by trying to apply each relevant rule type. The one that works best is the most accurate one.

Quick Exercise 5.1

Provide data (in the form of English words both spelled and transcribed at the surface level) that suggests the silent letters at the end of each of the following words aren't always so silent.

[dæm]	"damn"
[kəndɛm]	"condemn"
[krʌm]	"crumb"

Allomorphic Variation with Affixes

The allomorphy example above dealt with allomorphs of a free, root morpheme. Many morphophonological analyses focus on an affix, rather than a root. What follows is another example dealing with a prefix, specifically the morpheme "in-/im-" (a negating prefix):

[ɪŋkəmplit]	incomplete	[ɪmprabəbəl]	improbable	[kəmplit]	complete
[prabəbəl]	probable	[ɪnvɛriyəbəl]	invariable	[pasəbəl]	possible
[ɪmpasəbəl]	impossible	[ɪndəpɛndənt]	independent	[vɛriyəbəl]	variable
[ɪŋkamprəbəl]	incomparable	[kamprəbəl]	comparable	[əpropriyət]	appropriate
[dəpɛndənt]	dependent	[ɪnəpropriyət]	inappropriate		

The process is the same as before. Because we need to isolate the morpheme before we can analyze it, the first step is to separate all multi-morphemic words into their individual morphemes. If we compare the unprefixed form of each word to the prefixed form, we can easily draw morpheme boundaries like the following:

[kəmplit]	complete	[ɪŋ / kəmplit]	incomplete
[prabəbəl]	probable	[ɪm / prabəbəl]	improbable
[dəpɛndənt]	dependent	[ɪn / dəpɛndənt]	independent

In one of these words ("incomplete"), the prefix "in-/im-" is composed of the sounds [ɪŋ], in another ("improbable") it's composed of the sounds [ɪm], and in another ("independent") it's composed of the sounds [ɪn]. Because the morpheme has three phonetic realizations, we say that it has three allomorphs and represent them with the following graphic.

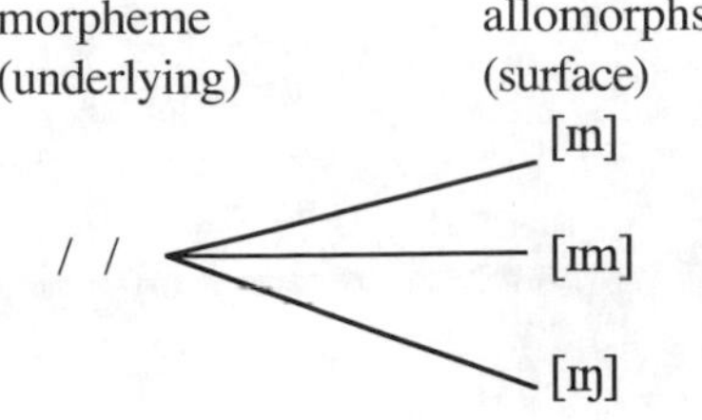

In this graphic representation of the three allomorphs, we have left the morpheme unnamed. An important part of the analysis, however, is determining the basic form of the morpheme. We know from our previous study of phonology and from earlier in this chapter that the basic form is the one that is used in the most environments. Based on the three words analyzed earlier, it's impossible to determine which allomorph is used in the most environments. All we can determine so far is that [ɪŋ] is used before a velar sound, [ɪm] is used before a bilabial sound, and [ɪn] is used before an alveolar sound.

If we analyze two other words from the original data set, however, we will find that the picture becomes clearer:

[vɛriyəbəl]	variable	[ɪn / vɛriyəbəl]	invariable
[əpropriyət]	appropriate	[ɪn / əpropriyət]	appropriate

Here we have [ɪn] being used before the labiodental sound [v] in one word ("invariable") and the vowel sound [ə] in another ("inappropriate"). Thus, we see two additional environments for the allomorph [ɪn]. Add these new environments to the one we discovered earlier, before alveolar sounds, and we see three distinct environments for this allomorph. For each of the other two allomorphs, however, there is just a single environment, the ones mentioned previously.

Based on this observation, we can determine that [ɪn] is the basic form of the three allomorphs, and we represent them all as follows (with the morpheme on the left and the allomorphs on the right):

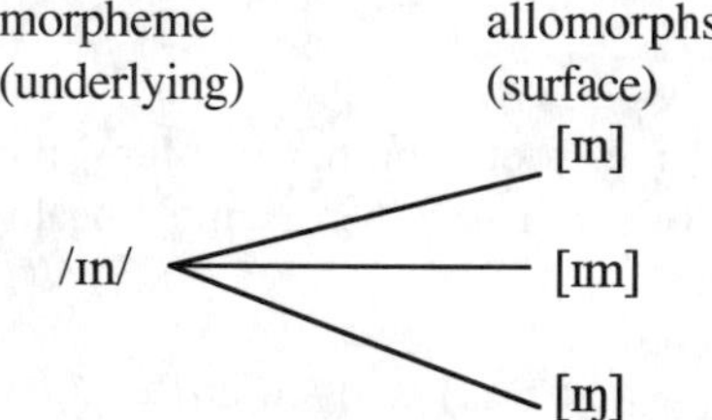

Here, unlike the previous example with "hymn," the choice for the basic form is immediately clear. As with the previous example, we know allomorphic variation is 100% systematic and rule governed and that there is something that leads a native speaker of English to use each of these three allomorphs in the appropriate environment. In this case, it is the following sound that determines which allomorph a speaker will use. Specifically, the consonant of the prefix assimilates to (becomes more like) the following sound. In each of the three examples given previously, the consonant of the prefix is identical to the following consonant in its place of articulation. Rules such as this one, in which neighboring sounds become more alike are called **rules of assimilation**. We can now state a rule that describes the phenomenon we observed in the data:

/ɪn/ → [ɪm] before bilabial consonants
/ɪn/ → [ɪŋ] before velar consonants

It is understood from such a rule that the basic form of morpheme does not change at the surface level in all other environments.

Quick Exercise 5.2
For each of the following *hypothetical* morphophonological rules in a language *unknown* to you (i.e. *not* English), determine which type of rule (assimilation, insertion or deletion) is being exhibited.

/ip/ → [ipə] before bilabial stops

/b/ → [p] after voiceless consonants

/tis/ → [ti] before alveolar fricatives

/v/ → [f] before voiceless consonants

/lɛv/ → [ɛv] after [l]

Morphophonological Analysis Resource

Analyzing morphophonological data involves the same type of analysis that we learned in the phonology chapter and combines it with elements of the kinds of morphological analyses we learned in the morphology chapter. If you understand each of these types of analysis, you should be able to perform a morphophonological analysis. Again, beginning with the *goals* will help:

A) Determine the number of phonetic forms (allomorphs) a morpheme can take.
B) Describe the rule(s) that condition the allomorphic variation—when is each allomorph used?

Next, follow these steps to help keep yourself on the right track:

1. Break all the words down into their individual morphemes, looking specifically for the morpheme(s) the problem asks you to focus on. You can do this by drawing lines between morphemes.
2. Write down all the forms that this morpheme takes (these are the *allomorphs*).
3. Determine the *environments* in which each allomorph appears. This may require generalizing to natural classes.
4. The allomorph that appears in the most environments (not necessarily the one that appears the highest number of times in the data) is the *basic form* of the morpheme (this is then the name of the morpheme).
5. Determine what phonological process(es) (rule types) determine(s) which allomorph is used.
6. Then state the rule(s) that explain(s) when the basic form changes to become an allomorph that is different from the basic form.

Common Types of Morphophonological Rules:

Assimilation: a morpheme becomes like a neighboring sound
- this makes it easier to pronounce a word (ease of articulation)

Insertion: a sound is inserted between two morphemes
- this makes it easier to pronounce a word (ease of articulation)
- this makes it easier to hear every sound in a word (ease of perception)

Deletion: a sound is deleted from a morpheme
- this makes it easier to pronounce a word (ease of articulation)

Hint: If the morpheme and its allomorphs have the same *number* of sounds, then you must have a rule of assimilation. If, however, the morpheme and its allomorphs have a different *number* of sounds, then you must have a rule of insertion or deletion. It's also possible to have a combination of these possibilities if there are more than two allomorphs.

These steps were modeled earlier in this section on morphophonological analysis and will be modeled again in the next section on rules of English morphophonology. If this kind of analysis isn't completely clear to you yet, pay attention to how it's modeled in the next section.

Some Rules of English Morphophonology

As in our study of phonology, our goals in this chapter can be viewed at several levels. First, and most generally, it's important to practice thinking as a linguist does in order to develop the analytical skills that will be required in a classroom setting. At a more specific level, we need to begin to identify morphophonological patterns that recur in the production of language. At an even more specific level, we need to familiarize ourselves with some of the more common rules of English that will be an important part of the language arts curriculum. To achieve all of these goals, it makes sense to perform analyses of data that will lead to a description of some rules of English morphophonology. Specifically, we will analyze data that illustrate two rules of inflectional morphophonology in English—the past tense and the plural suffixes.

The Past Tense in English

Most native English speakers learn fairly early on in their elementary school career that there is a rule for making an English verb past tense. This rule states that English verbs are made past tense by adding "-ed." As we have already seen, however, the language rules we learn in elementary school do not give an accurate picture of the reality of language. Through an analysis of the following data, we will evaluate this rule for accuracy and completeness and revise it as necessary.

1.	[rab]	rob	[sim]	seem	[briz]	breeze
2.	[rabd]	robbed	[simd]	seemed	[brizd]	breezed
3.	[θa] or [θɔ]	thaw	[plaw]	plow	[bre]	bray
4.	[θad] or [θɔd]	thawed	[plawd]	plowed	[bred]	brayed
5.	[hæk]	hack	[res]	race	[blʌš]	blush
6.	[hækt]	hacked	[rest]	raced	[blʌšt]	blushed
7.	[blɛnd]	blend	[fæst]	fast	[bust]	boost
8.	[blɛndəd]	blended	[fæstəd]	fasted	[bustəd]	boosted

A good place to begin in any morphophonological analysis is to isolate the morphemes; that is, for past tense verbs, draw a boundary between the root verb and the past tense suffix by comparing the inflected form (past tense) with the uninflected form (present tense). For example, by comparing the forms in rows 1 and 2 above, we can isolate the morphemes in row two as follows:

Row 2. [rab/d] robbed [sim/d] seemed [briz/d] breezed

What we see, then, is that with some verbs, when we want to make them past tense, we add a [d]. Already, our elementary school rule is called into question.

Continuing with this strategy, we can isolate the morphemes in row 4:

Row 4. [θa/d] or [θɔ/d] thawed [plaw/d] plowed [bre/d] brayed

Again, the data indicates that, contrary to the rule we learned, English verbs seem to be made past tense by adding a [d]. We need to look further, however, to see if the rest of the data presents the same surface level form for the past tense morpheme. When we isolate the morphemes in row 6, it yields the following:

Row 6. [hæk/t] hacked [res/t] raced [blʌš/t] blushed

Now we see that some English verbs are made past tense by adding a [t]. Our original rule seems even less accurate now. Before we attempt to describe a rule of our own, however, we need to consider the past tense verbs in row 8 and compare them to their uninflected forms. Isolating their morphemes results in the following:

Row 8. [blɛnd/əd] blended [fæst/əd] fasted [bust/əd] boosted

In this row, all of our past tense forms consist of two syllables. Their corresponding present tense forms in row 7, however, consist of only a single syllable. Thus, we know we added a syllable and, therefore, a vowel when we added the past tense morpheme. Because the syllable we have added is unstressed, we represent its vowel as schwa [ə]. We still hear the [d] at the end of the word, though, so what we've done is to add both a vowel and a consonant to create the past tense. The words in row 8, then, make it clear that with some English verbs, we add [əd] to make them past tense.

We can now represent our preliminary findings graphically:

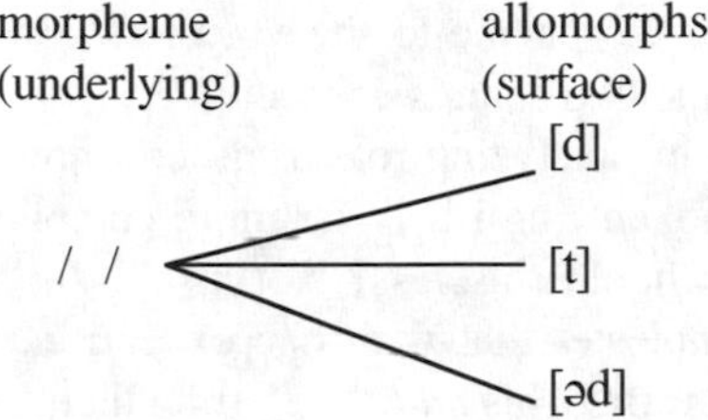

As we know from our study of phonology, when we have variation at the surface level, there is some systematic rule that leads us to produce each of the surface forms, and this rule is based on the environment in which we use the morpheme. The only relevant aspect of environment in this analysis is the preceding sound. We can conclude this because we are analyzing an inflectional *suffix*, and it must, therefore, be used *after* a root with no sounds following it. The data reveals the following sounds preceding each allomorph:

b, m, z, a, aw, e [d]
k, s, š [t]
d, t [əd]

As before, rather than stating our rule in terms of the individual sounds that precede each allomorph, we want to try to identify natural classes for each environment. The [d] and [t] preceding the [əd] allomorph share the features *alveolar* and *stop*, which makes them the natural class of alveolar stops. The [k], [s] and [š] preceding the [t] allomorph all share only one feature, namely *voicelessness*, so we can hypothesize that they represent part of the natural class of voiceless consonants. The sounds before the [d] allomorph, however, do not share any feature; some are vowels and some are consonants. If we separate the vowels from the consonants, however, we can identify two natural classes—the natural class of voiced consonants *and* the natural class of vowels. We can now express the environments of each allomorph in terms of natural classes:

b, m, z, a, aw, e [d] used after *voiced consonants* and *vowels* (two environments)
k, s, š [t] used after *voiceless consonants* (one environment)
d, t [əd] used after *alveolar stops* (one environment)

These natural classes lead us to our selection of *one* of the allomorphs as the basic (underlying) form. Because one of the allomorphs—[d] —[is used in two different environments, while each of the other allomorphs is used in only one environment, we can conclude that the basic form is [d]. We can now fill in the space in our earlier graphic of the levels of representation of the past tense morpheme by naming that morpheme /d/. The natural classes we identified also allow us to state our rule more succinctly. The new graphic and succinctly stated rule follow.

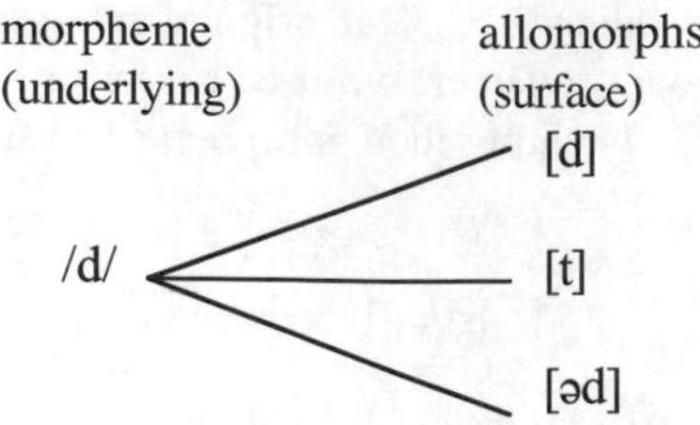

/d/ → [əd] after alveolar stops {rule of insertion}
/d/ → [t] after voiceless consonants (except /t/) {rule of assimilation}

This is the past tense rule in English. Notice that when the present tense form of a verb ends in an alveolar stop, we separate this alveolar stop from the alveolar stop in the past tense morpheme by *inserting* the vowel schwa [ə]. This makes it easier to hear both alveolar stops distinctly. When the present tense form of a verb ends in a voiceless consonant, we assimilate the morpheme to the voiceless consonant by removing the voicing. This makes it easier for us to pronounce the two sounds consecutively.

Having described a rule for making English verbs past tense by analyzing real data, let's now return to the rule we learned in elementary school. Clearly, the rule in spoken English is far more complicated than adding "-ed." Does this mean, then, that the rule we learned in school is useless? Not at all. As a spelling rule, it actually works quite well. A quick look at the data set indicates that with one exception, all of the past tense verbs are *spelled* by adding "-ed" to the present tense form. This *add "-ed"* rule, then, as long as it's presented as a spelling rule, and *not* a pronunciation rule, can be very useful.

One final point that needs to be made is that the morphophonological rule we described applies only to *regular* verbs in English. As we saw in the previous chapter, some words are irregular in their inflectional morphology. The verb "feed," for example, does not follow the rule we described because it is irregular. Instead of adding a suffix to make it past tense, we change the vowel. Table 5.1 contrasts the inflection of two phonetically similar verbs, one of which is regular and the other irregular.

	regular	irregular
spelling	"seed"	"feed"
present tense	[sid]	[fid]
past tense	[sidəd]	[fɛd]

Table 5.1: Regular and Irregular Verbs

Quick Exercise 5.3

For each word below, complete the surface level transcription by adding the allomorph that belongs in that environment.

[koč] coached   [fray] fried   [wɚd] worded   [ro] rowed

[kod] coded   [slæp] slapped   [hɛlp] helped   [praym] primed

The Plural in English

For our next rule of inflectional morphophonology in English, we begin once again with a rule that we probably learned in elementary school. Most American school children learn that the rule for making an English noun plural is to add "-s" or sometimes "-es." Again, we need to perform an analysis of real English data before we can accurately evaluate this rule. The following data will lead to the description of our rule.

1. [ræk]	rack	[not]	note	[blʌf]	bluff
2. [ræks]	racks	[nots]	notes	[blʌfs]	bluffs
3. [ræg]	rag	[nod]	node	[bɪn]	bin
4. [rægz]	rags	[nodz]	nodes	[bɪnz]	bins
5. [sa] or [sɔ]	saw	[bi]	bee	[plaw]	plow
6. [saz] or [sɔz]	saws	[biz]	bees	[plawz]	plows
7. [mæč]	match	[bʌs]	bus	[blez]	blaze
8. [mæčəz]	matches	[bʌsəz]	buses	[blezəz]	blazes

As we did with our past tense data, we will begin here by isolating the roots from the suffix row by row.

2. [ræk/s] racks [not/s] notes [blʌf/s] bluffs

Based on this row of data, our rule looks good. We see that each of these nouns is made plural by adding [s] to the singular form of the noun. Before declaring our rule accurate, however, we need to consider all the data in our set.

4. [ræg/z] rags [nod/z] nodes [bɪn/z] bins

6. [sa/z] or [sɔ/z] saws [bi/z] bees [plaw/z] plows

Here in rows 4 and 6 we see that some nouns are made plural by adding a [z] to the singular form. Now our elementary school rule doesn't seem so good. Before we can describe a more accurate rule, however, we need to finish looking at all the data.

8. [mæč/əz] matches [bʌs/əz] buses [blez/əz] blazes

This row of data indicates that to some words we add [əz] to form the plural, and this third surface level form makes the initial rule seem even more incomplete.

We can now represent our preliminary findings graphically:

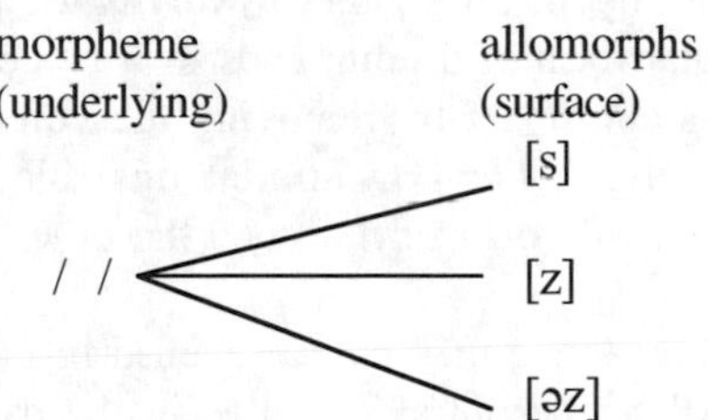

The next step, as before, is to identify the environment of each allomorph. We do this simply by listing all the sounds that precede each allomorph.

k, t, f	[s]
g, d, n, a, i, aw	[z]
č, s, z	[əz]

Now we're ready to start identifying natural classes in our environments. We see that the [k], [t] and [f] before the [s] allomorph all share the feature of voicelessness. The [č], [s] and [z] before the [əz] allomorph, however, do not seem to share any single feature that we've studied up to this point. The reason for this is that so far we have been identifying natural classes of sounds based on *articulatory* features, such as frontness for vowels and voicing for consonants. Articulatory features refer to how a sound is produced. The natural class we're identifying now is different in that it is based on an *acoustic* feature. Acoustic features refer to how a sound sounds; thus, how they are *perceived* is what's relevant, rather than how they are *pro-*

duced. The acoustic feature that they share is a hissing sound. Other consonants that share this hissing quality are [ǰ], [š] and [ž]. All six of these sounds comprise the natural class of **sibilants**.

Con tinuing with the analysis, when we try to identify a natural class for the sounds that precede the [z] allomorph, we have less success. If we separate the six sounds into two separate sets, however, it becomes possible to identify two natural classes. Specifically, the [g], [d] and [n] are all voiced consonants, and the [a], [i] and [aw] are all vowels. We can now express the environment of each allomorph using natural classes:

k, t, f	[s] used after *voiceless consonants* (one environment)
g, d, n, a, i, aw	[z] used after *voiced consonants* and *vowels* (two environments)
č, s, z	[əz] used after *sibilants* (one environment)

With our natural classes identified, we are prepared to determine the basic form of the morpheme. Because the [z] allomorph is used in two different environments, while the [s] and [əz] allomorphs are used in only one each, we conclude that [z] is the basic form. Our picture begins to become even clearer:

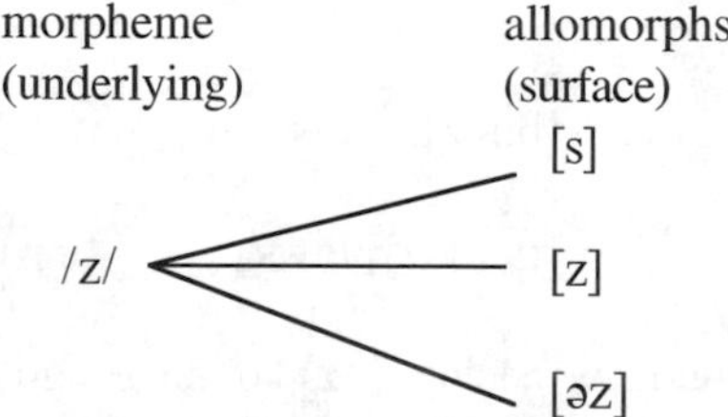

Now we can write the rule that predicts the allomorph of the plural morpheme that a native speaker of English will use in any plural noun:

/z/ → [əz] after sibilants {rule of insertion}
/z/ → [s] after voiceless consonants (except sibilants) {rule of assimilation}

This is the plural rule in English. Notice that when the singular form of a noun ends in a sibilant, we separate this sibilant from the sibilant in the plural morpheme by inserting the vowel schwa [ə]. This makes it easier to hear both sibilants distinctly. When the singular form of a noun ends in a voiceless consonant, we assimilate the morpheme to the preceding voiceless consonant by removing the voicing. This makes it easier for us to pronounce the two sounds consecutively. Notice how similar this rule is to the past tense rule. Each rule consists of two parts, one of which is a rule of insertion, and the other a rule of assimilation.

As we did after describing the past tense rule, we should reexamine the rule we learned in elementary school. Again, we see that as a spelling rule, it works well. All of the plural spellings in the data are, in fact, created by adding an "-s" or "-es" spelling. As a pronunciation rule, however, it, like the past tense spelling rule, falls far short of being accurate.

Another similarity between this rule and the past tense rule is that it applies only to regular nouns. Table 5.2 illustrates the difference between a regular and an irregular noun.

	regular	irregular
spelling	"house"	"mouse"
singular	[haws]	[maws]
plural	[hawsəz]	[mays]

Table 5.2: Regular and Irregular Nouns

Quick Exercise 5.4
For each word below, complete the surface level transcription by adding the allomorph that belongs in that environment.

[koč] coaches	[fray] fries	[wɚd] words	[ro] rows
[kod] codes	[mæp] maps	[wɛlt] welts	[daym] dimes

Relevance at Three Levels

Before we move on, it would be wise to reflect upon what we've done and see its significance at three different levels. First, and most generally, we have studied a way of thinking about language, a new kind of analysis. As has been noted before, to deal effectively with linguistic issues in a classroom setting, educators need to be aware of the linguistic production around them in a very conscious way. After making keen observations, the instructor's task is then to analyze the data and identify the process or phenomenon at work. Participating in analyses like the ones presented here is an important step towards acquiring the skills necessary to work with linguistically diverse student populations.

At a more specific level, we have seen some of the common processes that can change the form of an underlying morpheme when it's used on the surface level. Rules of assimilation, insertion and deletion are common in languages throughout the world, so by familiarizing ourselves with these processes, we have gained a certain amount of insight into the linguistic competency of any person, not just an English speaker.

At the most specific level, we have learned in detail two very common rules of inflectional morphophonology in English—the past tense and the plural. These are rules that all English language learners must face early in their quest to master the language, and their task is much more manageable if they have an instructor who understands them well. Thus, while having the skills to tackle any situation that might arise is of primary importance, a certain amount of specific knowledge is certainly useful.

Spelling and Morphophonology in English

The final point that needs to be made in this chapter regards spelling. As we noted in the phonetics chapter, English spelling is not very phonetic; that is, we cannot necessarily predict how a word is spelled based on its sounds, nor can we predict exactly how a word is pronounced by looking at its spelling. In the phonology chapter, however, we noted that English spelling is, to a great extent, phonemic, with a single symbol used for a single underlying phoneme. Recall that all words pronounced with an allophone of the phoneme /t/ are spelled with the letter "t." Using the same letter "t" to represent the aspirated /t/ in "top," the regular /t/ in "stop" and the alveolar flap in "hitter" makes sense because even though these sounds are different on the surface, they're allophones of the same phoneme and, therefore, the same in our minds.

We see the same kind of underlying spelling system at work with the past tense in English. Regardless of whether the allomorph used in a past tense is [d], [t] or [əd], the spelling is always the same—"-ed." Again, this agrees with the psychological reality in our minds. If we unconsciously view all of these allomorphs as being the same morpheme, it makes sense to spell them all the same way. The only exception to this rule is a word that already ends in the letter "e." With such words we do not need to repeat the letter "e" when we add the past tense morpheme in writing. This corollary to the *add "-ed"* rule can easily be taught and learned.

Unfortunately, the spelling of the plural morpheme is a little more difficult to explain. Clearly it's not accurate at the *surface* level because we add a letter "s" in writing to both "seat" and "seed," even though the first requires the [s] allomorph while the second requires the [z] allomorph. However, it is not accurate at the *underlying* level either, as is evidenced by the fact that the spelling changes to "-es" when the [əz] allomorph is used. Here, we account for the additional spoken syllable by using an additional vowel letter. Because this spelling rule isn't true to either the underlying or surface levels, it might present more problems in literacy instruction than the past tense rule.

What we've presented here is, of course, just a small part of the English spelling picture. A more thorough treatment would be advisable for those planning on teaching literacy. However, between these examples and the "silent" letter examples discussed earlier, you should at least have an increased awareness of the system of spelling in English.

Summary

In this chapter we explored the interface between morphology and phonology. We saw that morphemes, like phonemes, can be analyzed at two different levels of representation—the underlying level and the surface level. While we have just the idea of the single underlying morpheme in our head, that morpheme can take multiple surface level forms, or allomorphs, depending on the environment in which we use the morpheme. When there is variation at the surface level, it is *always* 100% systematic; that is, there is a rule that leads us unconsciously to produce each allomorph in a specific environment. We approached these rules on three levels by 1) modeling the kind of analysis that leads us to a description of such rules, 2) identifying some common rule types, or processes, that languages exhibit and 3) describing two specific rules for English. As we have done before, we've addressed the relevance of the material in an educational setting.

Exercises

English Morphophonology Practice

Using your knowledge of two of the English morphophonological rules discussed in this chapter (the plural morpheme, and past tense morpheme), transcribe the following English words at *both* the underlying level (morphemic) and the surface level (allomorphic). This means that, as with the English phonology practice exercise at the end of Chapter 3, you will write *two* transcriptions for each word—both an underlying transcription and a surface one. Also, when the underlying and surface forms are different, write the type of rule (e.g, assimilation, insertion) that led to the change. Focus mainly on the past or plural morpheme; that is, you should feel free to practice the phonological rules we studied earlier, but it's not a requirement in this exercise. Use the first two as examples.

"hooks" /hʊkz/ → [hʊks] rule type: assimilation	"raided" /redd/ → [redəd] rule type: insertion
1. tutors rule type:	11. slipped rule type:
2. packets rule type:	12. prayed rule type:
3. classes rule type:	13. passed rule type:
4. tests rule type:	14. weakened rule type:
5. quizzes rule type:	15. seated rule type:
6. grades rule type:	16. clapped rule type:
7. majors rule type:	17. snorted rule type:
8. papers rule type:	18. fumed rule type:
9. speeches rule type:	19. forced rule type:
10. spots rule type:	20. pretended rule type:

English Morphophonology Problems

Negative Prefix in English (“un-”)

The following data contains English words with “un-“ and the roots/stems of the words.

[əŋk^{h}ʌmftɚbəl]	uncomfortable	[əmbəlivəbəl]	unbelievable
[plɛzənt]	pleasant	[əsumɪŋ]	assuming
[ənfæšənəbəl]	unfashionable	[ənɪntɛləǰənt]	unintelligent
[ənəsumɪŋ]	unassuming	[ənsʌŋ]	unsung
[bəlivəbəl]	believable	[fæšənəbəl]	fashionable
[əmplɛzənt]	unpleasant	[əŋgrešəs]	ungracious
[ɪnt^{h}ɛləǰənt]	intelligent	[næčərəl]	natural
[ənæčərəl]	unnatural	[k^{h}ʌmftɚbəl]	comfortable
[sʌŋ]	sung	[grešəs]	gracious

1. How many allomorphs of the negative morpheme are there? List them.

2. Describe the environment in which each allomorph appears. Which is the basic form?

3. Write the rule(s) that determines which allomorph of this morpheme is used. What type of rule(s) is/are this?

4. Based on your analysis of the data, which of the following words is/are phonologically possible in English?

[əmsɚtən] derived from the root [sɚtən]
[ənfæðəməbəl] derived from the root [fæðəməbəl]
[ənpælətəbəl] derived from the root [pælətəbəl]
[əŋgarnɪšt] derived from the root [garnɪšt]
[əmæpətayzɪŋ] derived from the root [æpətayzɪŋ]

The Out-Meaning Prefix in English ("ex-")

The following data contains English words with "ex-" and the roots/stems of the words.

[ɛksprɛs]	express	[poz]	pose
[æsərbet]	acerbate	[ɛgzækt]	exact
[ɛksayt]	excite	[sid]	cede
[prɛs]	press	[ɛkskəmyunəket]	excommunicate
[ɛmplɚi]	emplary	[tɚmənet]	exterminate
[ɛksid]	exceed	[sayt]	cite
[kəmyunəket]	communicate	[ɛkspoz]	expose
[ɛgzæsərbet]	exacerbate	[ækt]	act
[ɛgzɛmplɚi]	exemplary	[ɛkstɚmənet]	exterminate

1. How many allomorphs are there? List them?

2. Describe the environment in which each allomorph appears. Which is the basic form?

3. Write the rule(s) that determines which allomorph this morpheme is used. What type of rule(s) is/are this?

4. Based on your analysis of the data, which of the following words is/are phonologically possible in English?

[ɛgzæmən] derived from the root [æmən]
[ɛgzpɛl] derived from the root [pɛl]
[ɛkstɛnd] derived from the root [tɛnd]
[ɛkssayz] derived from the root [sayz]
[ɛgzfoliyet] derived from the root [foliyet]

The Morpheme "bomb" in English

The following data contains words with bomb as their root and some affixes that can be added to the root. Accents have been included to indicate stress.

[bam]	bomb	[bambədír]	bombardier	[bámɪŋ]	bombing
[bamd]	bombed	[bambǽstək]	bombastic	[bambárd]	bombard
[ǽstək]	adj suffix	[ədír]	noun suffix	[ɪŋ]	pres part suffix
[bamz]	bombs	[bámɚ]	bomber	[ɚ]	noun suffix
[ard]	verb suffix	[z]	{plural}	[d]	{past tense}

1. How many allomorphs are there of the morpheme "bomb" in English?

2. Describe the environment in which each allomorph appears.

3. Describe the possibilities for the rule(s) that determines which allomorph this morpheme is used. What type of rule(s) is/are this/these?

   A)

   B)

4. Which of these possibilities do you think is more accurate? Why?

Additional English Morphophonology Problem

Up to this point, we have been looking at individual words in isolation in our study of phonology and morphonology. In fact, however, when we speak, we rarely pronounce individual words in isolation. Instead, we generally pronounce strings of words together with no breaks. The result of this is that sound can affect each other across word boundaries. The next data set illustrates that phonological processes are at work across word boundaries.

The Indefinite Article in English

[əmæn]	a man	[ənæpəl]	an apple	[mæn]	man
[əwʊmən]	a woman	[əgɚl]	a girl	[æpəl]	apple
[ək^{h}læs]	a class	[ənopənɚ]	an opener	[yæk]	yak
[ənəmbrɛlə]	an umbrella	[ənævəlænč]	an avalanche	[opənɚ]	opener
[ənəvɛnt]	an event	[əyæk]	a yak	[k^{h}læs]	class
[wʊmən]	woman	[gɚl]	girl	[əvɛnt]	event
[əmbrɛlə]	umbrella	[ævəlænč]	avalanche	[ay]	eye
[ənay]	an eye				

1. How many allomorphs are there of the indefinite article in English?

2. Describe the environment in which each allomorph appears.

3. Write the possible rule(s) that determine(s) which allomorph of this morpheme is used. What type of rule(s) is/are this?

4. Based on your analysis of the data, which of the following combinations of words is/are phonologically possible in English?

   [əəgzæmpəl] from [əgzæmpəl]   [əpɚsən] from [pɚsən]

   [ənčɛr] from [čɛr]   [ənpɛg] from [pɛg]   [əful] from [ful]

Addtional Morphophonology Problems

Egaugnal

1. [kuftin]	run	9. [ɛsčɔm]	succeed
2. [ugdogin]	will impeach	10. [ugəkuftin]	will run
3. [šačmo]	arrest	11. [ugɛsčɔm]	will succeed
4. [dogin]	impeach	12. [tašmili]	confide
5. [uktašmili]	will confide	13. [ŋaŋ]	solicit
6. [ugəginǰi]	will faint	14. [ginǰi]	faint
7. [ugəŋaŋ]	will solicit	15. [ukšačmo]	will arrest
8. [umu]	harass	16. [ugumu]	will harass

1. How many allomorphs are there of the future tense morpheme in Eguagnal?

2. Describe the environment in which each allomorph appears.

3. State the rule(s) that determines which allomorph of the future morpheme is used.

4. What type(s) of rule is applied to this morpheme to change its surface form?

5. Based on this data, which of the following transcriptions of future tense verbs could be accurate in Egaugnal?

[ugədini] from [dini]	[ukǰamin] from [ǰamin]
[ugonon] from [onon]	[ukfimin] from [fimin]

Luiseño (a southern California Native American language)

[Adapted from Department of Linguistics (1994), p. 154]

1. [pewum]	wife	7. [kamayum]	sons
2. [ki]	house	8. [tana]	blanket
3. [tanam]	blankets	9. [kapim]	pipes
4. [pewumum]	wives	10. [tukwutum]	mountain lions
5. [kamay]	son	11. [kapi]	pipe
6. [tukwut]	mountain lion	12. [kim]	houses

1. How many allomorphs are there of the plural morpheme in Luisen)o?

2. Describe the environment in which each allomorph appears.

3. State the rule(s) that determines which allomorph of the plural morpheme is used.

4. What type(s) of rule is applied to this morpheme to change its surface form?

5. Based on this data, which of the following transcriptions of plural nouns could be accurate in Luiseno?

[tunaym] from [tunay]   [papum] from [papu]
[fiwanum] from [fiwan]   [timaum] from [tima]

Egaugnal:

[zumi]	flash	[pʊspos]	fight	[pʊsposk]	fights
[faysufk]	offenses	[faysuf]	offense	[mækəg]	homes
[ayɔduvg]	pills	[ayɔduv]	pill	[zumig]	flashes
[pragəg]	piles	[hamaŋg]	overdoses	[minap]	bottle
[hamaŋ]	overdose	[šomug]	illnesses	[minapk]	bottles
[šomu]	illness	[prag]	pile	[mæk]	home

1. What are the allomorphs of the plural morpheme in Egaugnal?

2. What is the environment of each allomorph?

3. Which is the **basic form** of the plural morpheme?

4. State the rule(s) that is/are applied to the morpheme to arrive at each surface level allomorph.

5. What **type**(s) of rule is applied to this morpheme to change its surface form?

6. Based on this data, which of the following transcriptions of plural nouns could be accurate in Egaugnal?

[maŋəg] from [maŋ] [sæmagk] from [sæmag]
[minag] from [mina] [pivivg] from [piviv]

<u>Turkish</u> (very difficult):

[ɛlma]	apple	[ɛtlɛr]	meats	[ɪplɛr]	ropes	[ɛlmalar]	apples
[ɪp]	rope	[kəzlar]	girls	[sɔplar]	clans	[adamlar]	men
[kəz]	girl	[ɛt]	meat	[adam]	man	[kɔyʊnlar]	sheep (plural)
[kɔyʊn]	sheep	[sɔp]	clan				

1. What are the allomorphs of the <u>plural</u> morpheme in Turkish?

2. What is the environment of each allomorph?

3. Which is the **basic form** of the plural morpheme?

4. State the rule(s) that is/are applied to the morpheme to arrive at each surface level allomorph.

5. What **<u>type</u>**(s) of rule is applied to this morpheme to change its surface form?

6. Based on this data, which of the following transcriptions of plural nouns could be accurate in Turkish?

[kɪtaplar] from [kɪtap]

[bɪralɛr] from [bira]

[dɔnlɛr] from [dɔn]

[ɔsʊrʊklɛr] from [ɔsʊrʊk]

6

Syntax: English Phrase and Sentence Structure

Having studied the sounds and words of language, we are now ready to move on to a larger unit—the sentence. We will add to what we know about word classes and study the structure of phrases, clauses and sentences. Here, we will return to the notion of grammaticality that we discussed briefly in Chapter One. Our goals in this chapter will be as follows:

- to learn some of the more common terminology of grammar
- to identify various phrase and sentence types
- to draw diagrams to represent the structure of these phrases and sentences
- to be able to explain the grammaticality or ungrammaticality of sentences in English

We began our study of the structure of English by focusing on the smallest units of language—sounds. Then we moved on to a larger unit—words. Now we are going to look at an even larger unit—sentences. The study of sentences and sentence structure is called **syntax**. Because sentences are made up of smaller units coming together, we will need to spend some time addressing those smaller units, including words, phrases and clauses, in our study of syntax.

More Word Classes

Recall that in Chapter 4 we defined word classes in terms of their function and their form. By function we meant the type of "meaning" each word class represented. In terms of form, we focused mainly on the inflections the word classes could take. What we discovered, however, was that while our function and form definitions were useful, they weren't complete. A noun like "information," for example, doesn't fit the form definition of a noun perfectly because it can't be inflected for number. Similarly, an adjective like "unpleasant" does not fit the form definition of an adjective perfectly because it cannot be inflected for comparison. However, these observations don't mean that our function and form definitions are worthless. Rather than toss out everything we've already observed about word classes, we need to *add* a new component to our word class definitions. We'll refer to this new component as the **co-occurrence** features of word classes. Co-occurrence refers to the other kinds of words a given type of word can occur together with. What we'll see is that with this new component, we can justify placing words like "unpleasant" and "happy" together in the same category, even though they don't fit the same form definition.

Also, because our focus now is on sentence structure and grammaticality, our functional definitions for each word class will need to be more grammatical, and less meaning based.

We'll begin by adding several new classes to the list we covered in Chapter 4 before revisiting those familiar word classes. All of the new classes are minor/closed classes to which new members cannot be added. You'll notice that there is nothing we can say about these closed classes in terms of their form. This is because, with the exception of pronouns, no minor classes in English can be inflected to indicate any meaning.

Determiners (Examples: a, the, this, my)

The first new class to add to our list is called **determiners**. Determiners, as the name suggests are used functionally to "determine" a noun. By this, we mean that determiners allow us to make clear *which* noun we're talking about. Often this is in terms of the noun's specificity. Examples such as (1) and (2) illustrate this function:

```
    det N          det  N            det  N
(1) A student in my class visited the Pentagon.
```

(1) <u>A</u> student in <u>my</u> class visited <u>the</u> Pentagon.

```
     det adj    N
(2) This short example illustrates determiner usage.
```

(2) <u>This</u> short example illustrates determiner usage.

Each use of a determiner tells us something about the noun it precedes. Notice that "my" and "the" in (1) identify very specific nouns, whereas "a" does not identify a definite or specific entity in the world. Because of their different function, "a" and "the" are called indefinite and definite, respectively. These words also belong to a subcategory within determiners called **articles**. Thus, "a' is often referred to as the indefinite article and "the" the definite article. Other subcategories within determiners are **demonstratives**, such as "this" and "that," and **pronominal determiners**, such as "my" and "your." This last term indicates that these words are derived from pronouns.

The function of determiners suggests their co-occurrence features; that is, if determiners tell us something about nouns, we might expect to see them being used with nouns. This intuition is confirmed by the data. Notice that each of the determiners used is followed by a noun, either immediately, as in the uses in (1), or shortly thereafter, as in (2).

We can define determiners then as words that "determine" nouns and occur before nouns.

Quantifiers (Examples: one, two, many, few)

The next class, **quantifiers**, is very similar to determiners. This similarity is illustrated by (3) and (4).

```
     Q   N              Q   N
(3) Two hearts can beat as one heart, according to a popular song.
```

(3) <u>Two</u> hearts can beat as <u>one</u> heart, according to a popular song.

```
   det Q  adj       N                  det Q    N
(4) A few helpful examples can illustrate the many uses of quantifiers.
```

(4) A <u>few</u> helpful examples can illustrate the <u>many</u> uses of quantifiers.

In each case, the underlined quantifier tells us something about the quantity or amount of a following noun. We can say, then, that quantifiers quantify nouns. Predictably, they occur together with nouns, either immediately or shortly before them, just as determiners do. Because quantifiers and determiners seem so similar, one might wonder why they aren't lumped together in the same category. A closer look at (4), however, indicates an important difference between them. In this example we see quantifiers being used with preceding determiners. As the ungrammatical sentence in (5) indicates, this is not a feature that determiners share (note that an asterisk preceding an example indicates that the example is ungrammatical).

```
     det det                               det det
(5) * A the helpful examples can illustrate the these uses of quantifiers
```

(5) * A <u>the</u> helpful examples can illustrate the <u>these</u> uses of quantifiers

Prepositions (Examples: in, on, with, by)

Prepositions are a difficult class to define. Students often learn that they are words that indicate location or direction. To a certain extent this is true. In (6), for example, the prepositions tell us about the location of some information and a book.

```
                       P det N   P det N
(6) The information is in the book on the table.
```

(6) The information is <u>in</u> the book <u>on</u> the table.

We see in (7), however, that prepositions do not always have a locational or directional meaning. Neither of the prepositions in this example has a physical meaning at all.

P det N P N
(7) I'm thrilled with the book by Nabokov.

If we look for a more syntactic function of prepositions we might find something more useful to add to our definition. Note that in all the uses, the prepositions indicate some relationship between a noun and some other element in the sentence. In (6), "in" relates "book" to the information it contains, and "on" relates "table" to the book located there. In (7), "with" relates "book" to the feeling of thrill that it evokes, and "by" relates Nabokov to the book he authored. As with the two previous classes, because prepositions work with nouns, we expect to see them used with nouns, and again the data confirms our suspicions. In each case, the prepositions are followed immediately or closely by a noun.

Quick Exercise 6.1
So far we've looked at three closed word classes that can be described by their occurrence before nouns—determiners, quantifiers and prepositions. Because they're so similar, functionally, we need some co-occurrence feature to distinguish them from each other. To do this, try filling in the blanks in each of the sentences below with a word from one of these classes (determiner, quantifier and preposition).

1. The president drank beer __________ __________ __________ daughters.

2. The sultan conversed __________ __________ __________ wives.

In what order did you use the three types of words?

Auxiliaries (Examples: might, should, will, be, have)

The next category is probably better known by its common name as "helping verbs." The more technical term, **auxiliary verb**, or just auxiliary, also implies a helping function. We can say, then, that auxiliaries help, or add "meaning" to, verbs. As we've seen before, however, we have to define "meaning" rather loosely, because different auxiliaries add very different kinds of meaning. Consider the range of meanings in (8) through (10).

aux V aux V
(8) You might teach word classes someday, so you should know them well.

aux V
(9) The sun will come up tomorrow (bet your bottom dollar on it).

aux V aux aux V
(10) We are enjoying linguistics because we have been studying word classes.

In (8), "might" adds a meaning of *possibility* to the verb "teach," and "should" adds a meaning of *advisability* to the verb "know." In (9), "will" adds time reference, or *tense*, specifically *future*, to the verb "come." These words belong to a subclass of auxiliaries known as **modals**. In (10), the auxiliaries add *aspect*, *perfect* and *progressive*, respectively, to the verbs. Recall that aspect is similar to tense in that it refers to time, but different in that it refers to the time of an event within a certain time frame.

Again, we might predict co-occurrence features based on function, and again we would be correct. The data confirm that auxiliaries do, in fact, precede verbs, though not always immediately. In (10), for example, we see two auxiliaries being used with the same verb, the result being that only one of them directly precedes the verb.

Quick Exercise 6.2
Use the following sentence to determine the kind of meaning each of the underlined auxiliary verbs adds.

"We were told that because we had taken a linguistics class we could teach English effectively, but first we must become fully certified."

had:

could:

must:

Conjunctions (Examples: and, or, but, if, because)

The final new category we need to add to our list was popularized by the ABC TV musical cartoon called School House Rock in a song called "Conjunction Junction, What's your Function?" The refrain of this song states that **conjunctions** "hook up words and phrases and clauses." This is a fairly useful definition. In examples (11) through (13) we see conjunctions performing as advertised.

N C N [clause] C [clause] adj C adj
(11) [Conjunctions and auxiliaries are closed word classes], but [they aren't unimportant or useless].

[clause] C [clause]
(12) [Beans cause painful gas] if [you eat them in large quantities].

[clause] {phrase} C {phrase} C [clause]
(13) [Beans cause {painful gas} and {severe bloating}] because [they contain a lot of fiber].

In (11), the conjunction "and" hooks up, or conjoins, the nouns "conjunctions" and "auxiliaries," and "or" conjoins the adjectives "unimportant" and "useless." This example also contains the conjunction "but," which is conjoining two clauses here. We'll define a **clause** as a group of words with some kind of meaning and *both* a subject and a verb. The subject and verb of the clause preceding "but" in (11) are "conjunctions and auxiliaries" and "are," and the subject and verb of the clause following the conjunction are "they" and "aren't."

The conjunction "and" is used again in (13), this time to conjoin the phrases "painful gas" and "severe bloating." We'll use the term **phrase** to refer to groups of words that come together to create some kind of meaning. Later we'll see, however, that some phrases are made up of only single words. Note that unlike a clause, a phrase does *not* have both a subject and a verb. The three conjunctions covered so far, "and," "or" and "but," are subclassified as **coordinating conjunctions** for reasons that will be explained shortly.

The conjunctions "if" and "because" in (12) and (13) are behaving similarly to "but" in (11) in that they're conjoining clauses. The exact way in which they conjoin phrases is a little different from "but." The conjunction "if," like the conjunction "because," is subclassified as a **subordinating conjunction**. This distinction between coordinating and subordinating conjunctions will be discussed in more detail in the next section.

We've seen from the data that conjunctions conjoin a variety of grammatical elements. The ungrammatical sentence in (14), however, indicates that we need to tighten our earlier functional definition somewhat.

N C [phrase]
(14) * Beans and [cause painful gas] contain a lot of fiber.

This example suggests that the grammatical elements being conjoined by a conjunction must be like each other. (14) is ungrammatical because the conjunction is being used to conjoin a noun—"beans"—and a phrase with a verb—"cause painful gas." Our revised functional definition, then, is that conjunctions conjoin not just any elements, but *like* elements, meaning grammatically equivalent elements. And once again, our functional definition leads us to our co-occurrence features. Specifically, as we would expect, we find conjunctions being used with like elements on either side.

Combining the new classes just covered in this section with the familiar ones from Chapter 4, our inventory of word classes now numbers ten. Table 6.1 lists them all.

Open/Major:	**Closed/Minor:**
nouns	pronouns
verbs	determiners
adjectives	quantifiers
adverbs	prepositions
	auxiliaries
	conjunctions

Table 6.1: Inventory of Word Classes Discussed

Now that we've rounded out our inventory of word classes, we can return to the ones we studied in Chapter 4 and revise our definitions as necessary. For each category, we will quickly review the form definition we arrived at previously, reevaluate the functional definition to provide a more syntactic one when necessary, and finally describe their co-occurrence features.

Nouns (Examples: student, linguistics, class, hair)

Recall that we described nouns as words that could be inflected for number (singular vs. plural) and case (specifically the possessive case). Our functional definition of nouns as representing persons, places and things was very meaning based and is, therefore, inadequate for our current purposes. Instead, we will describe the function of nouns with regard to their relationship to verbs. What we see from (15) is that nouns can function as **subjects** and **objects** of verbs.

```
      N        V        N
(15) Students love linguistics.
```

The noun "students" is serving as the subject of the verb "love." The subject can be thought of as who or what "does" the verb. The noun "linguistics" can be thought of as the object of the verb. The object is who or what receives the action of the verb. This functional definition is more syntactic in nature. To see the usefulness of this observation, contrast the grammatical sentence, (15), in which nouns function as the subject and object of the verb, with the ungrammatical, (16), in which verbs attempt to serve these functions.

```
          V          V      V
(16) * Complains love acquires.
```

Clearly, our functional definition helps distinguish nouns from verbs.

Finally, we can complete our definition of nouns by describing their co-occurrence features. We can begin by recalling that we described certain minor classes, most notably determiners and quantifiers, as co-occurring with nouns. Based on this observation, we expect to see nouns co-occurring with these same words. The data in (17) confirms this.

```
      Q      N           det   adj      N
(17) Many students love this difficult class.
```

We see the noun "students" being preceded by a quantifier, and we see the noun "class" being preceded by a determiner. We also see an adjective between the determiner and "class," which shouldn't surprise us if we recall from Chapter 4 that adjectives modify nouns. These observations suggest a syntactic test for identifying noun. Simply try to plug a word into the syntactic frame in Figure 6.1, and if it fits to form a phrase, then you have a noun.

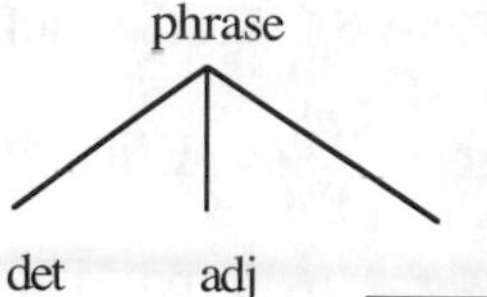

Figure 6.1: Syntactic Frame for Testing Nouns

If, for example, we were to use the word "hair" in this frame along with the determiner "her" and the adjective "purple," we would have the phrase "her purple hair," which is perfectly acceptable grammatically. We would conclude, then, that "hair" was a noun. Because "hair" is the most important word in the resulting phrase, meaning the one that carries the bulk of the meaning, we will name this phrase after the noun and call it a noun phrase (NP). Notice that this NP could be used as the subject of a verb, as in (18).

det adj N
(18) Her purple hair disgusted her mother.
NP

While we can analyze the noun "hair" by itself as one kind of subject of the verb "disgusted," namely the **simple subject**, we must also acknowledge that the entire phrase is also the subject of the verb. We will call this the **complete subject**.

Quick Exercise 6.3
For each sentence below, underline the NP that is the complete subject and circle the word that serves as the simple subject.

1. The pathetic team lost another game.
2. My funny Valentine told a good joke.
3. The rain in Spain falls mainly on the plain.
4. Football is a violent sport.
5. Cheap beer is the official drink of football.
6. Our players drink too much beer.

Verbs (Example: disgust, leak, approach)

Previously we noted that the form definition for verbs was complicated because they took several inflections in English. Specifically, verbs can be inflected for tense, number, person and aspect. Our functional definition, that verbs represent actions and states, was meaning based, so we need to revise it now because our focus in this chapter is more structural. To do this, we will return to the sentence in example (18). While the sentence is made up of six words at one level, it is comprised of two larger units at another level. One of these units is the subject NP. Another way of thinking about the subject using traditional terms is to consider the subject to be who or what the sentence is about. The other is the phrase that follows the NP. This phrase expresses what the speaker of the sentence wants to say about the subject. In grammar terms, this is known as the **predicate** of the sentence. Because the most important word in this phrase is the verb "disgusted," we will call this type of phrase a verb phrase (VP). We are now beginning to classify phrases, as we have words. Example (19) breaks the sentence in (18) down into its two main parts, the subject NP and the predicate VP.

(19) Her purple hair disgusted her mother.
NP VP

We see that functionally, a verb serves as the main word, also known as the **head**, in a predicate, just as a noun (or a pronoun) serves as the main word in, or the head of, a subject. This is a more scientific functional definition of a verb. To further illustrate the verb's importance in a predicate, consider (20), in which the verb is the *only* word in the predicate. This VP is an example of the kind of single word phrase that was mentioned earlier.

```
      det  N      V
(20) The roof   leaks.
        NP       VP
```

For our co-occurrence definition of verbs we can return to the definition for auxiliaries and reverse the order. Because auxiliaries precede verbs, we expect to see verbs following auxiliaries, and as we see in (21), this is the case.

```
              aux      V
(21) A storm  is  approaching from the ocean.
```

At this point, a word about co-occurrence *requirements* vs. *possibilities* is in order. The data for verbs indicates that a verb *can* follow an auxiliary, as in (21), but doesn't *have* to follow one, as the verb in (20) does not. The same is true for nouns, which *can* follow determiners and adjectives, as in (17), but don't always *have* to, as in (15). These can be described as co-occurrence *possibilities*. Contrast these situations with that of a determiner, which *must* be followed by a noun to be used grammatically, or the result is the kind of ungrammatical sentence in (22). For determiners, then, this co-occurrence feature is a requirement.

```
        det
(22) *  A is approaching rapidly.
```

Quick Exercise 6.4

In each of the sentences below, underline the entire predicate (VP) and circle the head verb of that VP.

1. The pathetic team lost another game.
2. My funny Valentine told a good joke.
3. The rain in Spain falls mainly on the plain.
4. Football is a violent sport.
5. Cheap beer is the official drink of football.
6. Our players drink too much beer.

Adjectives (Examples: leaky, serious, unfortunate, favorite, hungry)

The definitions we used for adjectives in Chapter 4 will serve us well here, too. Specifically, the form observation that adjectives can be inflected for comparison holds true for many of the words in the category, and the functional definition as words that modify nouns is more structural than the other meaning based functions we described initially for nouns and verbs in Chapter 4. All that remains to be done is to provide the co-occurrence features of adjectives. Predictably, these words that modify nouns can also occur together with nouns, as in (23). Note also the *possibility* of a determiner or quantifier preceding the adjective.

```
     adj   N      det  adj     N           Q       adj          N
(23) Leaky roofs are a serious problem that many unfortunate people face.
```

However, the picture is not quite as simple as this one example would lead us to believe. As the sentence in (24) illustrates, adjectives are not *always* used before nouns.

det adj N adj
(24) My favorite player [is hungry]
[predicate]

In this example, rather than being used with the noun it modifies, the adjective "hungry" is used in the predicate of a sentence to modify the noun in the subject. When adjectives are used in a **predicative** way, as "hungry" is here, they occur after certain verbs, one of which is the verb "to be." When adjectives are used with nouns, as "favorite" is in (24), they are said to be used in an **attributive** way. Thus, we see two ways in which adjectives can modify nouns in two different kinds of phrases.

Quick Exercise 6.5

For the most part, any given adjective can be used both attributively and predicatively. There are, however, a few exceptions. Generate data (create sentences) to determine if each of the following adjectives can be used both attributively and predicatively or only one or the other. If only one use is allowable, state which one that is.

immense

asleep

previous

Adverbs (Examples: unfortunately, very, quickly, extremely)

Adverbs were described in Chapter 4 as the garbage category because of their many functions. We observed four different functions in one sentence alone. This sentence is repeated in (25).

adv V adv adv adv adj N
(25) Unfortunately, [some motorists drive very quickly and create extremely dangerous roads].
[sentence]

Adverbs like "unfortunately" which modify entire sentences are called **sentence adverbs**. Adverbs like "quickly," which modify verbs, are called **manner adverbs** because they describe the manner in which a verb is "done." Adverbs like "very" and "extremely," which modify adjectives and other adverbs are called **intensifiers** because they intensify the meaning of the word they modify.

With regard to co-occurrence, there is little we can say about most adverbs. As we see in (26) through (28), sentence and manner adverbs (in these examples the words "unfortunately" and "quickly") are very flexible in terms of where in a sentence they're used. In fact, we see the sentence adverb "unfortunately" going from the first word in a sentence to the last. Intensifiers, on the other hand are more fixed. They stay with the adjective or adverb they modify, specifically right before it. Note that in all of the examples, the intensifiers "very" and "quickly" move with the word they modify wherever that word goes.

adv adv adv adv adj
(26) Unfortunately, my favorite player ate his dinner very quickly and now he feels extremely ill.

adv adv adv adv adj
(27) My favorite player very quickly ate his dinner and now, unfortunately, he feels extremely ill.

adv adv adv adj adv
(28) Very quickly, my favorite player ate his dinner and now he feels extremely ill, unfortunately.

What this data suggests is that the traditional category known as adverbs probably shouldn't be a category of its own at all. Instead, sentence adverbs, manner adverbs and intensifiers really ought to be separate categories of their own.

Quick Exercise 6.6

Using functional and co-occurrence clues, determine the subcategory (type) of each of the underlined adverbs in the sentence below. Use SA for sentence adverbs, MA for manner adverbs and INT for intensifiers.

"Hopefully, we'll learn adverbs completely by the time this highly difficult chapter is nearly over."

hopefully   completely

highly   nearly

Pronouns (Examples: he, she, it)

Finally, we need to return to the one minor class that we discussed in Chapter 4—pronouns. As we saw earlier, pronouns can be inflected for case, as is illustrated by the subject cases (he, she) and object cases (him, her) in (29).

```
     pro   V        pro        pro  V  pro
(29) She despises him, but he loves her.
```

Functionally, we described pronouns as taking the place of, or substituting for, nouns, though it was suggested that this definition would need to be revised. We will, in fact, prove this description to be inaccurate, but assuming for the time being that this is the case, then pronouns, like nouns, should serve as subjects and objects of verbs. This is, indeed, exactly what we see in (29).

Also, if pronouns substitute for nouns, we might expect to see them used with the same kinds of words. Specifically, we could hypothesize that they can be used in the frame det + adj + ______ , as nouns are. This is where reality does not meet our expectations. The ungrammatical sentence in (30) proves our intuitions wrong.

```
       det  adj     pro         det adj  pro
(30) * My favorite he likes the purple it.
```

The most useful observation we can make about the co-occurrence feature of pronouns, then, is that they can *not* be used with the same kinds of words that nouns are. This helps us distinguish pronouns from nouns and prompts us to wonder whether, in fact, they really *do* substitute for nouns. We'll return to this point shortly.

Sentence Types

Now that we've dealt with words, phrases and clauses (all of which constitute the building blocks of sentences), it's time to start analyzing sentence structure. What we'll see is that, while all sentences share certain features such as a subject and a predicate, they can differ in important ways. We'll consider four types of sentences in this section—**simple sentences**, **coordinate sentences**, **complex sentences** and **complex-coordinate sentences**.

Simple Sentences

Earlier in this chapter we discussed the two essential components of a sentence—its subject and its predicate. We also used these terms in our discussion of a clause. It seems, then, that the definition of a sentence and a clause are very similar. In fact, this is true. There are some sentences, such as the one in (31), that are both a clause and a sentence at the same time.

```
        N            V
(31) My students   like big shoes.
     subject       predicate
```

Sentences like this one are called simple sentences because they contain the bare minimum that a sentence needs—one subject and one predicate. They are, therefore, sentences in their simplest possible form. A simple sentence is also, by definition, a clause, specifically an **independent clause**. An independent clause is one that can stand alone grammatically as a sentence.

Coordinate sentences

Not all sentences, however, are simple. Others, like the one in (32), go beyond simple sentences because they contain more than just the bare minimum that a sentence requires. Here, we see *two* subjects and *two* predicates in the sentence.

```
        N            V                CC       N              V
(32) My students   like big shoes,   but   their parents   prefer small shoes.
     subject       predicate               subject         predicate
```

This sentence uses two independent clauses, each with its own subject and verb, and combines them in a grammatically *coordinate* way. For this reason, this sentence is considered a **coordinate sentence**. By grammatically coordinate, we mean that the two clauses are equal to each other grammatically. If we break the word "coordinate" down, we will discover the stem "ordinate" which has to do with placement, and the prefix "co-," which mean together. The two clause are thus placed together at the same grammatical level. To illustrate this, imagine how you would respond if someone were to ask you what the subject of the *whole* sentence was. You could just as easily answer "my students" as "their parents." This is because they both have equal grammatical status in the sentence. In a coordinate sentence, two or more independent clauses are linked by one or more coordinating conjunctions, such as "but." We will now start labeling conjunctions as either coordinating conjunctions (CC) or subordinating conjunctions (SC).

Complex Sentences

Just as not all sentences are simple, not all sentences with multiple clauses are coordinate. In example (33), we see a sentence with two clauses, but the way those clauses are combined is not coordinate. Instead, the clauses are combined in a **subordinate** way. The prefix "sub-" means "beneath" or "under," which suggests that one clause is placed beneath the other grammatically.

```
        N            V                 SC          N          V
(33) My students   [like big shoes,   because   big things   are cool].
     subject                                    subject      predicate
                          [predicate]
```

Even though we have two subjects in this sentence, the first one, "my students," is clearly the one that the entire sentence is about. This is the grammatically super-ordinate subject. The other subject, "big things," is buried, or **embedded**, along with its predicate within the predicate of the entire sentence. It is subordinate to the other subject. Because the clause with the grammatically subordinate subject and verb is inside the predicate of the entire sentence, it is said to be subordinate.

Notice that the conjunction in this sentence is a subordinating one, not a coordinating one as in (32). Subordinating conjunctions attach to clauses that follow them to create **dependent clauses**. A dependent clause is one that cannot stand alone grammatically as a sentence. The ungrammatical example (34), which consists of *only* the clause that follows the SC in (33), illustrates this.

```
         SC          N       V
(34) * Because  big things  are cool.
                  subject   predicate
```

This sentence is ungrammatical because it needs, or *depends* on, something else added to it to make it a sentence. It feels unfinished. Complex sentences, then, are ones in which at least one dependent clause is embedded within part of the larger sentence.

Complex-Coordinate Sentences

Having covered both coordinate and complex sentences, we should have no trouble anticipating what a **complex-coordinate sentence** consists of. As you might have guessed, such sentences contain multiple clauses that are combined in both a coordinate and a subordinate way. The sentence in (35) illustrates this kind of clause combining.

```
         N            V               CC      N          V                 SC          N         V
(35) Some folks  dislike big shoes,  but  my students  [like them, because  big things  are cool].
      subject       predicate              subject                           subject   predicate
                                                              [predicate]
```

In this sentence, what's to the left of the coordinating conjunction "but" is an independent clause. What's to the right of "but" is a subject and a predicate that has embedded within it a dependent clause set off by the subordinating conjunction "because." An easier way to think of this sentence is to view it as a simple sentence and a complex sentence being conjoined in a coordinate way. As the label suggests, complex-coordinate sentence are more complicated than the other sentence types.

Quick Exercise 6.7

Combine the following three independent clauses to form a complex-coordinate sentence. Feel free to add conjunctions where necessary, but don't alter the clauses in any significant way.

"I love linguistics. My roommate hates it. I don't understand why he feels that way."

Coordination vs. Subordination

Before we move on, we need to address the distinction between coordination and subordination in more detail. What we've stated here is that, in a coordinate structure, two perfectly independent clauses are conjoined by a coordinating conjunction, which is part of neither clause, but merely links the two. In subordination, however, we have stated that the subordinating conjunction is actually part of the clause that follows it, and by attaching to the following clause it makes that clause dependent. If we analyzed subordinating conjunctions, like coordinating conjunctions, as *not* being part of either clause the distinction between coordination and subordination would be lost. Why, for example, do we have two separate independent clauses in (36) but not in (37) when, at first glance, they appear to be the same?

	N	V	CC	N	V
(36)	Big shoes	are cool	but	small shoes	are uncool.
	subject	predicate		subject	predicate

	N	V	SC	N	V
(37)	Big shoes	will be uncool	when	current trends	change.
	subject	predicate		subject	predicate

There are two ways to answer this question, one of which is more intuitive and the other of which is more scientific. We begin with the more intuitive approach. Recall our earlier discussion of which subject feels like the subject of the *whole* sentence. In (36), it's not clear which of the two subjects is the main subject. The sentence feels like it is about both "big shoes" and "small shoes" at the same time. In (37), however, the sentence feels like it's about "big shoes," not "current trends." This intuitive test is somewhat useful, but we always want to test our intuitions empirically. Remember, the whole point behind our study of language is to be able to explain our intuitions.

The best test for proving the difference between coordination and subordination is a syntactic test called a **movement test**. If a group of words belong together as a single unit, it makes sense that they would move together as a single unit. If we try to attach the conjunction "but" to the following clause in (36), we see that it doesn't work. The conjunction, then, is not part of the clause. Example (38) illustrates this inability of the conjunction to attach to, and move with, the following clause.

	CC	N	V	N	V
(38) *	But	small shoes	are uncool,	big shoes	are cool.
		subject	predicate	subject	predicate

If, however, we try the same test with the sentence (37), we see that it *does* work. What this tells us is that the conjunction "when" belongs together with following clause as part of that clause. Example (39) illustrates this.

	SC	N	V	N	V
(39)	When	current trends	change,	big shoes	will be uncool.
		subject	predicate	subject	predicate

This is very convincing evidence for saying "when fashion trends change" *is* a single unit (a dependent clause) while "but small shoes are uncool" is *not* a single unit. Being able to recognize the difference between coordination and subordination is important in determining sentence types.

Quick Exercise 6.8

For each of the sentences below, determine if the clauses are combined in a subordinate or coordinate way by applying the relevant movement test. Then label it subordinate or coordinate.

"We learned the golden rule when we were mere children."
after movement:

"We learned the golden rule but we prefer to live by our own rules."
after movement:

"Life is easier if we follow the golden rule."
after movement:

"We should follow the golden rule because people appreciate polite behavior."
after movement:

A Different Kind of Subordination

Up to this point, all of the subordination we've seen so far has involved dependent clauses being embedded in a predicate and serving an adverbial function. By this, we mean that the dependent clause modifies the head verb of the verb phrase it's embedded in. In (37), for example, the dependent clause tells us *when* big shoes will *be* uncool. Any element that answers a how, when, where or why question performs an adverbial function. In (40), however, the dependent clause that is introduced by the subordinating conjunction "that", does *not* answer a how, when, where or why question. Instead, it tells us *what* I think. In this way, it's more like a direct object than an adverbial clause. We can say, then, that it's performing a nominal (like a noun) function. This sets dependent clauses like the one in (40) apart from the others we've seen thus far. Predictably, because this kind of dependent clause is not adverbial, it's not as free to move around in the sentence as an adverbial clause.

(40) I think that big shoes are an embarrassment.
dependent clause

(41) ? That big shoes are an embarrassment I think.
dependent clause

(42) That big shoes are an embarrassment is what I think.
dependent clause

To illustrate this, we can use an example like (41), in which we try to move the embedded noun clause to the sentence initial position. For many people, this is ungrammatical; for others, it might be acceptable but also awkward. Because its grammaticality is questionable, we mark it with a "?" to indicate that it's somewhere between grammatical and ungrammatical. We could move the noun clause to the front of the sentence, as we've done in (42), but it would require adding additional elements. So, while dependent clauses like the nominal one in (40) are similar to their adverbial counterpart in that they are embedded in a predicate, they are different in the exact function they serve in that predicate.

The Purpose of Syntax

With some important terms and concepts under our belts, we are now prepared to dive into the study of syntax. First, we need to understand our overall goal. As always, our overarching goal is to be able to consciously articulate our unconscious understanding of English. For example, any native or fluent speaker of English knows that the sentences in (41), (42) and (43) are ungrammatical. As soon as we hear or read them, we know they're bad. This does not, however, mean we have conscious understanding of what makes them ungrammatical.

(43) * Teachers know that them have an important job.
(44) * Know that they have an important job teachers.
(45) * Good teachers put their work.

Anyone who has ever taught a foreign language has encountered ungrammatical sentences from students, perhaps ones similar to these examples. When you, as a teacher, tell the student the sentence is ungrammatical, the next logical question from the student is "why?" Without a conscious understanding of what makes the sentence ungrammatical, you will be unable to explain it to the student, which will make the student unable to correct the mistake in the future. Understand that telling him or her how to correct a *particular* sentence, by changing a word or two, for example, will not give that student a rule to use in the future. Our goal, then, will be to develop theories of syntax that will help us explain the ungrammaticality of ungrammatical sentences, like those in (43) through (45), as well as the grammaticality of grammatical sentences. We should then be able to apply these theories systematically to new sentences.

Interestingly, we already have a theory to help us explain ungrammaticality of (43). All we need to do is recall the form component of our word class definitions. Specifically, we described pronouns as words that were inflected for case. In this sentence, the pronoun "them" is inflected for the object case, but in the sentence it is being used as the subject of the verb "have." Because this sentence violates the rules governing the inflection of pronouns, it is ungrammatical. If we were to change the pronoun to a subject case ("they"), the sentence would be perfectly grammatical.

While this form component of our word class definitions helps us explain the ungrammaticality of (43), it does *not* help us with (44) and (45). We cannot correct either of these sentences simply by changing the form of any of the words, which tells us that we need to go beyond our word class definitions and develop additional theories to explain their ungrammaticality. Much of the rest of this chapter will be devoted to developing these theories.

Constituents

We'll begin our exploration of syntax by asking the basic question, "What are sentences made up of?" Your initial answer is most likely to be "words," and while this is technically accurate, it's not the best answer. Recall that in Chapter 4 we discovered that words were made up not of letters or sounds, but of morphemes. Similarly, it's most useful to think of sentences as being made up of **constituents**. A constituent can be thought of as a group or "chunk" of words that belong together as a unit.

Basic Constituents

Although we are just now introducing the term "constituent," you already know something about them. To illustrate this, we'll use the sentence in (46).

(46) The man with the toupee shocked the woman at the bar.

To begin, this entire string of words qualifies as a constituent because all the words work together to form one unit, namely a sentence. We can also, however, break the largest constituent, the sentence, into smaller constituents. Recall that the main components of a sentence are its subject and predicate. If we use the traditional definition of a subject as who or what the sentence is about and the predicate as what we want to say about the subject, we can easily separate the subject, "the man with the toupee," from the predicate, "shocked the woman at the bar." We can represent these constituents graphically with the simple diagram in Figure 6.2.

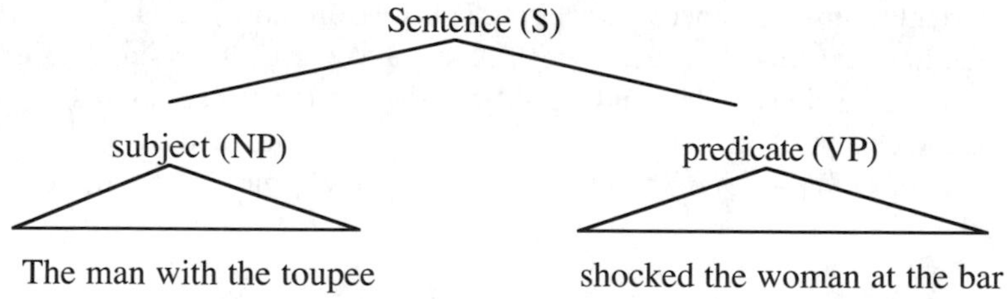

Figure 6.2: Basic Constituents

In addition to identifying our constituents, we also want to classify them. Notice that we've labeled the subject "NP" for noun phrase. This is because, as we determined earlier, the most important word in the subject is the noun. Notice also that we've labeled the predicate "VP" for verb phrase because the verb is most important word in it. This verb is the head of the verb phrase. We'll return to this example later.

The Importance of Hierarchical Structure

The tree diagram in Figure 6.2 illustrates the *hierarchical* structure of the sentence. In Chapter 4, we saw how words had a hierarchical structure, in addition to their linear structure, and that it was the hierarchical structure that helped us really understand how the word was put together. The same importance of hierarchical structure rather than linear structure holds true with sentences. In Figure 6.2, we see the sentence being represented as two constituents, the subject NP and the predicate VP, coming together to form the sentence at the next level of the hierarchy.

To illustrate the importance of hierarchical structure in analyzing phrases and sentences, consider the example in (47), a phrase taken from a radio advertisement.

(47) big stereo sale

What, exactly, is the advertiser describing as big, the stereo or the sale? Intuitively, you probably want to say "sale," but there is nothing in the grammar of the phrase to tell you that. You make this assumption only because you can't imagine a retailer putting only big stereos on sale. There is really no way to determine from this phrase alone what its meaning is. This phrase, then, is **ambiguous** because it has more than one possible meaning.

This observation presents a problem, however, because it doesn't make sense that a single structure could have multiple meanings. To reconcile this problem, we have to show that the two meanings do, in fact, have different structures. To do this, we turn to the hierarchy of the phrase, the way the words are grouped, or "chunked," at different levels. Figure 6.3 illustrates the two different structures.

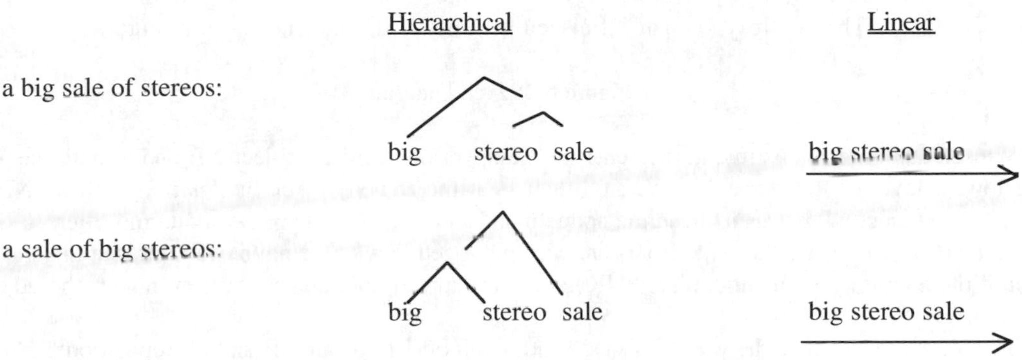

Figure 6.3: Hierarchical Structure vs. Linear Structure

Linearly, these two phrases are identical. Each one begins with "big," which is followed by "stereo," which is followed by "sale." Hierarchically, however, they are different in that "stereo" is grouped with "big" at the lowest level of the hierarchy in one meaning but it is grouped with "sale" at the lowest level of the hierarchy in the other meaning. So we see that the two different meanings really *do* have different structures. Without hierarchical structuring of constituents, we would not be able explain how "big stereo sale" could be ambiguous.

Quick Exercise 6.9

For each structurally ambiguous phrase below, provide a paraphrase and hierarchical diagram to represent each possible meaning.

Lebanese history teachers Lebanese history teachers

old taxi drivers old taxi drivers

Determining and Representing Hierarchical Structure

Because we're interested in sentence structure, we need to be able to determine the hierarchical combining of constituents in a sentence, and we must be able to represent the structures we've identified. We do this through **tree diagrams**. Tree diagrams allow us to represent the hierarchical grouping of constituents graphically. An accurate tree diagram indicates the hierarchical structure of a sentence.

In Figure 6.4, we see an example of a tree diagram.

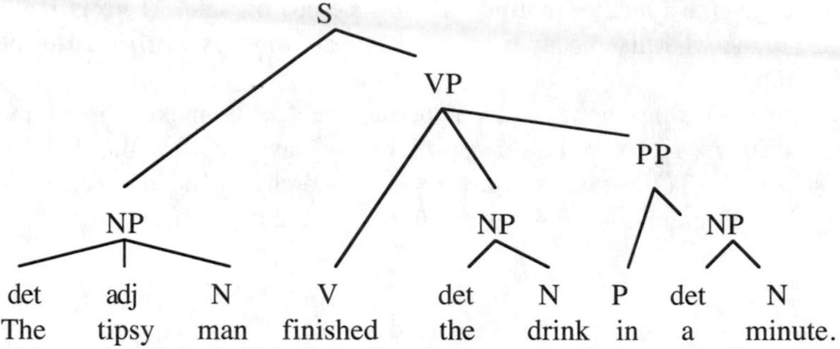

Figure 6.4: Tree Diagram #1

We see the largest constituent, the sentence, being made up of a subject NP and a predicate VP at the next lowest level of the hierarchy. We say, then, that the S node *directly dominates* these NP and VP nodes. The subject NP has as its head the noun "man" and also consists of two noun modifiers, a determiner and an adjective. Because these modifiers are working together with the noun, we represent them at the same level of the hierarchy as the noun. This NP node, then directly dominates the determiner, the adjective and the noun[1].

The VP has as its head the verb "finished" and also consists of an NP and a prepositional phrase (PP). These three elements express the complete predicate by working together to tell what the sentence says about its subject. Because they all work together, they are represented at the same level of the hierarchy, directly dominated by the VP node[2]. The PP has another constituent, an NP, within it. Thus, it directly dominates both the preposition and the NP.

Figure 6.5 provides another example of constituent structure. Note the structural differences, especially within the predicate.

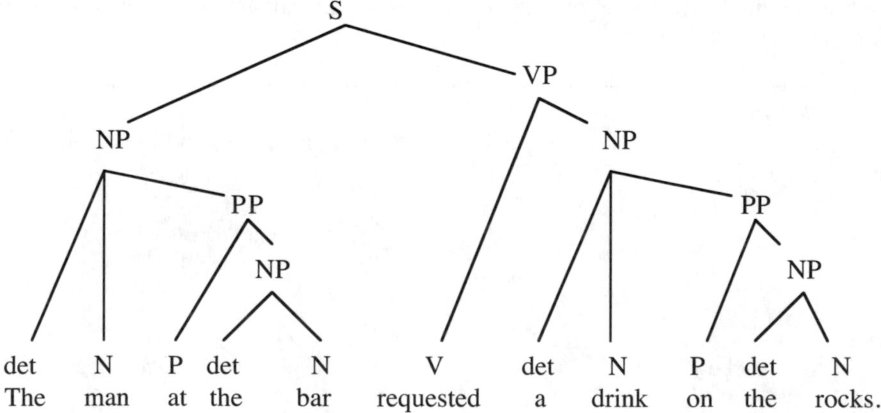

Figure 6.5: Tree Diagram #2

[1] Note that this treatment of the NP as being made up of the determiner, adjective and noun at the same level of the hierarchy is, to a certain extent, simplified.

[2] Note that while there is evidence for positing two VPs in the sentence in Figure 6.4, one directly dominated by the other, this approach does not address that.

In the previous sentence, the PP in the predicate was directly dominated by the VP node because it worked together with the verb to complete the predicate. Here, however, the PP "on the rocks" doesn't work the verb at all; instead, it works with the noun "drink" to complete the NP. We also see a PP that performs the same kind of function within the subject NP. It describes which man is being discussed.

Grammatical Relations

When diagramming sentences, it can be useful to consider the grammatical function of the various elements in the sentence. In particular, we will focus on the **grammatical relations** of NPs. Every NP in a sentence has an important relationship to some other element in the sentence, and these relationships are what the term grammatical relations refers to. For example, in the previous sentence, the important relationship that the NP "the man at the bar" has is with the verb "requested;" specifically, it's the **subject** of that verb, meaning it is who or what *does* the verb. Hierarchically, we see that NPs that have the grammatical relation of subject are directly dominated by the sentence node. Also related to the verb is the grammatical relation **direct object**. The direct object is who or what receives the action of the verb. In the previous sentence, the NP "a drink on the rocks" has this grammatical relation. Note that it is directly dominated by the VP node. The other two NPs in the sentence are not related to the verb. Instead, their important relationship is with the prepositions that precede them. An NP that has this relationship and is directly dominated by a PP node is called the **object of a preposition**.

Quick Exercise 6.10

As we saw, each grammatical relation has a certain place within the hierarchy of a sentence. Using the sentence and diagram below, for each NP determine what kind of node directly dominates the NP and what grammatical relation the NP is.

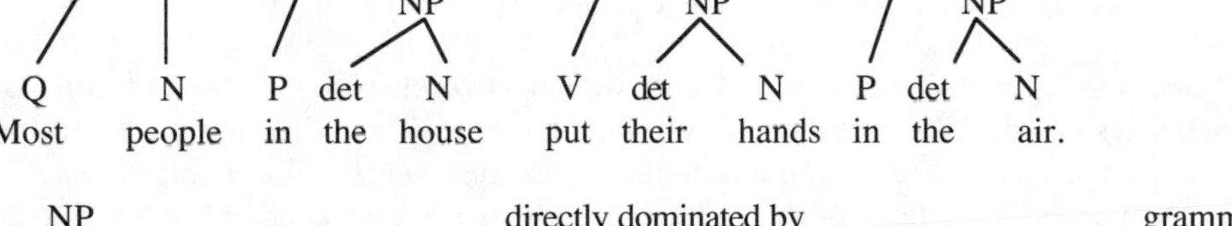

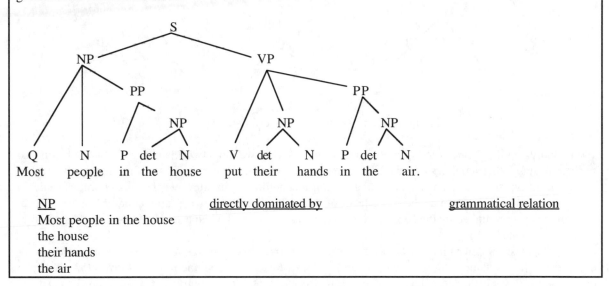

NP	directly dominated by	grammatical relation
Most people in the house		
the house		
their hands		
the air		

Constituent Structure of Complex and Coordinate Sentences

Each of the sentences we have diagrammed so far has been a simple sentence with a single subject and a single predicate. As we saw earlier, however, there other sentence types in English. Figure 6.6 illustrates the constituent structure of a complex sentence, and Figure 6.7 illustrates the structure of a coordinate sentence.

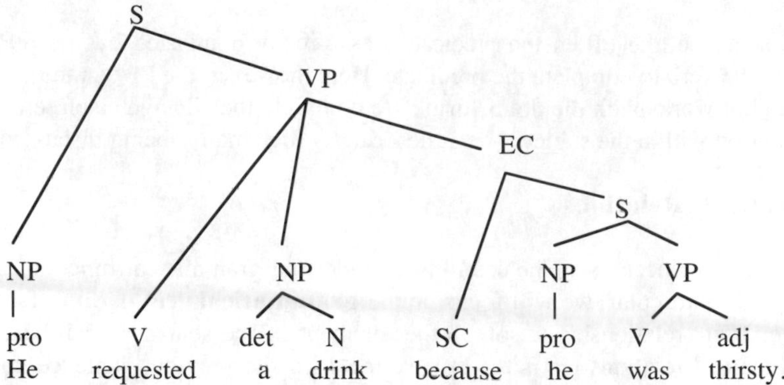

Figure 6.6: Tree Diagram #3 (complex sentence)

In this sentence, we have two clauses, one of which is an embedded clause (labeled "EC") consisting of a sentence with a subordinating conjunction attached to it. Like all embedded clauses, this one is dependent, meaning it must be part of another grammatical element. We see that it is embedded within the VP of the larger sentence. It works together with the verb and the NP to complete the predicate. Because this clause is hierarchically lower than the larger sentence node, we say it is subordinate.

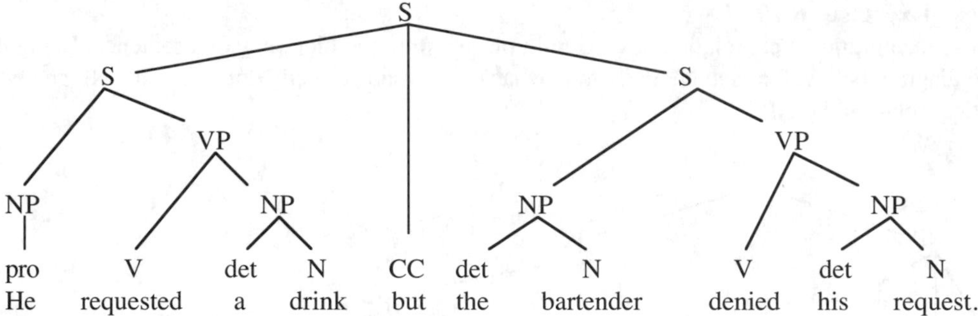

Figure 6.7: Tree Diagram #4 (coordinate sentence)

In analyzing the diagram in Figure 6.7, again, we see that we have two clauses with two subjects and two predicates. What separates this sentence from the previous one, however, is the fact that neither clause is dependent on the other. Thus, rather than having a subordinate structure, we have a coordinate one in which the two sentences are at the same level of the hierarchy. These two grammatically equal and independent clauses are linked by the coordinating conjunction "but" at the same level of the hierarchy to form the larger sentence.

The best test for determining whether a sentence with multiple subjects and predicates is coordinate or complex is the movement test we studied earlier. Recall that if the conjunction can move along with the clause that follows it to the beginning of the sentence, the sentence is complex. On the other hand, if the conjunction can *not* move with the following clause, the sentence is coordinate.

Quick Exercise 6.11

By using the relevant movement test, prove that the sentence in Figure 6.6 is complex, while the one in Figure 6.7 is coordinate.

Diagramming Ambiguous Sentences

Let's now return to the sentence we began this section with in Figure 6.2 and begin to represent its hierarchical structure in Figure 6.8.

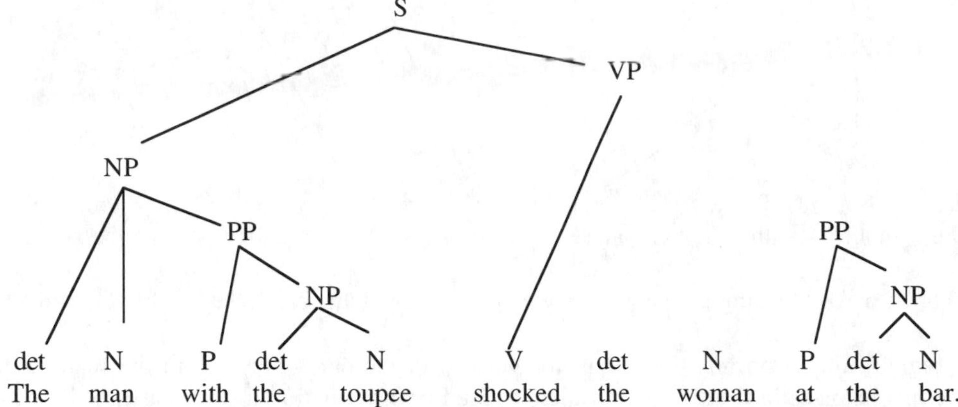

Figure 6.8: Partial Diagram of an Ambiguous Sentence

Determining the structure of the subject NP is relatively easy but the predicate VP presents a problem. Does the PP go together with the noun "woman" to complete the direct object NP or does it go together with the verb "shocked" to complete the VP? The answer is that it depends on how the sentence is interpreted. This is a structurally ambiguous sentence, which means that it has multiple meanings that are based on multiple structures. One meaning has one structure and the other meaning has another structure. The different meanings and structures are presented in Figures 6.9 and 6.10.

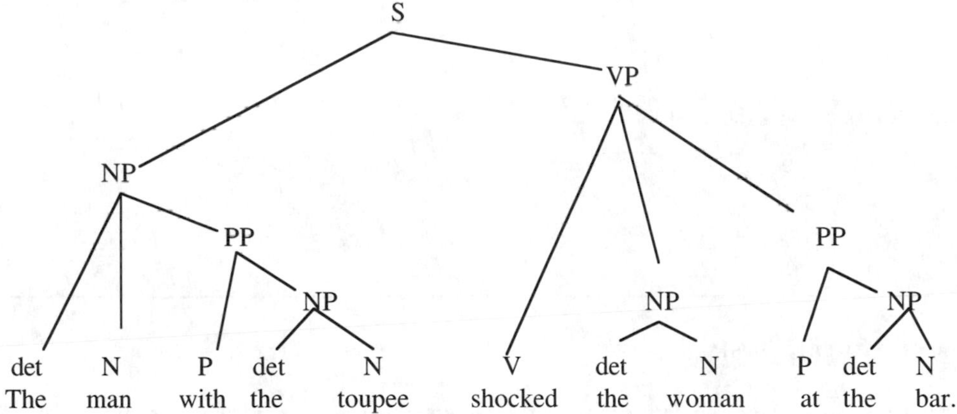

Figure 6.9: Meaning A (at the bar is where he shocked the woman)

In this meaning, we know that the event took place at the bar, but the location of the woman at the time of the utterance is unknown. The speaker could be talking about a woman who has left the bar but at one time was there, at least long enough for the man to shock her.

In the next meaning, however, the situation is reversed. In Meaning B (see figure 6.10) the speaker does *not* specify where the event took place. For all we know, the shocking happened out on the street. What we do know, however, is the location of the woman at the time of the utterance. Specifically, she's at the bar.

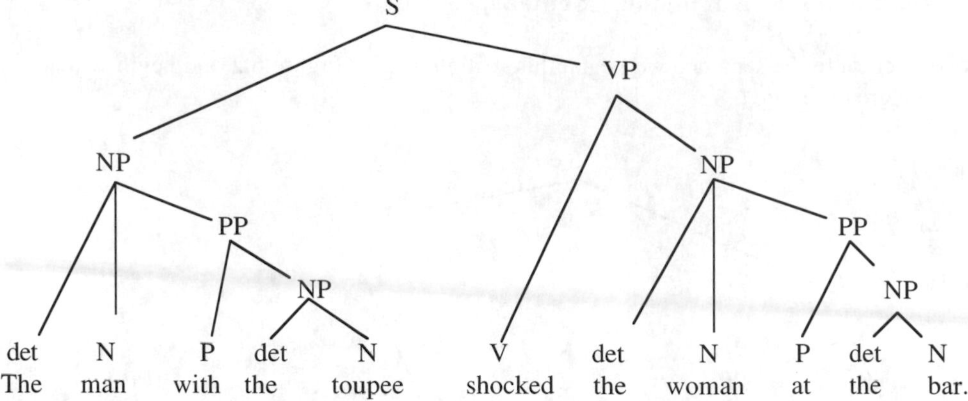

Figure 6.10: Meaning B (the woman who is currently at the bar is the one he shocked)

The ambiguity hinges on how the PP is combined with the other elements in the sentence hierarchically. Notice that its place in the hierarchy, which is based on its function in the sentence, is the only difference between the structures of the two sentences.

Quick Exercise 6.12

For each of the ambiguous sentences below, provide two different paraphrases that clearly distinguish the two meanings. You can use the paraphrases in Figures 6.9 and 6.10 as models, though there are other kinds of paraphrases that will also work.

"The governor of Minnesota bodyslammed the lobbyist in his office."

A.

B.

"I like the chairs against the wall."

A.

B.

Constituent Tests

When determining the hierarchical structure of a sentence, it's a good idea to test whatever hypotheses you have regarding constituents. This is especially useful with constituents in a predicate because this is where questions tend to arise. The first kind of test is more meaning based and, therefore, less scientific, but it can be a useful place to start. The two sentences in Figures 6.11 and 6.12 have PPs in the predicate that can be distinguished by using a meaning-based test. This test involves determining what other grammatical element the PP modifies in the sentence. In the sentence in 6.11, it tells us something about the noun "drink;" specifically, it tells us *which* kind of drink we're talking about. Because it modifies the noun, we can say that it is performing the function of an adjectival element, which supports placing it together with the noun at the same level of the hierarchy.

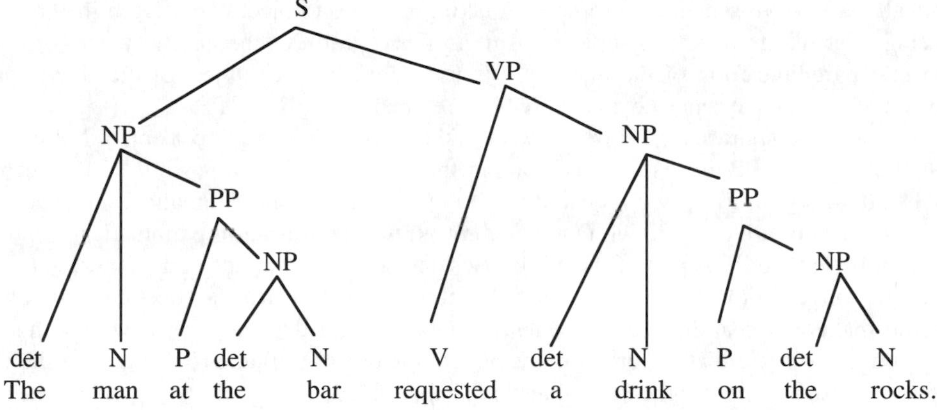

Figure 6.11: Adjectival Prepositional Phrase (PP)

In the sentence in 6.12, however, the situation is different. Here, the PP "in a minute" does not tell us anything about the noun "drink;" instead, it modifies the verb "finished." Specifically, it tells us *when* the drink was finished. As we saw earlier, any element that answers a *how*, *when*, *where* or *why* question about a verb is performing an adverbial function. Because this PP modifies the verb, we place it together with the verb at the same level of the hierarchy.

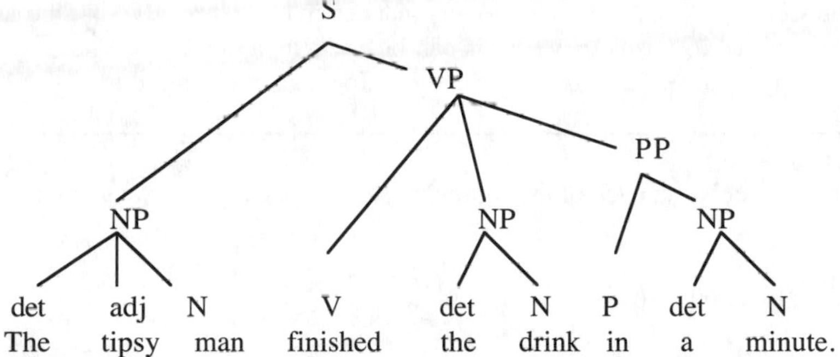

Figure 6.12: Adverbial Prepositional Phrase (PP)

While these meaning-based tests can be useful initially, it's always a good idea to employ more scientific syntactic tests. These are tests in which you manipulate the constituents of a sentence to test their constituent status. The most effective kinds of syntactic tests are movement tests, like the one we used earlier to distinguish coordinate structures from subordinate ones. If, as we stated earlier, a constituent is a "chunk" of words that belong together as one unit, it stands to reason that a constituent should be able to move together as one unit. We can test the structure of a direct object NP by moving it to the subject position and creating a **passive** sentence. A passive sentence is one in which the grammatical subject is the logical, or real world, direct object. In an active sentence, the grammatical subject is also the logical subject. Examples (48) and (49) illustrate passive paraphrases of active sentences. In each sentence, the real world object is underlined.

(48) active: The man at the bar requested <u>a drink on the rocks</u>.
passive: <u>A drink on the rocks</u> was requested by the man at the bar.
* A drink was requested by the man at the bar on the rocks.

(49) active: The tipsy man finished <u>the drink</u> in a minute.
passive: <u>The drink</u> was finished in a minute by the man at the bar.
* The drink in a minute was finished by the man at the bar.

Grammatically, a passive sentence is formed by taking the direct object of the verb in the active sentence and placing it in the grammatical subject position. Then a form of the auxiliary verb "to be" is inserted and the past participle form of the main verb is used. Finally, the subject of the active sentence is moved to the end of the passive sentence, in the predicate, embedded in a "by" PP.

What these passive paraphrases tell is what, exactly, the structure of the direct object NP of the active sentence is. Notice how the PP moves with the noun in the first example, (48), while in the second, (49), it does not. Also, if we try to leave the PP behind in (48) the result is an ungrammatical sentence, and if we do the opposite and try to move the PP with the noun in (49) the result is an ungrammatical sentence. This test indicates clearly that the PP is part of the NP in one sentence, (48), but not in the other, (49).

Another useful movement test is a *fronting* test. Fronting a sentence with a constituent involves moving it from its normal position at the end of a sentence to the front of the sentence. If we try this with the two sentences above, we'll see that it works for one but not the other. (50) and (51) illustrate the results of a PP fronting test. In each sentence, the PP in question is underlined.

(50) regular PP: The man at the bar requested a drink <u>on the rocks</u>.
fronted PP: * <u>On the rocks</u>, the man at the bar requested a drink.

(51) regular PP: The tipsy man finished the drink <u>in a minute</u>.
fronted PP: <u>In a minute</u>, the man at the bar finished the drink.

In (50), the result of the PP fronting is an ungrammatical sentence. This is because the PP is part of the NP, and as an adjectival PP, it needs to stay with the noun it modifies. In (51), however, the PP is *not* part of the NP and can easily move away from the noun because it doesn't modify the noun. Instead, consistent with what we've seen for other adverbials, namely manner and sentence adverbs, the adverbial PP has a certain amount of flexibility in terms of where it can be used in a sentence. These syntactic movement tests, when employed appropriately, are useful for determining constituent structure.

Quick Exercise 6.13

Identify the direct object NP in each of the following sentences by performing both a passive and a PP fronting test.

"We won the game by a touchdown."

Passive:

PP fronting:

"We crushed their spirit in the quarter."

Passive:

PP fronting:

"We ridiculed the emblem on their helmets."

Passive:

PP fronting:

Phrase Structure

Now that we're familiar with constituent structure, it's time to return to our overall goal in syntax, namely explaining grammaticality. Recall that we set out to explain the ungrammaticality of the following sentences:

(43) * Teachers know that them have an important job.
(44) * Know that they have an important job teachers.
(45) * Good teachers put their work.

We already accounted for the badness of (43) by focusing on the form definition of the word class called pronouns. However, because nothing was wrong with the form of any of the words in (44) and (45), we knew we needed to develop additional theories to account for the ungrammaticality of these two sentences. Clearly something is wrong with the structure of the sentence in (44), so our theory must focus on structure and not form. The theory we will use is the **theory of phrase structure**. Specifically, the theory states that every language has a set of **phrase structure rules** that govern how constituents can be structured in that language. To explain the badness of the sentence in (44), we can hypothesize that it violates the phrase structure rules of English. To confirm this hypothesis, of course, we must first describe a set of phrase structure rules for English. Then we'll compare the structure of our sentence to these rules. As always, our approach to determining these rules will be a very descriptive one; that is, we will describe a set of rules by analyzing real English language data.

Figure 6.13 shows three grammatical sentences in English. We will determine the constituent structure of each and then list all the possible structures of each constituent type. To do this, we will simply look to see what elements each constituent node directly dominates. After we've done that, we'll put all the different possibilities together and describe a single rule for each constituent type.

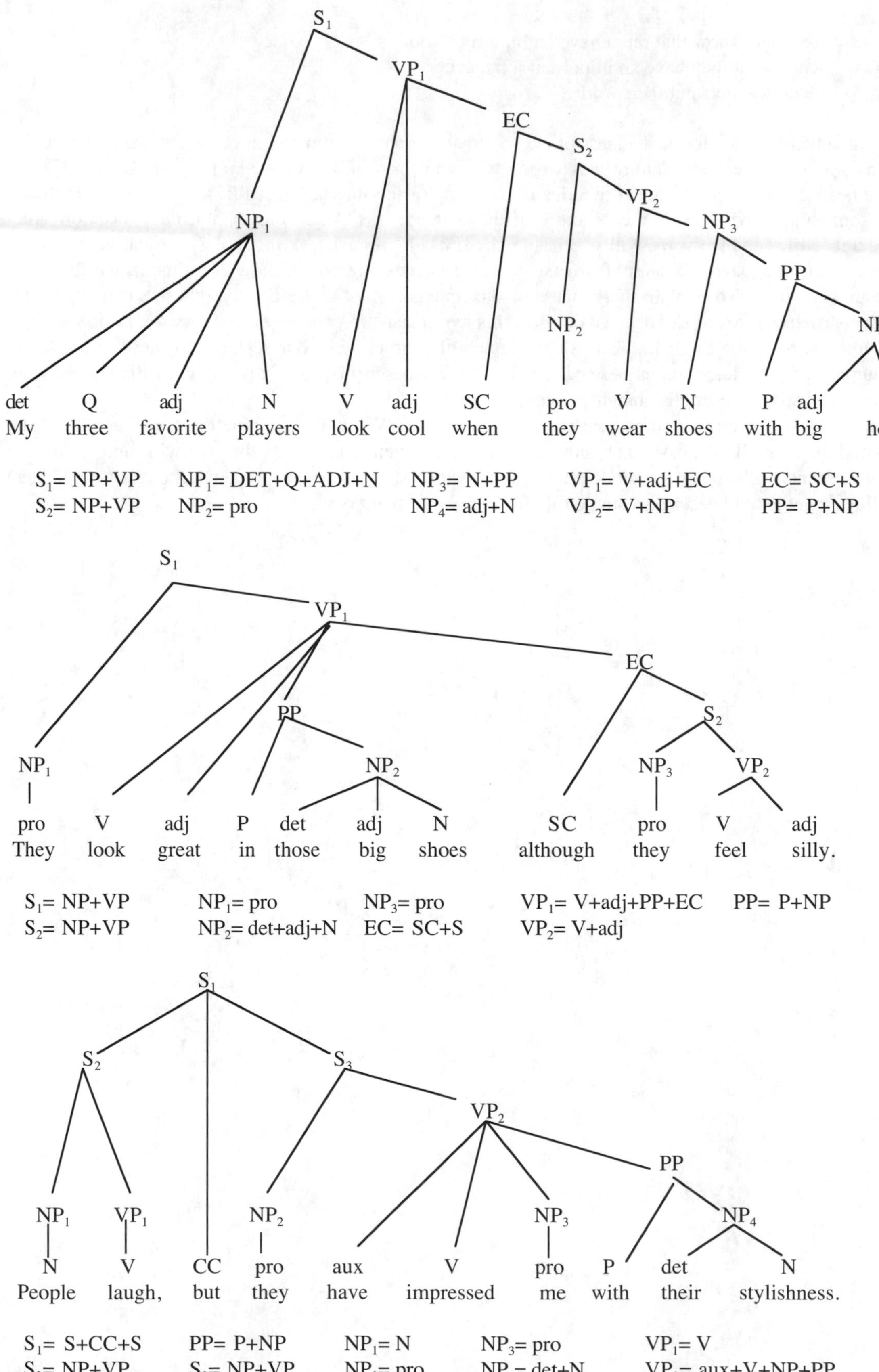

Figure 6.13: Sentences for Phrase Structure Rules

Now we need to list all the possibilities for each constituent type and then boil each set of possibilities down to a single rule for each type. We'll begin with the constituent *sentence*, for which we saw only two possibilities.

S= NP+VP (6 times)
S= S+CC+S

We can represent these two possibilities with a rule in fraction form to indicate an either/or situation.

S rule: $$S= \frac{\text{NP+VP}}{\text{S+CC+S}}$$

Next, we'll list all the possibilities for NP structures.

NP= N NP= det+N NP= det+adj+N NP= det+Q+adj+N NP= adj+N NP=pro (5 times)

What we see from this list is that all NPs have either a noun or a pronoun, and when they have a noun, they can have optional modifying elements before and after the noun, but when the NP has a pronoun, there can be no modifying element. Again, we'll use a fraction format to indicate the either/or situation.

NP rule[3]: $$NP= \frac{\text{(det)+(Q)+(adj)+N+(PP)}}{\text{Pro}}$$

The use of parentheses is to indicate that an element is optional. Either a noun or a pronoun is mandatory, which is why they are not enclosed in parentheses. All the modifying elements that can be combined with a noun, however, are optional. At this point we should return to the traditional definition of a pronoun as being a word that substitutes for a noun. If this description were true, the noun and the pronoun would be interchangeable in this rule. Clearly, however, this is not the case. A more accurate description would be to say that pronouns substitute for NPs.

Now for the VP possibilities:

VP= V VP= aux+V+NP+PP VP= V+PP+EC VP= V+adj VP= V+adj+EC VP= V+NP

The only common element, and therefore the only mandatory element, to all these possibilities is the verb. All the modifiers that precede and follow the verb are optional and are thus enclosed in parentheses. Here, the fraction is used to indicate that an adjective and NP are not *both* possible in the same VP (note that they're never used together in a predicate).

VP rule[4]: $$VP= \text{(aux)+V+} \frac{\text{(NP)}}{\text{(adj)}} \text{+(PP)+(EC)}$$

The embedded clauses and prepositional phrases in the data have only a single structure each, so they are relatively easy to describe with a phrase structure rule.

PP rule: PP= P+NP

EC rule: EC= SC+S

---

[3] Note that while the rule as presented does not explicitly reflect it, there is the possibility for multiple adjectives in an NP. Also, while there is evidence for positing a phrasal category for adjectives (AP), this approach does not address it.

[4] Note that while the rule as presented does not explicitly reflect it, there is the possibility for multiple auxes in a verb phrase, as was suggested earlier in the chapter.

The complete list of phrase structure rules generated by our data is provided in Table 6.2. It's important to note that this set of rules is by no means complete. The data that we used to describe them is very limited, which means our rules will necessarily be incomplete. This should not be a source of concern. To date, no one has written a complete set of phrase structure rules for English.

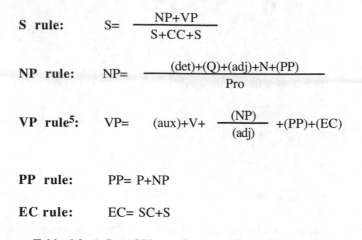

S rule:	$S = \frac{NP+VP}{S+CC+S}$
NP rule:	$NP = \frac{(det)+(Q)+(adj)+N+(PP)}{Pro}$
VP rule[5]:	$VP = (aux)+V+\frac{(NP)}{(adj)}+(PP)+(EC)$
PP rule:	PP= P+NP
EC rule:	EC= SC+S

Table 6.2: A Set of Phrase Structure Rules for English

Also, it's important to note that this set of rules was described by analyzing English language data. Any set of phrase structure rules for other languages will necessarily be different because the data will be different. In fact, differences in phrase structure rules are one of the many factors that make learning a second language so challenging.

We can now use these phrase structure rules of English to explain the ungrammaticality of the sentence in (44). The diagram in Figure 6.14 illustrates the constituent structure of the sentence.

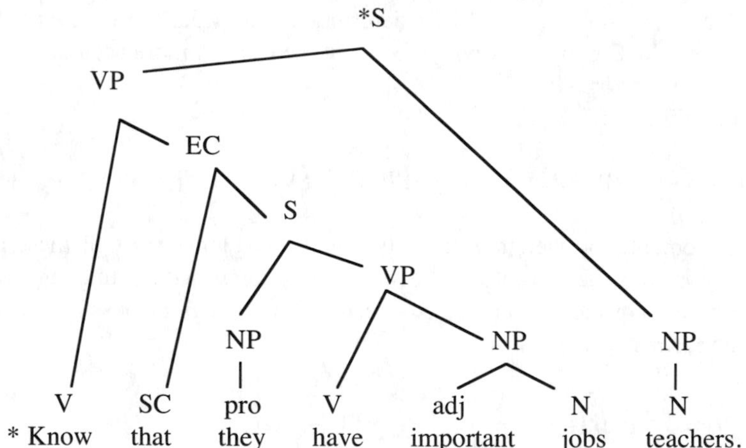

Figure 6.14: Constituent Structure of an Ungrammatical Sentence

We see that every constituent conforms to the phrase structure rules we described with one important exception. The higher of the two S nodes has the structure VP+NP, and we know that this is not an allowable structure in English. We can now explain the ungrammaticality of this sentence by citing the theory of phrase structure and noting that, specifically, it violates the rule for how a sentence constituent can be formed in English.

---

[5] Note that while the rule as presented does not explicitly reflect it, there is the possibility for multiple auxes in a verb phrase, as was suggested earlier in the chapter.

Quick Exercise 6.14

Determine which of the constituents in the following ungrammatical sentence is/are in violation of our phrase structure rules. Circle the node(s) of the bad constituent(s).

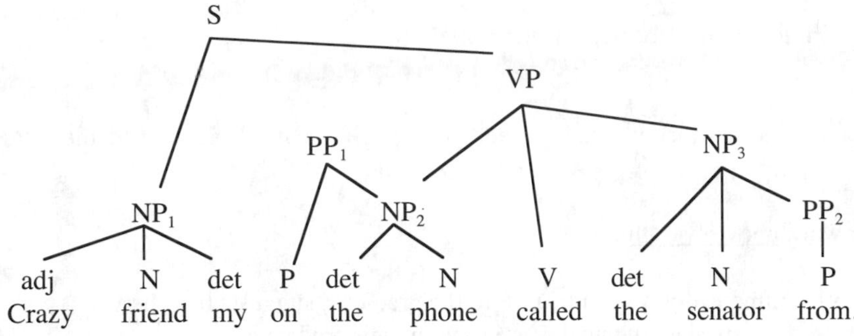

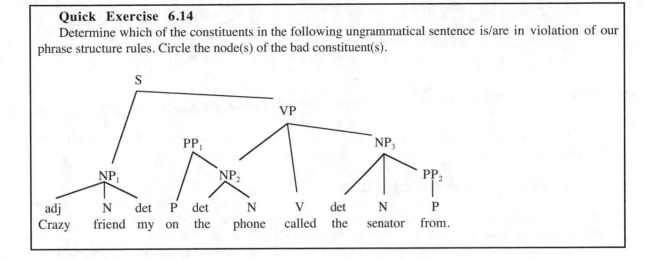

Subcategorization

With our theory of phrase structure, we now have a theory that enables us to explain the ungrammaticality of the sentence in (44). If this theory is all we need to explain structural ungrammaticality, it should also help us explain the badness of the sentence in (45); that is, this sentence, being ungrammatical, should also violate the phrase structure rules of English. Let's determine the constituent structure of this sentence in Figure 6.15 to see if this is indeed the case.

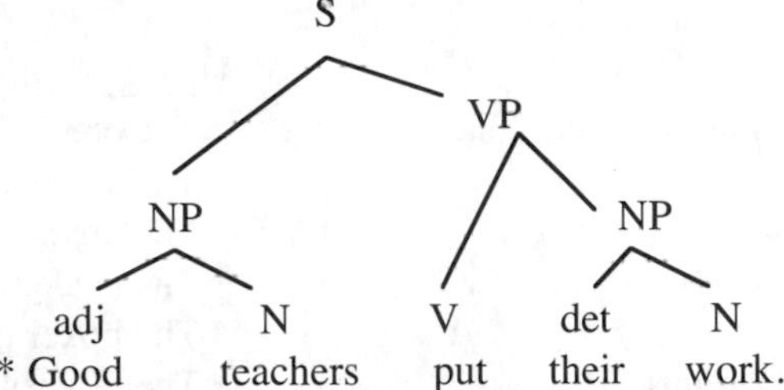

Figure 6.15: Constituent Structure of an Ungrammatical Sentence

Unfortunately, there is nothing wrong with the phrase structure of this sentence. Every constituent conforms to the phrase structure rules we described earlier. Also, every word is perfectly well formed. What this tells us is that the theories we have so far are inadequate to explain the ungrammaticality of this sentence, so we need an additional theory.

To determine what this theory should focus on, we can try to correct the sentence to make it grammatical. The easiest way would be to change the verb, as in (52).

(52) Good teachers <u>love</u> their work.

The fact that the verb "love" works grammatically in the original sentence, while the verb "put" does not, leads us to the conclusion that these two verbs are in some way different. We can say, then, that while they are both verbs, they are different kinds of verbs. This leads us to separate verbs into smaller categories of verbs, called **subcategories**. Figure 6.16 illustrates this.

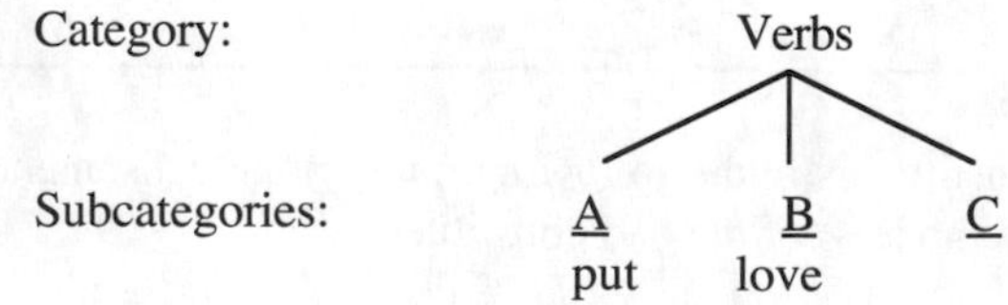

Figure 6.16: Subcategorization of Verbs

Another possibility for correcting the sentence would be to add another grammatical element to the VP, as in (53).

(53) Good teachers put their work above everything.

Now, the fact the "put" works grammatically if we add a PP to the predicate suggests that the way "put" and "love" differ is in terms of the grammatical elements that are used in their predicates.

These two observations have led linguists to a theory called **subcategorization restrictions.** This theory states that different types of verbs can be distinguished from each other based on the complements (other grammatical elements) that they take in their predicate. The verbs "put" and "love" help illustrate this concept because we can see that while "love" works perfectly well with just a single NP in its predicate, "put" requires both an NP and a PP.

Data Analysis 6.1

Using the data below, subcategorize the underlined verbs used by looking at the other grammatical elements that the verbs are combined with in their predicates.

Grammatical	Ungrammatical
The president put the cigar in his mouth.	* The president put the cigar.
The student laughed.	* The student laughed the teacher's jokes.
The unknown eater tasted the soup.	* The unknown eater tasted.
The student gave the apple to the teacher.	* The student gave the apple.
The boxer punched his opponent.	* The boxer punched.
The teacher created an educational exercise.	* The teacher created.
The child cried.	* The child cried the story.
The teacher yawned.	* The teacher yawned the student.
The police placed the player under arrest.	* The police placed the player.

Subcategory X	Subcategory Y	Subcategory Z

Subcategories of English Verbs

With the concept of subcategorization restrictions under our belts, we are now ready to describe some subcategories of English verbs based on an analysis of data. Our goal will be to separate English verbs into four subcategories by determining what grammatical elements they *must* take, *can* take and can *not* take in their predicate. The four subcategories we'll look at are *transitive*, *intransitive*, *ditransitive* and *linking* verbs.

Transitive Verbs

Table 6.3 illustrates grammatical and ungrammatical uses of three transitive verbs.

Grammatical Uses	Ungrammatical Uses
1. Lewis punched Holyfield.	7. *Lewis punched in the face.
2. Lewis punched Holyfield in the face.	8. *Lewis punched.
3. Holyfield wants a rematch.	9. *Holyfield wants.
4. Holyfield wants a rematch with Lewis.	10. *Holyfield wants with Lewis.
5. Tyson tasted Holyfield's ear.	11. *Holyfield wants a rematch good.
6. Tyson tasted Holyfield's ear in the third round.	12. *Tyson tasted.
	13. *Tyson tasted in the third round

Table 6.3: Transitive Verb Data (punch, want, taste—as an *action*, not a *state*)

The grammatical data indicates that an NP is essential for a **transitive verb** to be used grammatically. This observation makes sense if we consider what transitivity means. The prefix "trans-" means "across," which is useful because transitivity involves action *across* the verb from the subject to the direct object. We can illustrate this, as in Figure 6.16.

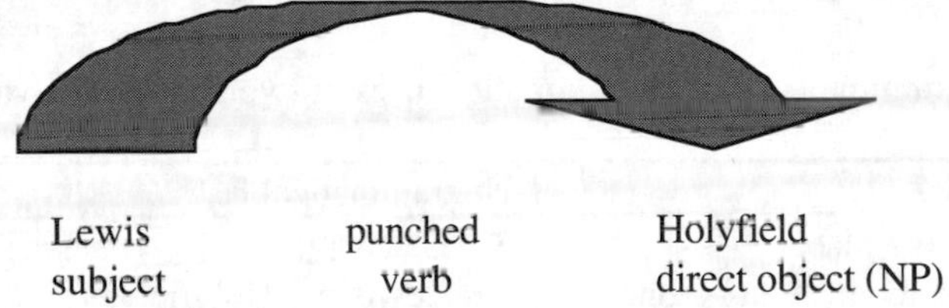

Lewis	punched	Holyfield
subject	verb	direct object (NP)

Figure 6.16: Graphic Representation of Transitivity

In Table 6.3, in addition to the mandatory NP, we see an optional PP working grammatically in some of the examples (#1, #4, #6). The ungrammatical data also indicates that an NP is necessary because every sentence without an NP in the predicate is ungrammatical. In addition, the ungrammatical data indicates that a predicative adjective does not work in a predicate with a transitive verb because the example with a predicative adjective (#11) is not good even though it has the necessary NP.

Quick Exercise 6.15

For each grammatical example in Table 6.3, identify the direct object NP.

1. 2. 3.

4. 5. 6.

Intransitive Verbs

Table 6.4 illustrates grammatical and ungrammatical uses of two intransitive verbs.

Grammatical Uses	Ungrammatical Uses
1. After the loss, Holyfield wept. 2. After the loss, Holyfield wept with his mother. 3. After the win, Lewis slept. 4. After the win, Lewis slept for hours.	5. *After the loss, Holyfield wept Lewis. 6. *After the loss, Holyfield wept Lewis with his mother. 7. *After the loss, Holyfield cried good. 8. *After the win, Lewis slept Holyfield. 9. *After the win, Lewis slept Holyfield for hours.

Table 6.4 : Intransitive Verb Data (weep, sleep)

As the negative prefix "in-" suggests, with **intransitive verbs** there is *no* action across the verb from the subject to a direct object. In fact, as the ungrammatical data indicates, there can be no direct object NP in the VP of an intransitive verb at all (see #8 and #9). The grammatical data indicates that it's possible for a PP to be in the predicate (#4), but a predicative adjective is *not* possible, according to the ungrammatical data (#7).

Ditransitive Verbs

Table 6.5 illustrates grammatical and ungrammatical uses of two ditransitive verbs.

Grammatical Uses	Ungrammatical Uses
1. Lewis put Holyfield in his place. 2. Lewis referred Holyfield to an ear surgeon.	3. *Lewis put. 4. *Lewis put Holyfield. 5. *Lewis put Holyfield good in his place. 6. *Lewis put in his place. 7. *Lewis referred Holyfield. 8. *Lewis referred to an ear surgeon.

Table 6.5 : Ditransitive Verb Data (put, refer)

Again, a morphological analysis of the name of the subcategory suggests the behavior of its verbs. The prefix "di-" means "two," which suggests transitivity in *two* ways, and the data confirms this. In the grammatical data, every sentence contains both a direct object NP and a PP in the predicate. When one of these elements is missing, as we can see from the ungrammatical data, the sentence is ungrammatical. The ungrammatical data also tells us that predicative adjectives do not work with ditransitive verbs (see #5).

Quick Exercise 6.16

For each grammatical example in Table 6.5, identify the direct object NP and the PP.

1. NP PP

2. NP PP

Linking Verbs

Table 6.6 illustrates grammatical and ungrammatical uses of two **linking verbs**.

Grammatical Uses	Ungrammatical Uses
1. Lewis looks big. 2. Lewis looks big in those trunks. 3. Holyfield's ear tastes bad. 4. Holyfield's ear tastes bad without ketchup.	5. *Lewis looks Holyfield. 6. *Lewis looks Holyfield in those trunks. 7. *Holyfield's ear tastes Tyson. 8. *Holyfield's ear tastes Tyson with ketchup.

Table 6.6 : Linking Verb Data (look, taste—both as *states*, not *actions*)

As their name suggests, linking verbs link two grammatical elements. In all of the grammatical examples, we see the verbs linking the subject NP with a predicative adjective that describes the subject. As the ungrammatical data indicates, without the predicative adjective, the sentence is ungrammatical. The ungrammatical data also indicates that a direct object NP does *not* work with a linking verb. In the grammatical data, we see an optional PP (#4).

Quick Exercise 6.17
For each grammatical example in Table 6.6, identify the predicative adjective.

1. 2. 3. 4.

Subcategory name	Transitive	Intransitive	Ditransitive	Linking
Must take	NP	---	NP+PP	adj
Can take	(PP)	(PP)	---	(PP)
Can *not* take	adj	NP/adj	adj	NP
Syntactic frame	VP: V NP (PP) ~~adj~~	VP: V ~~NP~~ (PP) ~~adj~~	VP: V NP PP ~~adj~~	VP: V adj (PP) ~~NP~~

Table 6.7: A Summary of Subcategories of English Verbs

Linking Verbs Revisited

While Table 6.7 is accurate for the data we've analyzed, there is another possibility for linking verbs that must be considered. The data in Table 6.8 illustrates this possibility with the linking verbs "be" and "become."

Grammatical Uses	Ungrammatical Uses
1. Lewis is a large man. 2. Lewis became the new champion. 3. Holyfield's ear is in bad shape. 4. Holyfield's ear became the talk of the town.	5. *Lewis is the heavyweight title. 6. *Lewis became high prices for gasoline. 7. *Holyfield's ear is. 8. *Holyfield's ear became Tyson with ketchup.

Table 6.8: More Linking Verb Data (be, become)

This data shows us that, contrary to what we found earlier, some linking verbs *can* have an NP in their predicate (#1, #2, #4), but don't always need to (#3). When they do have one, it must rename the subject, as the NP "a large man" does in the first grammatical sentence (#1). When an NP that does not rename the subject is used, as in the first ungrammatical example (#5), the sentence is bad. This makes sense when we consider that a linking verb's function is to link the subject with some element, often called a **complement**, in the predicate. We now have a new grammatical relation in these NPs that we will call a **subject complement**. The other things that this data tells are 1) that linking verbs must have *some* grammatical element in the predicate (see #7), and 2) that sometimes this element can be a PP (see #3). The first observation is predictable given the linking function of these verbs—there must be some complement in the predicate to be linked to the subject. The second one is not too surprising when we consider the adjectival function of many PPs; they do, in a sense, function as a predicative adjective would.

Quick Exercise 6.18

Mix and match the following subjects and subject complements to form sentences in which the subject complement renames the subject. Use the linking verb "to be" in your sentences.

subjects	subject complements
George Dubya Bush	one smooth beer
Pabst Blue Ribbon beer	a canine wonder
The act of underage drinking	a good-old boy
McGruff the crime dog	a crime in every state

sentences:

Transformations

Up to this point, the theories of syntax we've identified have been useful in helping us achieve our main goal—to explain grammaticality. If our theories are adequate, they should help us explain the grammaticality of all English sentences, including the three sentences in examples (54), (55) and (56).

(54) Will linguistics help us with our profession?
(55) What will linguistics help us with?
(56) Why will linguistics help us?

These sentences are different from the others we've looked at in this chapter because they are **interrogative** sentences, meaning they are questions. Every other sentence up to this point has been a **declarative** sentence, meaning a statement. Regardless of their interrogativity, each one is clearly grammatical, and as such, we expect them all to conform to the phrase structure rules of English. To test their phrase structure, we can attempt to represent their constituent structure with a tree diagram.

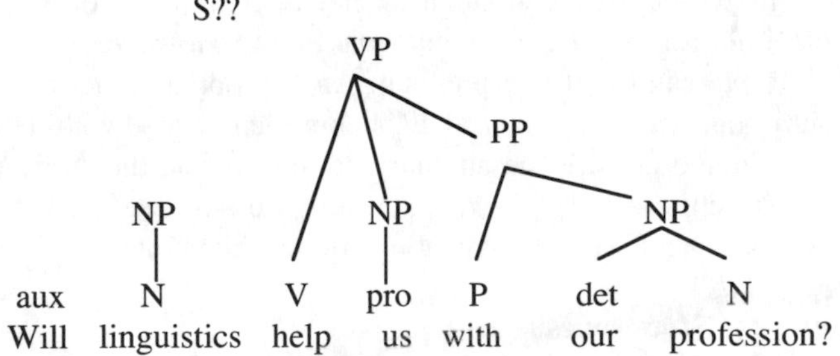

Figure 6.17: Constituent Structure of (54)

Unfortunately, this sentence does *not* conform to the phrase structure rules of English. With all sentences (excluding coordinate sentences), we saw that S=NP+VP, but here we have a sentence initial auxiliary verb. The structure of this sentence, then, appears to be S=aux+NP+VP, which violates the phrase structure rule for a sentence. We now have a problem in that the sentence is perfectly grammatical, yet it violates the phrase structure rules of English. This is a contradiction that must eventually be resolved.

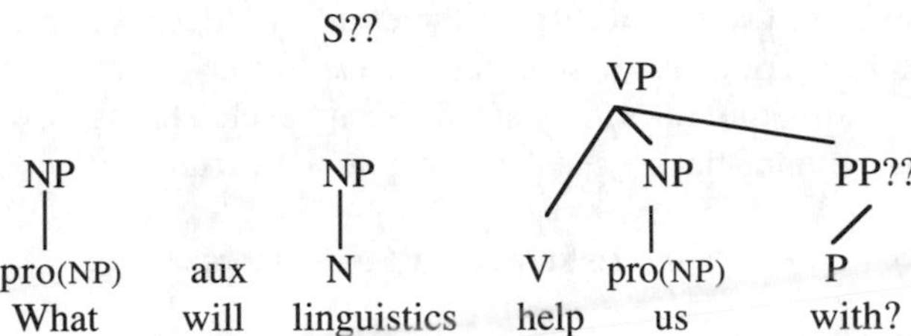

Figure 6.18: Constituent Structure of (55)

The first problem we have with this sentence is determining what type of word "what" is, since it is one we haven't seen before. A good way to determine this would be to answer the question that the sentence poses without forming a complete sentence, but instead just substituting a constituent for "what." Possible answers include "our profession" and "other classes," each of which is an NP. In our discussion of phrase structure at the beginning of this chapter, we determined that words that substituted for NPs were pronouns, and because "what" is substituting for an NP in this sentence, it makes sense to call it a pronoun. It's somewhat different from the other pronouns we've seen so far, however, so we'll subcategorize it as an **interrogative pronoun**, which sets it apart from the **personal pronouns**, such as "he" and "she," that we had been working with up to this point.

What this leaves us with is 1) an NP in the sentence initial position that is not the subject of the verb, 2) an auxiliary before the subject and 3) a PP without its required object (recall the rule PP=P+NP). These three features tell us that this grammatical sentence, like the previous one, does not conform to the phrase structure rules of English and it, therefore, leaves us with the same contradiction to resolve.

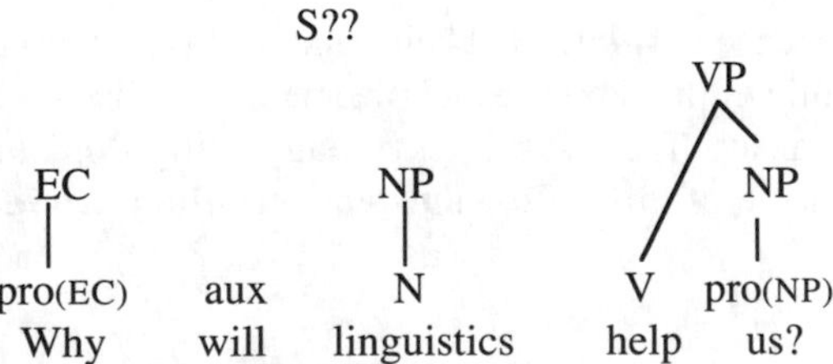

Figure 6.19: Constituent Structure of (56)

As with the previous sentence, we need to determine what type of word we have in the sentence initial position. Again, to do this, we can answer the question without using a complete sentence. Possible answers include "because it is a useful subject" and "because it is relevant to teachers," each of which is a dependent clause. "Why" is similar, then, to a pronoun in that it substitutes for a larger constituent. We'll call *all* such words that substitute for larger constituents **pro forms**. However, because "why" is substituting for an EC, and not an NP, we can't call it a pronoun. An appropriate label for the pro form "why" is "pro-EC." According to our phrase structure rules, an EC belongs embedded within the predicate, not in the sentence initial position, so this, along with the auxiliary coming before the subject NP, tells us that the sentence violates the phrase structure rules of English. Again, we will need to resolve this problem (this apparent contradiction) of a grammatical sentence violating our described rules.

Deep and Surface Structures

To reconcile the contradiction of a grammatical sentence violating phrase structure rules, linguists have proposed a **theory of transformations**, which states that these grammatical sentences may violate the phrase structures at one level, but at another level they actually *do* follow the phrase structure rules. These sentences, the theory states, have been *transformed*, or changed somehow, from **canonical** sentences, sentences that *do* follow the regular rules of structure, to **non-canonical** ones, sentences that do *not* follow the regular rules. This happens when we unconsciously apply transformational rules to change an unspoken canonical sentence in our minds, at a **deep** or **underlying level,** into a non-canonical, but perfectly grammatical, sentence that we then speak on the **surface level**. These concepts of underlying and surface levels should be familiar to you from chapters three and five. Because the surface and deep structures are really just two different forms of the *same* sentence, we can say that the non-canonical surface structure really *does* follow the phrase structure rules, only at a different level. This is how we can reconcile the apparent contradiction between grammaticality and incorrect phrase structure.

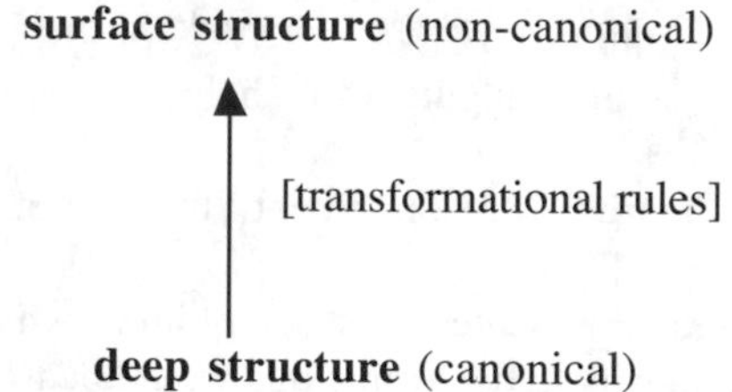

Figure 6.20: Graphic Representation of Transformational Rules

Transformational Rules

We can illustrate this process of transforming canonical structures into non-canonical ones using the sentences in (54), (55) and (56), and in the process we will describe the transformational rules that govern how these non-canonical sentences are formed.

Sub-Aux Inversion

Putting the elements of sentence (54) back in their canonical places involves returning the subject NP to its usual place at the beginning of the sentence and placing the auxiliary verb back in its canonical position at the beginning of the predicate. The result is essentially a flip-flopping of the subject and the auxiliary verb, which leads to the name of this rule—**subject-auxiliary inversion**. Figure 6.21 illustrates this inversion.

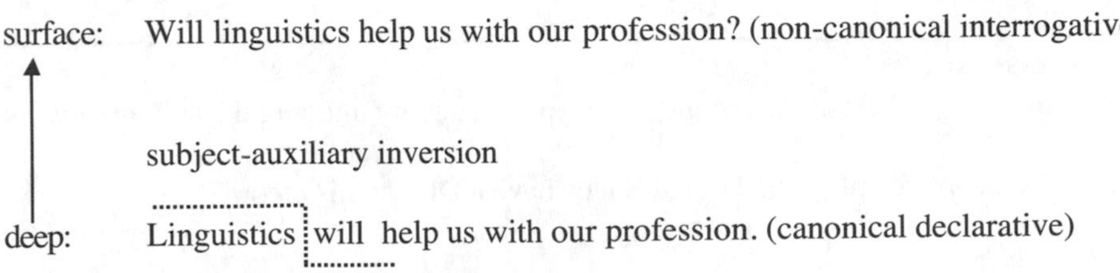

surface: Will linguistics help us with our profession? (non-canonical interrogative)
subject-auxiliary inversion
deep: Linguistics will help us with our profession. (canonical declarative)

Figure 6.21: Graphic Representation of Sub-Aux Inversion

It's essential for us to confirm that our proposed deep structure is truly canonical. If it's not, our whole theory of transformations, which states that non-canonical grammatical sentences are canonical at a deeper level, is useless. To confirm this, we can determine the hierarchical structure of the deep structure sentence in Figure 6.21. This is done in Figure 6.22.

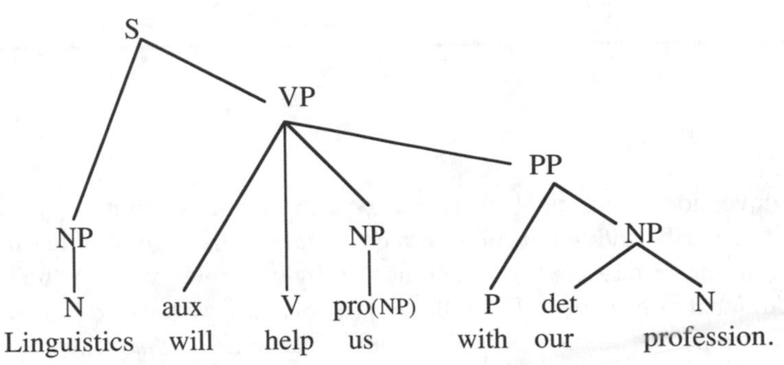

Figure 6.22: Canonical Constituent Structure of Deep Structure

Having confirmed that the deep structure is canonical, we now need to prove that this inversion is systematic, and not just an anomaly specific to this sentence. To do this, we need to see it repeated in the *same* pattern with other sentences of the *same* kind. This will involve first determining what kind of sentence we have. Notice that the possible answers to the question in this example are "yes" and "no." Based on this, we'll call this a **yes/no question** and use other yes/no questions to prove the systematicity of our rule.

surface: Should concerned teachers study linguistics?
deep: Concerned teachers should study linguistics.

surface: Can a teacher with training be effective?
deep: A teacher with training can be effective.

surface: Could it be true?
deep: It could be true.

Notice how in each case, the single underlined auxiliary and the double underlined subject NP simply change places at the surface level. Notice also that it's the *complete* subject that changes places with the auxiliary. In some sentences, the complete subject consists of several words, while in others it might just be a single word.

Quick Exercise 6.19
For each yes/no question below, determine the deep structure by undoing the sub-aux inversion.

surface: "Should the President of the United States have a DUI on his record?"

deep:

surface: "Can his constituency trust him if he does have a DUI on his record?"

deep:

surface: "Will his daughters have a DUI on their records?"

deep:

Wh-Movement

While sub-aux, inversion is sufficient to help us describe a rule for forming yes/no questions in English, we might need to describe additional rules because there are other types of questions. The question in (55), for example, can *not* be answered in a helpful way by a simple "yes" or "no." Instead, this kind of question requires additional information. Thus, these questions are often called **information questions**. With information questions, we see not only a sub/aux inversion, but also movement of a word from its canonical place within the predicate to the sentence initial position. Because this word and most of the others that function like it are spelled with the letters "wh-", this rule is usually called **"wh-" movement.** This spelling description has also led to the term **"wh-" question** for information questions. The transformations involved in forming "wh-" questions are illustrated in Figure 6.23.

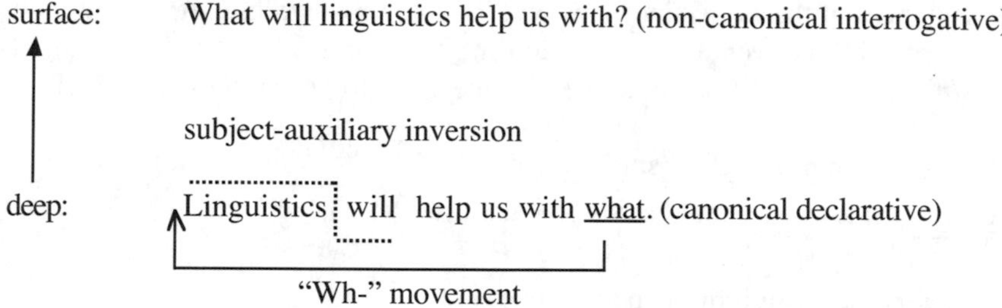

Figure 6.23: Graphic Representation of "wh-" Movement

Again, we need to verify that our deep structure is canonical. This is done in Figure 6.24.

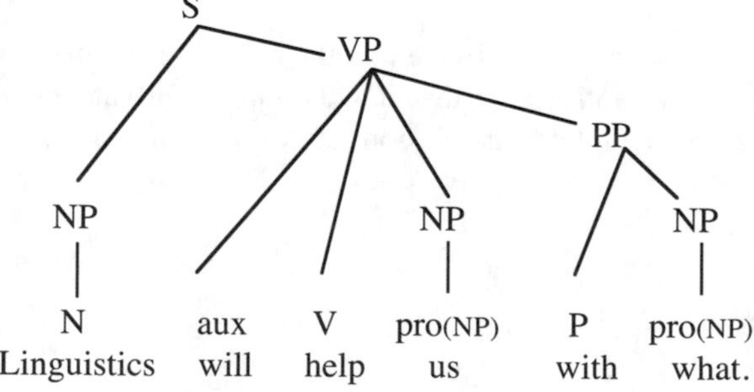

Figure 6.24: Deep Canonical Structure

ent clause that served a nominal (noun-like) function. Here, however, "that" can *not* be a subordinating conjunction because there is no sentence that follows it (recall the phrase structure rule EC=SC+S). Instead, in this sentence, "that" serves as the subject of the verb "provides." Because it is the subject of a verb, it must be an NP. Also, we know that because in the real world, there is some subject other than "that" (after all, what kind of meaning does "that" have on its own?), we can surmise that "that" is substituting for some other constituent, namely the NP "a profession." This leads us to classify "that" as a type of pronoun[6].

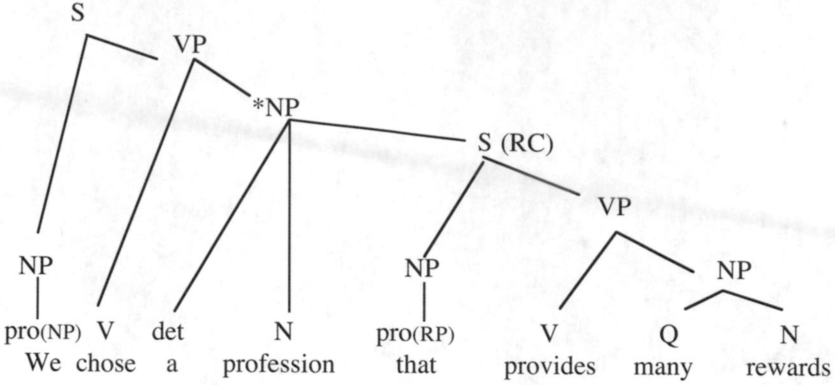

Figure 6.25: Non-Canonical Declarative

Also, we need to justify embedding the S within the NP in the predicate of the larger sentence. To do this, we need only perform a passive test. When we do this, as we have done in (58), we see that the S moves with the NP to the front of the passive sentence. Because this entire string of words is the subject of the passive sentence, we know this entire string of words must be the subject NP.

(58) <u>A profession that provides many rewards</u> was chosen by us.

Having justified our diagram, we can now address the non-canonical structure of the sentence. Notice that the direct object NP of the verb "chose" has the following structure: NP=det+N+S. A sentence embedded within an NP is clearly non-canonical according to the phrase structure rules we described. Such embedded sentences (also by definition clauses) that are embedded within NPs are called **relative clauses**. Relative clauses (or RC) serve an adjectival function, modifying the head of the NP in which they are embedded. In this case, the relative clause "that provides many rewards" is describing which profession we are talking about. A relative clause is introduced by a **relative pronoun** that refers to the noun that precedes it.

Relative clauses essentially allow us to take two separate sentences and combine them into one. It's a tool English speakers use to economize their speech. The rule is in two parts. First, we can analyze the deep structure as two separate, canonical sentences. Then, to avoid repeating an NP, we substitute a relative pronoun for the NP. In technical terms, we *relativize* the NP. Finally, we embed the relative clause within a NP of the larger sentence. This two-step process is illustrated in Figure 6.26. And again, we need to verify that our deep structure is canonical. Figure 6.27 shows that each of the two sentences in the deep structure is perfectly canonical.

[6]This treatment of "that" as a relative pronoun is not favored by most linguists, who instead view it as a complementizer.

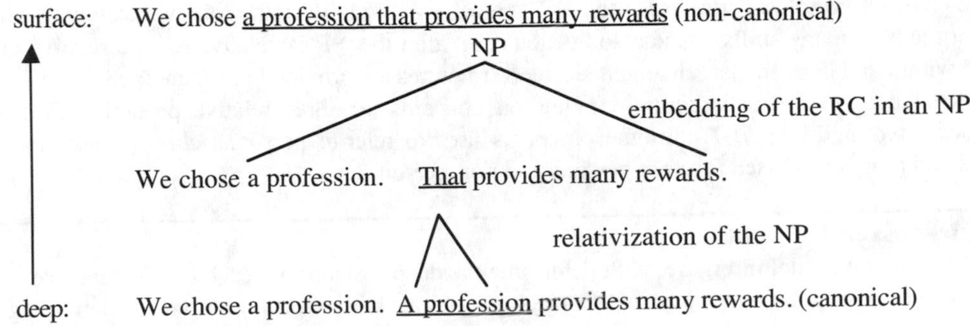

Figure 6.26: Graphic Representation of Relative Clause Transformation

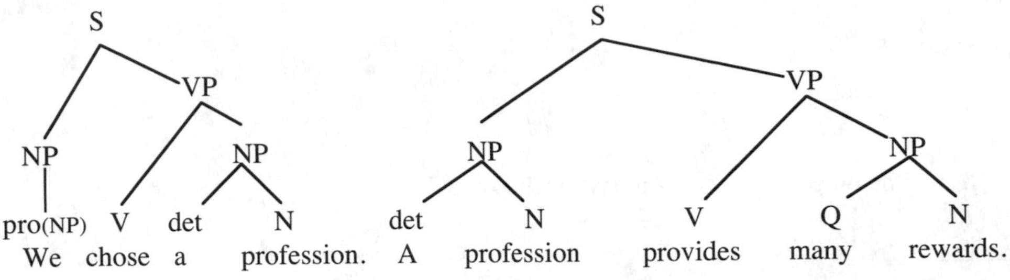

Figure 6.27: Canonical Deep Structure of a Sentence with a Relative Clause

As we have done for our other transformational rules, we need to prove systematicity for the relative clause transformation. Examples (59) and (60) are other sentences with relative clauses.

(59) Everyone needs a teacher *who knows linguistics*.
(60) Linguistics classes teach many skills *which benefit teachers*.

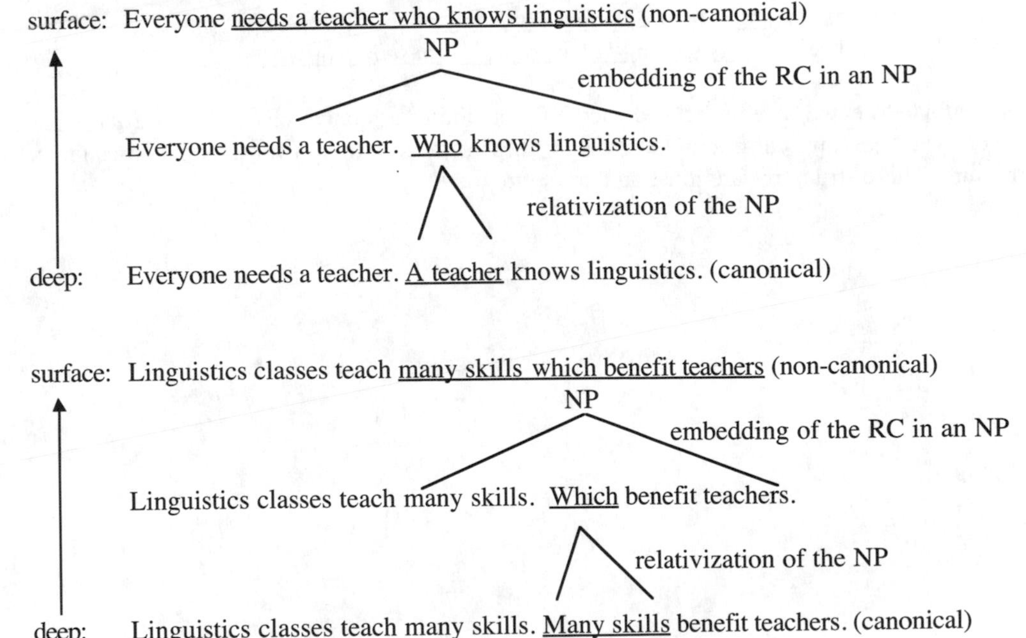

Figure 6.28: More Deep structures of Sentences with Relative Clauses

In each example, the NP with the embedded relative clause has been underlined and the relative clause has been italicized. Notice that in each case, there is a relative pronoun substituting for an NP. In (59), the relative pronoun "who" substitutes for the NP "a teacher," and in (60), the relative pronoun "which" substitutes for the NP "many skills." And also in each case, after the NP is relativized, the relative clause is embedded within an NP of the larger sentence. Deep structures are provided in Figure 6.28.

A final note to be made before moving on concerns the three relative pronouns used in this section—*who*, *that* and *which*. Traditionally, *who* is used to refer to persons, *which* is used to refer to non-persons and *that* can be used for both persons and non-persons.

Quick Exercise 6.21

Following the model in Figure 6.28, determine the deep structure of each of the sentences below. Start first by unembedding the relative clause to reach an intermediate structure before unrelativizing the relative pronoun to reach the deep structure.

surface: "I support the team that disappoints me."

[intermediate]:

deep:

surface: "I like the player who scores many touchdowns."

[intermediate]:

deep:

Movement of Relative Pronouns

Now that we have addressed sentences such as (59) and (60), we need to look at other, more complicated sentences with relative clauses, such as those in (61) and (62).

(61) We can diagram any sentence *that we can write*.

(62) We must justify each diagram *that we represent a sentence with*.

As we did before, we have underlined each NP containing a relative clause, and we have italicized each relative clause. Again, we can attempt to diagram these sentences to illustrate their non-canonical constituent structure. These structures are illustrated in Figure 6.29.

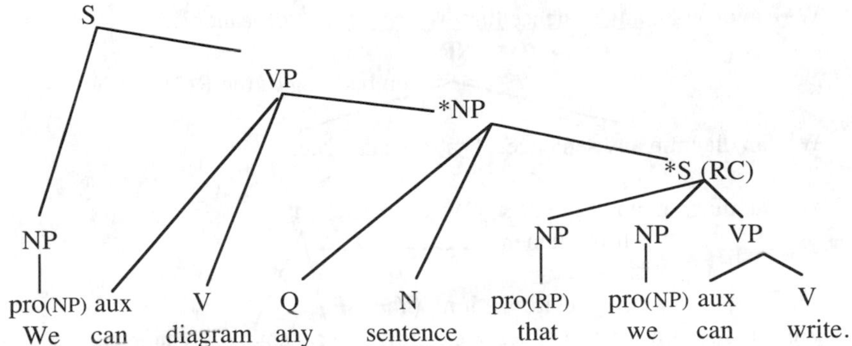

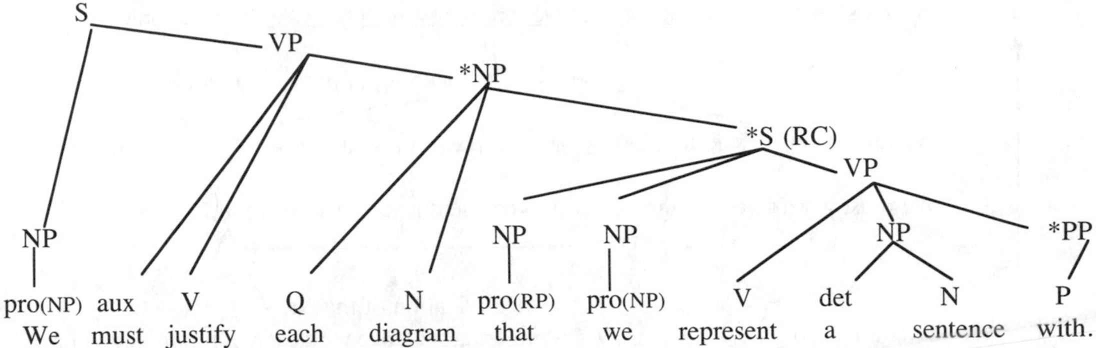

Figure 6.29: More Non-Canonical Declaratives

In each of these sentences, we see once again a relative clause being embedded within an NP of the larger sentence. These NPs, therefore, are non-canonical. In addition to the non-canonical NPs, however, we also see other non-canonical constituents within the sentences. In both sentences, the relative clause itself is non-canonical because each one has the structure NP+NP+VP. In the second sentence, we also see a non-canonical PP within the relative clause that lacks the necessary object NP to be canonical. Clearly, then, we are dealing with a different kind of relative clause and determining the deep structure of such sentences will require analysis beyond what we have already done.

To undo whatever transformations have been applied to reach the deep structure of these sentences, we would be wise to begin with what we already know, namely that a relative clause is a clause embedded within an NP. Our first step in undoing these transformations, then, should be to unembed, or pull the relative clause out of, the NP. When we do this, we notice that the relative clause is non-canonical, because the relative pronoun, which by definition introduces the relative clause, is not the subject of the verb in the clause. We know, however, that canonically, the NP at the beginning of a clause should be the subject of the clause, so before we unrelativize the relative pronoun, we need to determine where it belongs, canonically, in the relative clause. To do this, we need to determine what grammatical relation it serves in the relative clause. If it's not the subject, it must be either the direct object or the object of a preposition. Once we determine its grammatical relation, we can undo the wh-movement transformation that moved it to the beginning of the relative clause. Finally, we can unrelativize the relative pronoun to reach the deep structure. This three part process is illustrated for each sentence in Figure 6.30.

In arriving at our deep structure, we undid a wh-movement between the two steps of the relative clause transformation. In the first example, the relative pronoun is the direct object of the verb "write", so we put it back where it belongs canonically, directly dominated by the VP node. In the second sentence, the relative pronoun is the object of the preposition "with", so we put it back where it belongs canonically, directly dominated by the PP node. To check our work, we can confirm that the deep structures we've proposed are actually canonical. This is done in Figure 6.31.

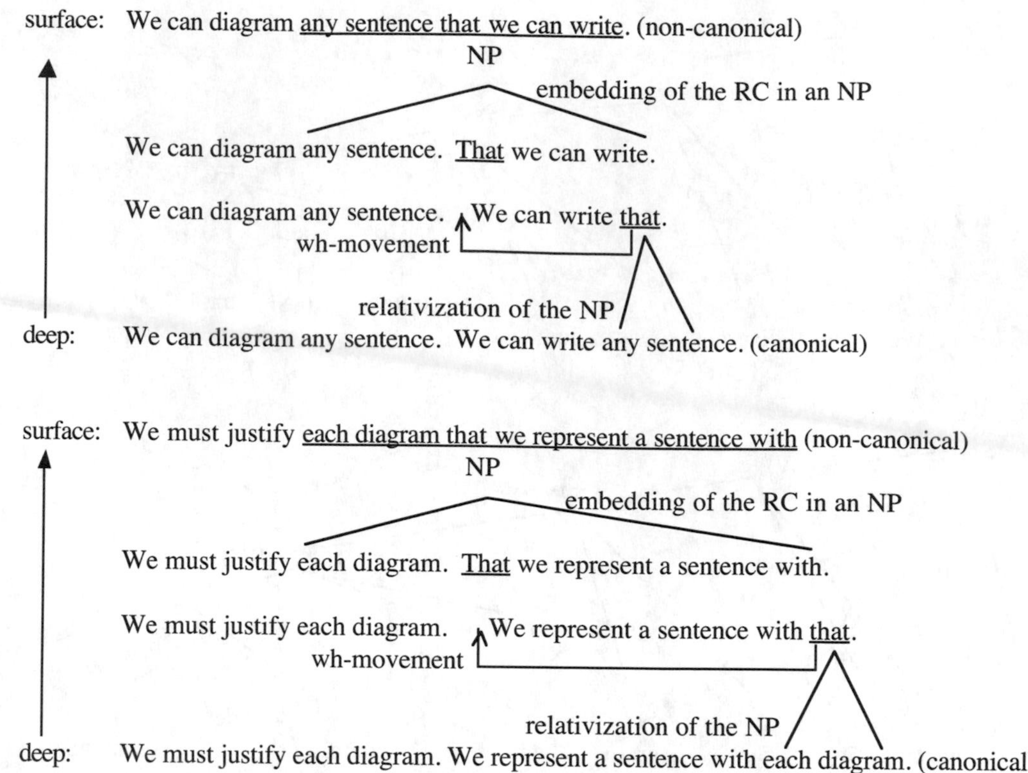
surface: We can diagram any sentence that we can write. (non-canonical)
NP
embedding of the RC in an NP
We can diagram any sentence. That we can write.
We can diagram any sentence. We can write that.
wh-movement
relativization of the NP
deep: We can diagram any sentence. We can write any sentence. (canonical)
surface: We must justify each diagram that we represent a sentence with (non-canonical)
NP
embedding of the RC in an NP
We must justify each diagram. That we represent a sentence with.
We must justify each diagram. We represent a sentence with that.
wh-movement
relativization of the NP
deep: We must justify each diagram. We represent a sentence with each diagram. (canonical)

Figure 6.30: Deep Structures of Relative Clauses with Wh- Movement

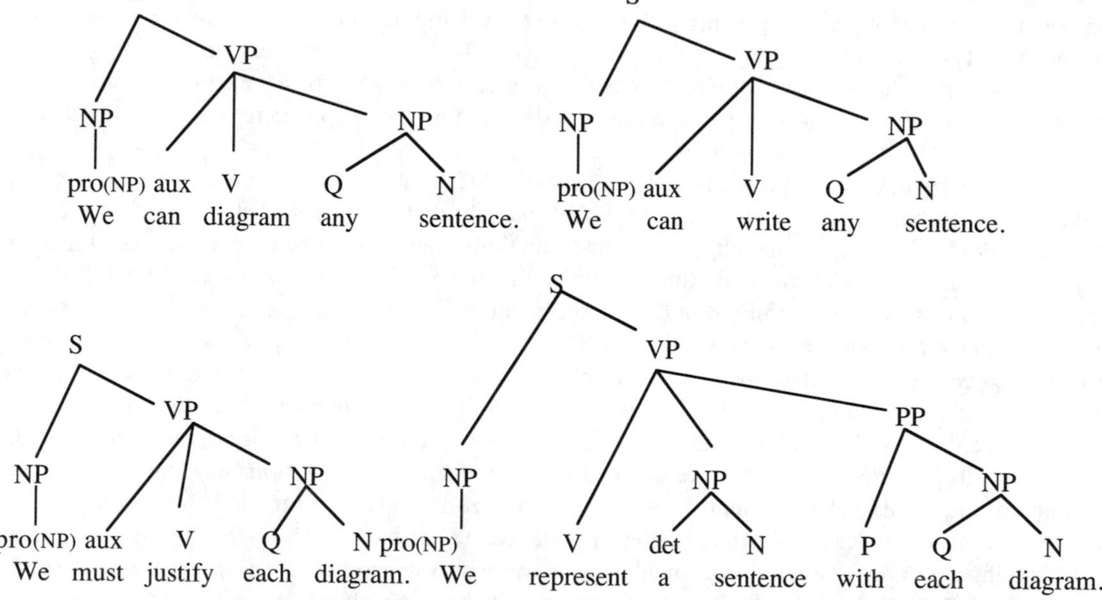
S
VP
NP
NP
pro(NP) aux V Q N
We can diagram any sentence.
S
VP
NP
NP
pro(NP) aux V Q N
We can write any sentence.
S
VP
NP
NP
pro(NP) aux V Q N
We must justify each diagram.
S
VP
PP
NP
NP
NP
pro(NP) V det N P Q N
We represent a sentence with each diagram.

Figure 6.31: Canonical Structures of Sentence with Relative Clauses with Wh- Movement

The key to determining whether there has been wh- movement in a relative clause is to determine the grammatical relation of the relative pronoun. If it's the subject of the relative clause, as in (59) and (60), there is no wh-movement within the clause. If, however, the relative pronoun is *not* the subject of the relative clause, as in (61) and (62), it has been wh- moved. To put the relative pronoun back in its canonical position in the deep structure, we need to determine exactly what grammatical relation it is. As we discovered in our study of phrase structure, each grammatical relation has it own place in the hierarchy of a sentence, and this connection between phrase structure and grammatical relations is an important one when analyzing certain transformations.

A Final Note Regarding Transformations

Much of what has just been covered in this section on transformations might seem inaccessible and perhaps irrelevant. It's easy to lose sight of broader goals when buried deeply in an analysis of data, as we must be when undoing transformed sentences. If we view these transformations as systematic applications of rules, and we see the rules being applied consistently, over and over again, they should be easier to make sense out of. And if we understand that thorough knowledge of sentence structure is an essential part of our overall goal, and that while English sentence follow a clear pattern of structure, not all grammatical sentences seem to conform to this pattern, we should be able to see the relevance in a study of transformations. Imagine being an English language learner who has just become comfortable with the basic subject-verb-object sentence structure; to then learn non-canonical structures that seem to violate the basic structure can be very difficult. If, however, students are able to learn rules which are grounded in the basic structure that they've already learned, the task becomes much more manageable. It's important for teachers to understand how their students respond to new material, and our study of transformations is a step in that direction.

Tying It All Together

Often, students have difficulty with syntax. This is probably due largely to the seemingly overwhelming amount of information. It's true that there's a lot to know, but if we're able to see the connections among the various parts of syntax, everything falls into place and the large amount of material becomes much more manageable. For example, when determining the deep structure of a sentence with a relative clause, we can use our knowledge of grammatical relations to determine where the relative pronoun belongs in the deep structure. This process might also involve understanding the subcategory of verb in the relative clause to determine which grammatical elements are a necessary part of the verb's predicate.

Also useful is to remember the overall goal of our study of syntax to provide some structure for the interrelated details. Our purpose here was to explain grammaticality and ungrammaticality. If, as teachers, we want to be able to teach aspects of language, it's not sufficient to simply recognize ungrammaticality when we hear it. Any native speaker, even those with no formal training in linguistics, can do this. Rather, the goal is to be able to *articulate* what makes an ungrammatical sentence ungrammatical. So if a student writes a sentence in a paper that we know is ungrammatical, but all we can do is highlight it and write "wrong" without explaining *why* it's ungrammatical, we won't be helping that student avoid the error in the future. The explanations of the errors, not the identification of them, are what language learners and users can use and apply systematically. The goal of this chapter has been to present theories of syntax that will enable us to articulate what we unconsciously know.

Summary

In this chapter we studied the phrase and sentence structure of English. Our goal was to be able to explain grammaticality and ungrammaticality; in other words, we looked at a number of theories that enable us to consciously articulate what makes a grammatical sentence grammatical and an ungrammatical sentence ungrammatical. We looked at a variety of sentence types and analyzed their structures in detail, identifying their constituents. We also studied a number of transformational rules that allow us to create structures that are different from the basic, or canonical, sentence structure of English.

Exercises

Word Class Exercise

Below is a list of made-up words and a paragraph that uses the words. Based on your understanding of the word classes discussed in class and how they can be defined for English, determine which word class (part of speech) each one belongs to. Use your knowledge of the form, function and co-occurrence of each class. Assume that all of the words follow the regular inflectional morphological patters (i.e., none of the made-up words is an irregular noun or verb).

plich: __________ klirt: __________ fesk: __________ borf: __________

wusk: __________ foft: __________ reest: __________ hirk: __________

According to unnamed sources, borf fesk was caught in the act of soliciting a prostitute near his home last night. Borf report hirks that at approximately 11:15 PM, borf fesk approached an undercover officer and asked if reest could take her home. Borf officer immediately slapped borf fesk klirt a citation and called for back-up. Borf officer hirks that while waiting for borf back-up, borf fesk fofted her by plich calling her names and threatening her. Borf fesk, however, denied that he fofted borf officer. Reest hirked that reest was wusk klirt borf way reest had been entrapped by borf officer. Borf fesk denied any wrong-doing in borf incident. Reest hirked that reest plich speaks to people reest meets and that sometimes this friendliness is misinterpreted. Reest added that fesks are bound by their duty to borf country to serve, not exploit, people. Borf fesk then hirked that although borf arrest was upsetting, reest was wuskest about borf fact that borf officer declined to use handcuffs, despite repeated requests. Plich, such force is used, authorities hirk, but in this case, it was not warranted

* Editor's note: After borf arrest was made, borf brave officer that made the collar was rewarded by her commanding officer.

Word Class/Sentence Type Exercise

Using the abbreviations below, identify the word classes (parts of speech) in each of the sentences below. Also determine the sentence type of each (simple, coordinate or complex).

aux = auxiliary
N = noun
V = verb
det = determiner (article/demonstrative/pronominal determiner)
adv = adverb
adj = adjective
Q = quantifier
P = preposition
pro = pronoun
cc = coordinating conjunction
sc = subordinating conjunction

det N V det N
1. The player choked his coach. (simple)

2. My favorite athlete is a murderer, but I love him.

3. The fans think that their heroes are thugs.

4. Our police caught the reckless driver quickly.

5. His account grew significantly after the verdict.

6. Some superstars think that he should take the money and run.

7. I believe that he should rot in jail unless he apologizes to PJ.

8. If he wants sympathy, he should go home to his mother.

9. The apologetic player hardly looks sincere.

<continued>

10. Chads hang from ballots if voters punch them incompletely.

11. The election exposed us to new words, but it bored us in the end.

12. Some voters want special consideration for their handicaps.

13. Many voters felt that they had no representation in the election.

14. The government might revise the electoral process after this absurd debacle.

15. The population of the country rode the roller-coaster for several weeks.

16. I exercised my rights and I voted for the candidate of my choice.

17. Dubya remained confident and achieved victory in the end.

18. The people preferred Al, but the election went to Dubya.

19. Many angry analysts accused Jeb of very unscrupulous acts.

20. They say that the spoils go to the winner and I agree with them.

Passivization

As we have seen, making active sentences passive can help us tremendously in determining the constituent structure of these active sentences. Remember, active sentences are ones in which the real world subject of the verb is the grammatical subject as well. In passive sentences, however, the real world object of the verb is its grammatical subject. The important ingredients of a passive construction are (a) a form of the verb "to be" before the main verb, (b) the past participle form of the main verb, and (c) a "by" phrase which includes the *real world* subject of the verb.

For each of the following active sentences, write its corresponding passive sentence. Remember, the direct object of an active sentence is the subject of the corresponding passive sentence, and subjects and direct objects are NPs. Therefore, what you move to the grammatical subject position of the passive sentence must be a noun phrase. The first one has been done for you, and labels have been added for clarity.

	real world subj.		real life object	
active:	Students	can create	passive sentences	with ease.

	real life object (NP)		"to be" verb	past participle	"by" phrase	
passive:	Passive sentences	can	be	created	by students	with ease.

active: Every teacher should understand the concept of passive verbs.

passive:

active: Elementary school textbooks use this concept with frequency.

passive:

active: Writers should use passive constructions in certain situations.

passive:

active: Many teachers of rhetoric have criticized overuse of passive constructions.

passive:

active: No one can deny the usefulness of this particular construction.

passive:

active: Each student should complete this exercise with great care.

passive:

active: The class will learn many important things from this exercise.

passive:

Beginning Syntax Trees

For each of the following sentences, in pencil, draw a tree identifying the constituents.

The proposition on the ballot confused the voters.

The team from Timbuktu loses with dignity.

Teachers of linguistics love examples about Timbuktu.

The mayor of this city befuddled the jury with her evidence.

Advanced Syntax Trees

For each of the following sentences, *in pencil*, draw a tree identifying the constituents.

All students in America love linguistics because the subject amuses them.

We believe that this class teaches topics of great importance.

The coach with the injury cuts his players if they choke him.

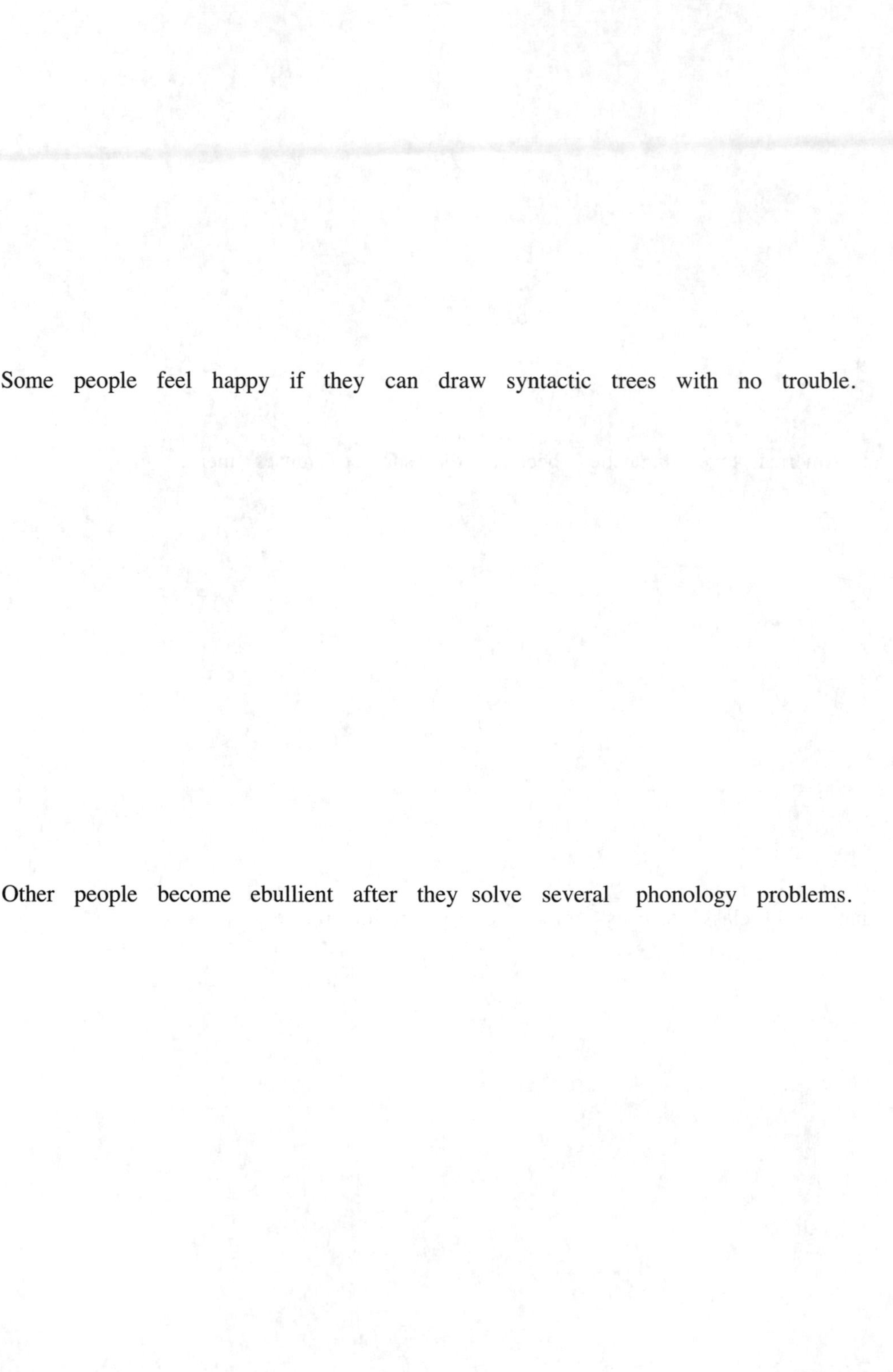
Some people feel happy if they can draw syntactic trees with no trouble.
Other people become ebullient after they solve several phonology problems.
I think that linguistics provides students with many hours of happiness.

Beans cause painful gas if you eat them in large quantities.

Tyson has many supporters, but he has the mind of an imbecile.

The coach put the childish player with a bad attitude in his doghouse.

The chef donned the hat with the puffy top when his best customer requested a tasty morsel.

A) The sinewy governor of Minnesota bodyslammed the helpless lobbyist in his office.

B) The sinewy governor of Minnesota bodyslammed the helpless lobbyist in his office.

Bart punched Milhouse in the face because he thought that Lisa kissed the nerdy fellow.

Grammatical Relation Practice

Using the two syntax tree exercises, list all the NPs that you found and determine their grammatical relation.

NP	grammatical relation
The proposition on the ballot	subject

NP	grammatical relation

NP	grammatical relation

Phrase Structure Practice

For each of the constituent candidates below, decide which, if any, constituent's phrase structure rule the candidate belongs to. You need to look at *every* level of each candidate's hierarchy. You might want to diagram each one. The first one has been done.

choices: S NP VP PP EC <none>

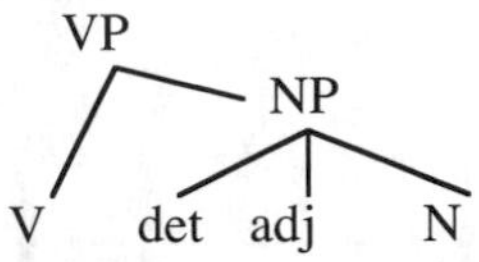

VP [V] [NP [det] [adj] [N]]

1. tasted the juicy apple VP
2. an evil serpent ______
3. in the huge cavern ______
4. wrote at home a letter ______
5. if I could write a book ______
6. this guy is strange ______
7. utter foolishness ______
8. and this time ______
9. although he likes the class ______
10. loves linguistics the man ______
11. homework is fun ______
12. some smelly children ______
13. for the love of linguistics ______
14. drinks large cans of beer ______
15. a crazy it ______
16. when the bell rings ______

Even More Syntax Tree Practice

Draw a diagram to represent the constituent structure of the following sentences.

A sad man lost his girlfriend when she discovered the good life without him.

This man became a jealous stalker and he trapped himself in a chimney.

The guy wanted his belongings but the chimney presented a problem for him.

He gave a bogus story to the police when they questioned him about his bizarre actions.

His girlfriend requested a protective order from the court after he stalked her on several occasions.

A reporter from the newsroom interviewed the man in the jailhouse after the cops arrested him.

The fool will get a sentence of many years unless he hires a lawyer with exceptional skills.

Subcategorization Exercise

Using the data in the chapter as a guide, place each of the following verbs in one or more of the subclasses we identified. Provide data, in the form of sentences, to support each subclassification.

work

drop

give

feel

communicate

speak

open

Transformation Exercise

For each of the non-canonical surface structure sentences,
a) write the deep (underlying) structure
b) determine which type(s) of transformation occurred to reach the surface structure
c) if you want to check your deep structures, you can draw trees for them

Theme: Syntax test

1. surface: What could our teacher ask us on this test?

deep: Our teacher could ask us what on this test. (sub/aux inversion, "wh-" movement)

2. surface: Should we study for this test which he will give to us?

deep:

3. surface: Will you know the questions that will be on the test?

deep:

4. surface: Why will you disregard the test which we must take?

deep:

5. surface: When should we buy the scantron sheets which the teacher requires?

deep:

6. surface: Can we get a good grade if we produce an effort that is sub-par?

deep:

Theme: Hanging chads

These are tough ones (hint: beware the complex sentence....)

7. surface: What can a voter do when chads hang from the ballots that he submits?

deep:

8. surface: How should voters clear the dimples after they make them?

deep:

9. surface: Where should voters file complaints if they have problems that are festering?

deep:

10. surface: What will the chads say when they face the voters whom they frustrated in November?

deep:

11. surface: How can voters trust the ballots after they see the dimples that the ballots left them with?

deep:

12. surface: What will Dubya do if the governor redesigns that ballot that the people had trouble with?

deep:

That Word

One of the most difficult words to analyze in English is the word "that." It has different uses and can therefore be classified several different ways. These complications have caused trouble for students. This exercise will help you classify "that" and recognize the different uses of "that" based on its syntactic environment.

A. Classifying "that"

Use the following data to determine the classes to which "that can belong. If you have difficulty, try drawing tree diagrams. Each pair of sentences illustrates one use of "that."

1. That class in linguistics is my favorite class.

2. I took that great class and I learned useful things.

word class:

---

3. That is a great idea.

4. I like that.

word class:

<continued>

5. I think that linguistics is a cool subject.

6. We feel that every student should take linguistics.

word class:

- -

7. I like classes that challenge me.

8. I aced the class that my counselor recommended.

word class:

<continued>

B. Tree practice using "that"

Draw trees for each of the following sentences using multiple "that"s, label each "that" correctly for its word class, and try to identify syntactic clues that will help you recognize the use of "that" in the future. Note that in some cases you might have a transformed sentence (you can recognize this by drawing a tree and noting that it's non-canonical); if so, undo the transformation(s) and diagram the deep structure of the sentence.

I believe that that is an issue that causes problems for people.

That student thinks that he can respond to any situation that he finds himself in.

7

Language Variation: English Dialects

Now that we've studied all the "core" areas of linguistics (phonetics, phonology, morphology and syntax) it's time to bring them all together in a study of **language variation.** We will have the opportunity to apply what we have learned in the core areas to an analysis of the linguistic production of a variety of English speakers. Here, we will revisit the notion of grammaticality and rethink our traditional approach to this complicated concept. The content of this chapter is especially relevant to classroom teachers, nearly all of whom are certain to encounter issues related to linguistic diversity at one time or another. Our goals in this chapter will be the following:

- to address the controversial issue of dialects
- to understand the distinction between linguistic correctness and appropriateness
- to classify variation according to the linguistic level at which it occurs
- to recognize and appreciate the systematicity of all linguistic varieties
- to learn some of the rules of a stigmatized variety of English

We will begin with a general discussion of the relevant concepts before moving into an analysis of real data. In that analysis, we will draw upon the knowledge and skills we've acquired in the preceding chapters. This chapter, therefore, serves as a review of familiar material in the context of new material.

The Language vs. Dialect Distinction

The concept of linguistic diversity is most familiar to people in the context of distinct languages. For example, we all can understand that English and Spanish are two different varieties of human language, each with its own set of linguistic rules. We recognize the foolishness of comparing the two languages with the idea of making evaluative judgments about their inherent superiority or inferiority. Neither one is better or worse than the other. We simply accept them as being different but equal.

This is probably not the case, however, when it comes to linguistic diversity in the context of two dialects of a single language. Would, for example, a highly educated person from a Boston suburb consider his own dialect of English and the dialect of English spoken by a poor farmer from Alabama to be different but equal? Probably not. Nearly every speaker of a language has certain ideas about what constitutes "good" or "proper" use of that language, the result being that people who speak a variety that differs from this "proper", or standard, variety are often considered to speak an inferior dialect. One of the main goals of this chapter is to illustrate that there is absolutely no linguistic basis for making such judgments. In fact, the relationship between the English dialects of the Boston suburbanite and that of the Alabama farmer isn't much different from the relationship between the two languages, English and Spanish.

To illustrate this blurred distinction, we can begin by trying to distinguish the relationship between two languages from the relationship between two dialects; that is, what specific criteria do we use to determine that two varieties of human language are different languages as opposed to different dialects of a single language? We all use these two terms regularly, but for the most part, we don't really know the difference between them. Let's use the following assumptions to guide our exploration. We'll look primarily at four varieties of language and assume that two of them, X and Y, are dialects of the same language, while the other two, P and Q, are different languages.

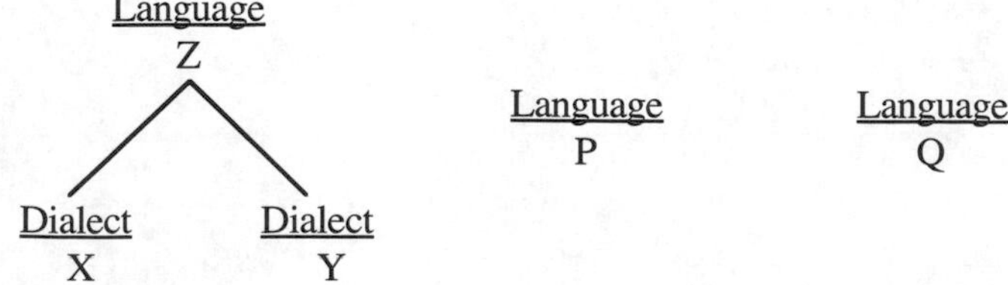

Figure 7.1: Graphic Representation of the Language-Dialect Distinction

What is it about X and Y that is different from P and Q? Most people would probably say that speakers of X and Y can understand each other, while speakers of P and Q cannot. This ability to comprehend in both directions is often referred to as **mutual intelligibility** and is the criterion most often cited when assigning two varieties dialect status. The true picture, however, is not as simple as this. Any American who has ever traveled to Scotland, where the majority of the citizens speak Scottish English (a dialect of English) can tell you that mutual intelligibility is not automatic, yet we all agree that Scottish English and American English are dialects of the same language. Consider also Spanish and Portuguese, which we all consider to be different languages. There is actually a fair amount of intelligibility between speakers of these two languages, especially among Portuguese speakers hearing Spanish, yet no one is likely to say they're dialects of the same language. What these examples tell us is that the language-dialect distinction is not as clear as we might think.

To further cloud the picture, we can consider the case of Mandarin and Cantonese, both of which are widely considered to be dialects of Chinese, despite the fact that there is virtually no mutual intelligibility between speakers of the two varieties. The same is true for different varieties of Arabic. For example, an Arabic speaker from Morocco is unlikely to understand an Arabic speaker from Iraq, and vice-versa. Clearly, then, there are other criteria that play a role in the language-dialect distinction. In the case of the Arabic dialects, feelings of ethnic identity are relevant. All Arabic speakers are Arabic people, regardless of their dialect, and language is an important part of culture, so it stands to reason that speakers of these two varieties would consider themselves to be speaking a common language. It's highly unlikely, however, that a Portuguese citizen and a Spanish citizen would feel the same cultural bond, which might account for their unwillingness to accept that they speak the same language. Also important in the case of the Chinese dialects is the fact that both varieties use the same writing system. So, while there is virtually no mutual intelligibility when the varieties are spoken, there is a great deal of mutual intelligibility when they're written.

We can see, then, that it is extremely difficult to distinguish languages from dialects. While mutual intelligibility is clearly important, it alone is not sufficient to make a determination. In fact, it has been said that this distinction does not really exist and that "every dialect is a language."[1] While this blurred distinction might be disconcerting at first, it will actually serve us well in our investigation of linguistic variation.

Dimensions of Language Variation

One of the most important facts to keep in mind when investigating language variation is that no language is static or uniformly used by all of its speakers. If language were static, it would never change over time, and if it were uniformly used by all of its speakers, everyone who spoke that language would speak it exactly the same way. Intuitively, however, we all know that language does, in fact, vary. It's helpful to think about this variation as occurring across three dimensions.

First, we can say that language varies across the *dimension of time*. That is, the English that is spoken today is different from the English that was spoken 50 years ago, which is different from the English spoken 100 years ago, and so on, continuing all the way back to the very first English spoken. We can think of this change as *historical change*. Perhaps the easiest way to illustrate variation across time is to think about slang expressions. In the 1960s, for example, expressions like "far out" and "groovy" were popular, but over time they ceased to be used. Later, in the 1990s, expressions like "phat", which no one used 30

---

[1] From Finegan (1990), p. 371.

years earlier, became popular. Over time, more old expressions will continue to be replaced by new ones. Just as life evolves, so, too, does language. This change, though bemoaned by many language "purists", is neither good nor bad; it's simply inevitable.

In addition to time, language varies across the *dimension of space*. This simply means that at any given time, the people in one geographic area speak differently from people in other geographic areas. To illustrate this kind of variation, we can return to the English vowel system that we discussed in Chapter 2. Recall that for most people who grow up in California, the mid, back, lax vowel, represented by the phonetic symbol /ɔ/, isn't a phoneme. In contrast, for many speakers who grow up in the eastern part of the U.S., it is a very real phoneme. People who grow up on opposite sides of the country, at exactly the same time, will speak differently. Again, we can invoke the analogy of evolving life. A survey of the wildlife in California reveals differences from the wildlife of the eastern part of the U.S. Just as we accept this as reality, we must accept regional linguistic variation as well.

Finally, we must consider the third dimension of language variation—variation across the *dimension of group*. This term is intentionally vague because it's meant to cover a wide range of groups. It can be used, for example, to refer to linguistic differences between gender groups, a topic that has been widely studied recently. These studies indicate that there are observable differences between the way men and women speak. Also, we can observe language variation across different socio-economic or ethnic groups. In very general terms, whenever people identify with different groups, regardless of what criteria distinguish those groups, there is the potential for linguistic variation. These differences can be with regard to sounds, words, sentences or, more likely, some combination of the above.

What this tells us, in a nutshell, is that *people who speak together tend to speak alike*.[2] So, if a male grows up in early 21st century Alabama in a poor area, he's very likely to speak in a way very similar to other males who grow up in early 21st century Alabama in a poor area, because these are the people he has contact with. He is far less likely, however, to speak like an affluent female who grew up in early 20th century London. Though this may seem fairly intuitive, it's an important point that is well worth mentioning.

Correctness vs. Appropriateness

Now that we've discussed the issue of dialects and the dimensions across which language varies, we're prepared to analyze data to describe variation. Before we do this, however, we need to address the perspective that our investigation will take. Our goal, as it has been from the outset of this text, is to take a descriptive approach. That is, we will describe differences without judging their relative worth. We will begin with the understanding that all native speaker production of a language, aside from the occasional slip of the tongue, is 100% rule governed. As was suggested earlier in this chapter, none of the rules that different people follow are inherently better or worse than any others. Our goal in analyzing data will be to describe some of the different rules that English speakers follow. Through our discovery of these rules, we will come to understand that every dialect of English is rule governed.

Before we move on, however, we need to address the reality of language politics. While we will view all linguistic rules as being equally legitimate, we will also acknowledge that not all rules are acceptable in all contexts. Most of us understand, for example, that the way we speak (meaning the rules we follow) in an informal situation, such as "hanging out" with old friends, would not be acceptable in a more formal setting, such as a job interview. We also understand that the way we write formal papers is different not only from the way we speak, but also from the way we write letters or emails to our friends. What we all unconsciously understand is that the linguistic rules we follow are, to a large extent, specific to the context in which we use language.

Let's illustrate this point by using a very common expression in English—"ain't." Most of us are taught in school or at home that "ain't" is *incorrect*. Certainly, it would be unwise to use this word in an interview with a principal for a teaching job. In such an environment, this word would never be used, so it does, in fact, seem to be incorrect. In other environments, however, such as a basketball court in an urban playground, it's very commonly used. How can we say it's *incorrect* if it's so commonly used by so many native speakers of English? Instead of *correct* and *incorrect*, more useful terms to use to describe the use of "ain't" would be *appropriate* and *inappropriate*. While it would be very inappropriate to use "ain't" in

---

[2] Adapted from Finegan (1990), p. 370.

the formal context of the job interview, it would be perfectly appropriate to use it in the informal context of the playground.

A clothing analogy can be useful in clarifying this point. Very few, if any, of us would be willing to declare certain articles of clothing, such as neckties and tank tops, flat-out *incorrect*. We understand that a tank top would be inappropriate to wear to a job interview; instead, a man should wear a neck tie. But we also understand that a necktie would be inappropriate to wear to a pick-up basketball game at a playground; in this case, it's the tank top that's more appropriate. Rules of language are not all that different from rules of dress. Different contexts call for different choices, and the savvy speaker, just like the savvy dresser, knows how to make different choices, depending on the context.

When discussing different linguistic contexts, it's important to understand the terms **standard** and **non-standard**, as applied to linguistic rules. Standard rules are the ones that are required in a formal context, such as the job interview. Non-standard rules are ones that, while perfectly acceptable in less formal contexts, are inappropriate in formal contexts. Every language has what is considered a **standard dialect**. The standard dialect is the one that is appropriate in formal contexts, the one that will not make a negative impression in educated circles. Non-standard dialects, on the other hand, are generally *stigmatized*, meaning people have negative feelings about these dialects and the people who speak them. The standard dialect in the US, generally referred to as **Standard American English** (SAE), is often presented to non-linguists as "newscaster English" because it is the variety that is generally heard in news reports on American television and radio. It is not a stigmatized dialect.

Because the only way to avoid being stigmatized linguistically is to be able to speak the standard dialect, it's in everyone's interest to know the standard dialect. Unfortunately, as anyone who has worked in a linguistically diverse classroom knows, not everyone comes to school with the rules of the standard dialect internalized. They do, however, come to school with the rules of their own, perhaps highly stigmatized and non-standard, dialect internalized. For many speakers, what they've internalized is what's correct in their minds; what they haven't internalized is incorrect in their minds. The challenge for the classroom teacher is to make sure all of his or her students, regardless of their first dialect, speak the standard dialect. In many cases this means teaching students to become **bidialectal** (able to speak two dialects). This is only possible if the teacher understands the linguistic realities of the students, and a *correct vs. incorrect* approach completely ignores reality.

Levels of Language Variation

Having covered the basic concepts of language variation, we are ready to analyze actual data. This data will illustrate variation mainly across the dimensions of space and group (socio-economic and ethnic). Our goals will be to identify the differences, classify them and describe rules whenever possible. Our classification will require us to draw largely upon the knowledge and skills emphasized in earlier chapters by determining the linguistic level at which the variation takes place. The five levels we will look at are:

1. <u>The lexical level:</u> Variation at this level refers to the use by different people of different words for the same meaning. An example would be the use of "lorry" among British English speakers versus the use of "truck" among American English speakers. We also see variation at this level among different dialects of American English. For example, in some parts of the country, particularly in the midwest, the word "pail" is used instead of "bucket," which is preferred throughout much of the country. While lexical variation can make for a fun exercise, as people try to think of as many alternate words to the ones they use as they can, it doesn't provide linguists in search of rules with much fodder for discussion. These differences don't really involve rules; instead, they simply illustrate different choices of expression for a given meaning.

Quick Exercise 7.1
For each British English word below, provide the corresponding American English word.

British English	American English
petrol	
queue	
lift	
boot	
bonnet	
biscuit	

2. The phonemic level: Variation at this level refers to different varieties having different phonemic inventories. The example of the mid, lax, back vowel, or /ɔ/, which exists in some eastern dialects of English but not most western ones, illustrates variation at this level. As with lexical variation, there are no real rules to uncover here; there are simply differences among the phonemes that different speakers use. This differs fairly significantly from lexical variation, however, in that it contributes to different accents. When we hear someone with an accent different from our own, the difference is due, in large part, to different phonemic inventories.

3. The phonological level: Variation at this level refers to the different phonological rules that different linguistic varieties have. The flapping rule, which American English has, but British English doesn't, can be used to illustrate variation at this level. While both dialects have the phoneme /t/, in American English there's a rule that leads speakers to flap /t/ in certain environments; this rule does *not* , however, exist in British English. To distinguish phonological variation from phonemic variation, note that in the phonological example, both varieties share the same phoneme, but not the same allophones, while in the phonemic example, the two varieties have different phonemes. Like variation at the phonemic level, phonological variation contributes to different accents.

4. The morphological level: Variation at this level refers to different processes of word formation. A good example is the differing past participle forms of the verb "to prove" among English speakers. For some, the sentence "He was proven wrong" is acceptable, while for others, the preferred verb form is "proved," as in "He was proved wrong." While variation at this level might seem similar to lexical variation , it's actually very different. When two speakers exhibit variation at this level, they are using the *same* word, but they are forming that word differently. At this level, the focus is on morphemes, often inflectional ones, and how they are combined.

5. The syntactic level: Variation at this level refers to the differences in how speakers form constituents (phrases and clauses). An example would be the different structure of the NP that is the object of the preposition "in" in the American English sentence "He is in *the hospital*" and the British English sentence "He is in *hospital*." The NP after the preposition in the American dialect requires a determiner, while the corresponding NP in the British dialect does not. Similar to variation at the morphological level, the focus here is on structure. The difference is that here we're concerned not with the way a single word is formed, but with the way entire constituents are formed.

Data Analysis 7.1

Below are some data pairs that illustrate variation across various levels. In each case, the data shows how the standard California English dialect differs from some other dialect of English. In most cases, the data illustrates regional differences (variation across the dimension of space), but in some cases there is an element of socio-economic status. Also, some of the examples illustrate non-standard forms.

Your goals in this exercise should be 1) to identify how the examples in each pair differ, 2) to classify the variation according to the levels presented in this section, and 3) to describe whatever process or processes the examples illustrate. When describing the processes, try to write rules that account for the variation whenever possible.

Examples A through D illustrate regional differences mainly (with some social differences).

	CA	working class NYC	level?
A. transcription of "youth"	[yuθ]	[yut]	________
transcription of "thick"	[θɪk]	[tɪk]	
transcription of "this"	[ðɪs]	[dɪs]	
transcription of "with"	[wɪð]	[wɪd]	

- description: ____

____

	CA	UK	level?
B. transcription of "little"	[lɪDəl]	[lɪtəl]	________
transcription of "title"	[tayDəl]	[taytəl]	

- description: ____

____

	CA	working class NYC	level?
C. transcription of "rare"	[rɛr]	[rɛ]	________
transcription of "cart"	[kart]	[kat]	

- description: ____

____

	CA	PA/NJ	Southeast	level?
D. transcription of "white"	[wayt]	[wʌyt]	[wat]	________
transcription of "wide"	[wayd]	[wayd]	[wad]	
transcription of "why"	[way]	[way]	[wa]	

- description: ____

____

Examples E and F illustrate standard vs. non-standard differences.

level? ____________

E. standard: If I had gone to class I would have gotten a better grade.
non-standard: If I had went to class I would have got a better grade.

- description: ____

____

level? ____________

F. standard: Julio and I [were] down by the school yard.
non-standard: Me and Julio [were] down by the school yard.
standard/non-standard: We [were] down by the school yard.
standard/non-standard: * Us [were] down by the school yard.

- description:

____

____

The Case of African-American English

Now that we've studied the general concepts of language variation and have analyzed some data that illustrates variation across various linguistic levels, we're ready to focus on a specific non-standard dialect of English, one that is highly stigmatized—**African-American English** (AAE). This particular dialect, which is known by a variety of names, including African-American Vernacular English, Black English, Black English Vernacular and Ebonics (to name a few) has been widely studied by linguists. This extensive study has enabled linguists to describe a substantial number of rules, specific to the dialect, which is one reason that AAE, rather than some other dialect, is chosen as a case study in many textbooks.

Most non-linguists first became aware of AAE in the wake of the Oakland School Board controversy in the mid 1990s. When the Board recommended a number of policies dealing with Ebonics, as they called it at the time, it set off a chain of reactions, many of which were extremely negative. Our goal here is not to support or denounce any of these proposed policies; rather it is to investigate the facts of the dialect so each individual can form his or her own opinion from an informed perspective.

Before analyzing actual data, it's useful to cover some basic facts about AAE. First, as was mentioned before, this dialect is highly stigmatized in many English speaking circles. Though it is every bit as rule governed as more standard dialects, it is not viewed favorably in many contexts, particularly formal business and academic ones. People who speak *only* AAE are at a disadvantage when operating in these contexts. Second, there is no biological basis to AAE; that is, not all African-American people speak AAE, nor is every speaker of AAE African-American. Recall that people who speak together tend to speak alike. It is the language that surrounds us that determines the language and dialect we speak, not the color of our skin or any other aspect of our genetics. Third, while we will be generalizing to describe features of a single dialect, which we will call AAE, there is actually a significant amount of variation among different varieties of AAE. In fact, AAE has been described as a term that is used to refer to "a continuum of varieties"[3] that, while similar, have certain differences. Finally, while there is some disagreement as to the origins of AAE, current research suggests that some of its features have their roots in the Western African languages spoken by the first generations of Africans to live in the U.S., while other features are similar to those of other American English dialects and appear to have developed *after* people of African descent began speaking English as their first language.

Phonological Features of AAE

Like any variety of human language, AAE is governed by a set of phonological rules. In most cases, these rules are identical to those of SAE. In some cases, however, the phonological rules of AAE differ from those of SAE, and it is these differences that cause an AAE "accent." One phonological area in which AAE differs from SAE is in the allophonic variation of diphthongs (two vowel sounds blended into one), which in certain environments become monophthongs (single sounds). This process is known as **monophthongization**, a mouthful of a term.

SAE	AAE
fine [fayn]	fine [fan]

Data Analysis 7.2

Using the data below, state a rule that describes when (i.e. in what environment) diphthongs are monophthongized in AAE.

	SAE	AAE
"now"	[naw]	[na]
"side"	[sayd]	[sad]
"time"	[taym]	[tam]
"doubt"	[dawt]	[dawt]
"bite"	[bayt]	[bayt]

Also common in the phonological system of AAE is the reduction of word final clusters of consonants through a process often called **consonant cluster reduction**. This process reduces clusters for ease of articulation.

SAE	AAE
cast [kæst]	cast [kæs]
told [told]	told [tol]
desk [dɛsk]	desk [dɛs]

Interestingly, though this process is stigmatized, nearly all speakers of English, including speakers of SAE, reduce consonant clusters. The process is the same in both dialects, but it is employed to a greater extent in AAE than SAE. This kind of similarity, with a difference of degree, between AAE and SAE is a theme that will recur throughout our analysis.

Quick Exercise 7.2

Think of three words that you think most English speakers, regardless of their dialect, pronounce with a reduced consonant cluster in casual speech. Write each word and transcribe it twice, once with the full consonant cluster, and once with the reduced cluster.

	Spelled Word	Full Cluster Transcription	Reduced Cluster Transcription
1.			
2.			
3.			

[3] From Department of Linguistics (1994), p. 380.

Morphological Features of AAE

As with its phonological rules, while AAE is very similar to SAE with regard to its morphological rules, their are some differences that distinguish the two dialects. One of the most stigmatized morphological features of AAE is the deletion of certain inflectional morphemes. Specifically, the possessive morpheme and the third person singular morpheme are often dropped. For simplicity's sake, we can call this process **inflectional morpheme deletion**.

SAE: The president's clothing looks expensive.
AAE: The president clothing look expensive.

While this kind of morpheme deletion does *not* take place in SAE, it's interesting to note that the absence of the morphemes in the AAE example doesn't interfere at all with the comprehension of the sentence. Clearly, these morphemes are not essential to communication, and the deletion of them serves to streamline the dialect without removing any of its potential for communication.

Data Analysis 7.3
If AAE allows for deletion of morphemes without a loss of meaning, then there must be some other way that these "meanings" are conveyed. Using the example above, suggest a way that hearers understand the possessive and third person singular meanings.

Another specific feature of AAE morphology that distinguishes it from SAE is the formation of certain **reflexive pronouns**. Reflexive pronouns are used when we want to use pronouns to refer to the same entity as both the subject and an object in a clause, as in "She hurt herself," with *herself* being the reflexive pronoun. While the formation of most reflexive pronouns is the same in AAE and SAE, for two of them, it's different.

SAE	AAE
himself	hisself
themselves	theirselves

This is a highly stigmatized feature of AAE, but is it somehow inherently inferior to SAE in this regard? A closer investigation reveals just the opposite, perhaps. In fact, the forms *hisself* and *theirselves* are actually more consistent with the rule for forming reflexive pronouns English, a rule that is shared by both dialects. The difference is that the SAE forms, *himself* and *themselves*, are actually irregular (meaning they don't follow the rule), while the AAE forms are regular (meaning they do follow the rule). This kind of **regularization**, contrary to being inferior, actually makes more sense from a rule perspective. Irregularities, as anyone who has ever studied a foreign language knows, make language learning difficult. Why not phase out exceptions to rules?

Data Analysis 7.4

Using the data below, state a rule that describes reflexive pronoun formation in English.

you	yourself	Rule:
we	ourselves	
I	myself	

Based on the rule you wrote, which forms would you expect to be "correct," the SAE forms *himself* and *themselves* or the AAE forms *hisself* and *theirselves*?

Syntactic Features of AAE

Again, there are far more similarities than differences between AAE and SAE, but it is the differences that cause the stigma. Here we'll address two specific syntactic features of AAE that are different from SAE, but through our analysis we'll see that even with regard to these differences, there is actually a striking similarity between the two dialects.

The first feature we'll address is one common to many non-standard dialects of English—**multiple negation**. Most children are taught in school that multiple (or double) negatives are ungrammatical. As we now know, however, what's grammatical depends on the rules of whatever variety of language a person speaks. Speakers who employ multiple negation do so in a very systematic, and therefore grammatical (for these speakers), way. By looking at some data of affirmative sentences and their corresponding negated forms, we can compare the rules for negation in AAE and SAE. To follow the ensuing analysis more easily, focus on the bolded words in each example. A "+" before a sentence indicates a positive (affirmative) sentence, while a "-" indicates a negative sentences.

SAE: + The president can afford to lose **some** more elections.
SAE: - The president ca**n't** afford to lose **any** more elections.

AAE: + The president can afford to lose **some** more elections.
AAE: - The president ca**n't** afford to lose **no** more elections.

SAE: + Ball players should know better.
SAE: - Ball players should**n't** know **any** better.

AAE: + Ball players should know better.
AAE: - Ball players should**n't** know **no** better.

What we see is essentially the same process in both dialects. Namely, a negator (the word "not") is inserted between the auxiliary verb and the main verb (in these cases in a contracted form), and whatever quantifying word is used in the affirmative sentence is changed. When there is no quantifying word in the affirmative sentence, a quantifying word is added. The *only* difference is the specific quantifying word that's used. AAE rules call for a quantifier with a negative meaning, while SAE does not. It's not only systematic, but consistent with the intended meaning as well. It's also a feature common throughout the world. Many languages employ multiple negation in their standard dialect. Interestingly, this was the case with English until a few hundred years ago, at which point the standard dialect's preference changed to the kind of "single" negation of SAE today.[4]

Another well-studied syntactic feature of AAE is known as **"be" deletion.** This involves the deletion of forms of the verb "to be" in certain environments. This last phrase should immediately signal systematicity in our minds. If it can be deleted in some environments but not in others, then there must be

[4] See Lester (1990), pp. 192–195, for a more detailed discussion of the history of the double negative "rule.".

some rule that governs the deletion. Again, by comparing AAE sentences with deleted "be" forms to SAE ones, we'll see that the rules of the two dialects are amazingly similar.

SAE: My team is the best team. <or> My team's the best team.
AAE: My team the best team.

SAE: California is a big state. <or> California's a big state
AAE: California a big state

SAE: I know what time it is in New York. <but not> *I know what time it's in New York.
AAE: I know what time it is in New York. <but not> *I know what time it in New York.

In two of the three sentences, AAE rules allow "be" deletion, but in the third they do not. Similarly, in the same two sentences, the rules of SAE allow contraction of the verb "to be" but in the third they do not. We see the exact same process at work in both dialects. We can think of it as a form of **syntactic reduction**, in that a constituent, in this case a VP, is being reduced in some way. Specifically, all or part of the verb is being reduced. Both dialects allow some kind of reduction in certain environments. The only real difference, syntactically speaking, is the degree of the reduction. That is, in SAE the verb is being partially reduced (contracted), while in AAE the reduction is more complete (deletion).

There are two main points that we need to take from this analysis. First, even highly stigmatized features of non-standard dialects are 100% rule governed. As soon as we acknowledge this, and we have no choice but to acknowledge it given the evidence, any notion of a non-standard dialect being somehow inherently inferior goes right out the window. A speaker of a standard dialect might not like the rules of AAE, and vice-versa, but this is merely a personal preference, not an objective determination of legitimacy. Second, because these stigmatized features of AAE are so remarkably similar to those of SAE, if we denounce AAE as an inferior dialect, then we have no choice but to denounce SAE as also inferior. What we have here are two dialects that are, ironically, very similar, even in their differences.

An Additional Feature of AAE

One last feature of AAE needs to be addressed, but it must be addressed outside of the context of phonology, morphology and syntax. This feature stands on its own because it's difficult to classify. It involves the use of a form of the verb "to be" in a way that differs significantly from anything in SAE. This verb is illustrated in the following examples:

SAE: Our linguistics teacher is always saying interesting things.
AAE: Our linguistics teacher always be saying interesting things.

SAE: With their new portable ovens, Domino's pizza is always hot.
AAE: With their new portable ovens, Domino's pizza always be hot.

AAE: *I be eating Domino's pizza right now.

The underlined "be" in the AAE sentences is known as the **habitual "be"** because of its meaning. It's used when referring to habitual or regular actions or states. Notice how the use of the habitual be is ungrammatical in the last AAE example. This is because the sentence is not intended to convey a habitual meaning; instead, it refers to a momentary action. Therefore, the use of the habitual "be" is ungrammatical in this sentence.

To further illustrate the limitations that the rules of AAE place on the use of the habitual "be" consider the following data gathered by Walt Wolfram, an expert in dialect studies. He surveyed 35 sixth grade African-American children to see when they preferred the habitual "be" and when they did not. The children were read each pair of sentences and asked which one they preferred. Overwhelmingly, they preferred the habitual "be" in sentences with a habitual meaning. The number in parentheses before each example indicates the number of students in the group who preferred that example in the pair.

1. (32) a. They usually be tired when they come home. (habitual meaning)
   (3) b. They be tired right now. (non-habitual meaning)

2. (31) a. When we play basketball, she be on my team. (habitual meaning)
   (4) b. The girl in the picture be my sister. (non-habitual meaning)

3. (4) a. James be coming to school right now. (non-habitual meaning)
   (31) b. James always be coming to school. (habitual meaning)

4. (3) a. My ankle be broken from the fall. (non-habitual meaning)
   (32) b. Sometimes my ears be itching. (habitual meaning)

From: http://www.cal.org/ebonics/wolfram.html [5]

Clearly, the habitual "be" is a rule governed linguistic feature.

Data Analysis 7.5
Looking at the habitual "be" data, what do you notice about the placement of "be" verbs in SAE and AAE relative to other grammatical elements? What similarities and differences do you see?

Implications of Dialect Study

At this point, students often become confused. They've gained a new perspective on the notion of grammaticality by analyzing data. They understand that grammaticality is relative to individual speakers and dialects. But as future teachers they wonder "What should we teach?" It would be unwise to think of this new understanding as a license to let "anything go." Regardless of the systematicity of non-standard dialects, they are still not accepted in most formal contexts. With very few exceptions, anyone who wants to participate in higher levels of business and academic society must know how to speak the standard dialect. For children growing up in the U.S., this means becoming fluent in SAE. Teachers who don't help their students become fluent in SAE do them a disservice. The answer to the question of what to teach must certainly be "SAE."

How to teach SAE, however, is a more complicated question. Whatever "method" a teacher chooses must be employed with an informed and enlightened approach. Specifically, teachers must understand that for some of their students, language production that follows the rules of SAE might sound "wrong." That is, if a student has grown up only with a non-standard dialect, then that dialect's rules are the only ones he or she knows (and even these are only known unconsciously). To such a student, a teacher who models SAE might sound "funny;" to such a student, that teacher might seem to be speaking incorrectly. These students who do not follow the rules of SAE are not doing so out of laziness or sloppiness; they are simply following the rules of their own dialect, just as everyone does. An informed teacher understands that linguistic rules are internalized by children at an early age and that these rules become a part of their being. They can't be denied or ignored, and instead must be acknowledged as a reality.

Perhaps the most helpful way of thinking about this is to return to the similarities between languages and dialects. If we consider a person trying to learn a different dialect to be tackling essentially the same task as a person trying to learn a different language, we'll be in a much better position to teach that person to be bidialectal, which is not very different from being bilingual. Being bidialectal means having a command of *two* dialects, both SAE *and* whatever the first dialect is. Bidialectal people, like bilingual people, have a

---

[5] For more links to information about AAE, see <http://www.cal.org/ebonics/>.

tremendous advantage over monodialectal people because they can comfortably move about in different contexts, switching back and forth between dialects, depending on what the situation calls for.

Expert Voices on Dialect Issues

Much has been written about the relevance of dialect study to education, and much more remains to be written. Here, we've provided just a sampling, focusing on brief selections of particular interest to teachers and future teachers.

A.

REDUCING LANGUAGE PREJUDICE

People without linguistic training are seldom aware that they have language prejudices. They commonly make assumptions about the inferiority of some dialects, like AAE, and the superiority of others, like British English. They may also draw unfounded connections between "correctness" of standard grammar and logic of thought. When they do this, they ignore decades of linguistic research which show us that "standard" English became the standard for historical and political reasons, not because it was better at communicating. That is, the group who speak a particular dialect have achieved power over groups who speak other dialects. It is the speakers who have power; the status of the dialect merely reflects the social and economic status of the group using it. People trained in linguistics, unlike lay people, generally consider that all dialects and modes of speech are equal. They are all adequate to communicate any message, at least among people who share the dialect. Even linguists, who are usually non-judgmental though, recognize that some contexts favor the use of a particular variety over another.

African-American children learn to speak as well as any children, but from a model that differs from SAE in systematic ways. In order to become competent speakers of AAE, they must internalize very subtle aspects of the language system, with complicated rules governing whether sentences are grammatical or not. The dialect that they are learning serves the same purposes of normal communication, as well as solidarity and in-group communication as other major varieties, like Scottish English or the dialect of southern white speakers. Just as Scottish is most useful within Scotland, AAE is less useful outside the AAE community.

THE NEED FOR BI-DIALECTALISM

Few people would deny that in 20th century America Standard English is the most useful dialect in the widest number of contexts. It is the language of literacy and power and economic opportunity. Like most African American spokespeople and parents, we feel children should be encouraged to learn SAE, but we favor having children ADD SAE to their repertoire of language competence, not subtract AAE. Like most people who learn a second language or dialect after a "critical age" (generally 5-8 years), AAE speakers of SAE will rarely eliminate all traces of their native dialect while speaking SAE. Therefore, at the same time as we encourage as much bi-dialectalism as possible, we recognize that language prejudice is not diminishing, so every child should also learn to be aware of and minimize his or her own negative judgments of other people based on dialect.

We agree with the educators and language teachers who say that instilling shame about the native dialect is a poor way to teach SAE. After all, no one is asked to disparage English in order to learn French. Likewise, there should be no need to eradicate the child's native dialect in order to add a new dialect. The true debate in Ebonics is, or should be, how best to achieve bi-dialectalism among African American children, in the inspiring tradition of the many African-Americans who have achieved success in America through that path. In John Rickford, a scholar at Stanford's, words, "The student who is led to greater competence in English by systematic contrast with Ebonics can switch between the vernacular and the standard as the situation merits, and as Maya Angelou (see her poem, "The Thirteens") and Martin Luther King and Malcolm X undoubtedly did too, drawing on the power of each in its relevant domain."

from: http://www.umass.edu/aae/position_statement_.htm (reprinted by permission of The AAE Working Group, principals: H.N. Seymour, T. Roeper, and J.de Villiers and B.Z. Pearson)

B.

Expressions: Studying Dialects in the Mountain State

By Kirk Hazen

I study dialects by listening to real people, I work in West Virginia where "the good of the earth" still exists, and I am fortunate to do both. I founded the West Virginia Dialect Project (WVDP) to learn more about language diversity in West Virginia and to share its fascinating beauty and complexity. Teaching and researching about dialects is a wonderful job because my laboratory is the entire state, and all I have to do is listen to what people have to say.

Dialects are often seen negatively, but this is one of the most unfortunate myths of our modern world. Dialects are something like snowflakes: all snowflakes contain water but no two snowflakes are alike. There is no meteorological reason why any one snowflake is better or worse than another. For dialects, no variety of any language is linguistically better or worse than any other. And that is not just a knee-jerk reaction of political correctness; that's nature.

All humans are born with a blueprint for language, and the languages people are exposed to become the building blocks that each young child builds from according to that blueprint. Whether it be Mandarin Chinese, Mexican Spanish, Swahili, or Appalachian English, they are all varieties of human language from the same blueprint, and they all function equally well as language.

Unfortunately, most of our attitudes towards dialects ignore their linguistic equality and enforce their social inequality. In the United States, some language varieties are stigmatized and the others are considered standard enough, both of which result from social attitudes towards the speakers. Outside and sometimes inside the state, West Virginia dialects are stigmatized, despite their linguistic equality, and the WVDP is actively battling that stigma.

The WVDP works with undergraduate and graduate students in researching and teaching about dialects in West Virginia, but language myths often stand in the way of our educational mission. For example, when I tell people I study dialects, the first thing I hear is that Elizabethan English is still spoken in West Virginia. For some people it makes a regal connection, and in one of the most unfairly badmouthed states in the union, it may give West Virginians a sense of pride. But it is simply not true.

With the myth of Elizabethan English no longer viable, is there any hope for West Virginia dialects? The WVDP believes a great deal that hope waits in the wings. With an understanding of how language works and why their dialects are as linguistically legitimate as any other dialect, West Virginians should feel proud of their language variation because it is part of their cultural heritage.

The dialect feature I hear the most about demonstrates a link to Scots-Irish heritage: The car needs washed vs. The car needs washing. Although upsetting to some, this is a perfectly normal process. A verb is the boss in a sentence and requires certain things to come after it. For example, the verb to kiss requires a following noun, as in The girl kissed the boy. The verb to need in areas outside upper West Virginia, eastern Ohio, and western Pennsylvania requires a verb, like washing or to be; inside this area, the verb to need only requires an adjective like washed or painted. This same bit of variation is found in parts of the British Isles, especially Scotland.

Another Scottish link is the similarity between the Appalachian mountains and the Outer Banks of North Carolina. They were both settled by Scots-Irish immigrants, and share a pattern of subject-verb concord that dates back at least six centuries. This pattern includes an -s in sentences like The dogs walks and The people goes. The two areas also share the famous a-prefixing, as in He went a-hunting; this process of a-prefixing is a complex linguistic process dating back four centuries. It originated in sentences like She is at working which meant that the action was going on at that moment.

Some of our research focuses on West Virginia dialects from a vastly different angle. The WVDP is currently studying whether or not people can speak two dialects the same way they can speak two languages. This study of bi-dialectalism is intimately linked to successful language education in our schools. In formal education, many teachers want their students to learn the standard regional dialect (standard English is simply a non-stigmatized dialect). The most popular approach in the last two decades has been the additive method: The teacher adds a second dialect to the student's first dialect, and this approach respects the local variety while helping the student achieve a regional standard. We know people can learn a standard form of a language, but does their local dialect stay intact? Until now, no linguistic study has ever been conducted to see if this approach works.

Part of the WVDP teaching effort in local communities will focus on students studying their own dialects. For example, students could interview their older relatives to gather words that were once popular but are now out of fashion. As a class, we could then incorporate those words into exercises and dialect quizzes like the one here. In other regions such as the Outer Banks where these dialect curricula have been tried for several years, both the teachers and the students have reacted enthusiastically to learning about their cultural heritage through dialect study.

- originally published in the West Virgina University Alumni Magazine (reprinted by permission of the author and publisher)

Summary

In this chapter we studied how language varies across the dimensions of time, space and group. Within each dimension, we analyzed variation at five linguistic levels—lexical, phonemic, phonological, morphological and syntactic. We addressed relevant issues of standard and non-standard dialects, focusing our attention on a single non-standard dialect of English—African-American English (AAE). Finally, we addressed the implications of dialect study for classroom teachers.

Exercises

Language Variation Survey

Read each of the sentences below and decide if you think it's grammatical or ungrammatical. Don't think about any rules that you think apply; just respond with your intuitions (your gut feelings). After you have decided, circle your choice.

1) That player has a big mouth.

grammatical or ungrammatical

2) Player that has a mouth big.

grammatical or ungrammatical

3) If he had kept his mouth shut, he would be more popular now.

grammatical or ungrammatical

4) If he would have kept his mouth shut, he would be more popular now.

grammatical or ungrammatical

5) If I were Rocker, I'd shut up and play baseball.

grammatical or ungrammatical

6) If I was Rocker, I'd shut up and play baseball.

grammatical or ungrammatical

7) I believe that OJ was proved guilty.

grammatical or ungrammatical

8) I believe that OJ was proven guilty.

grammatical or ungrammatical

Practice with AAE

For SAE sentences #1–4, provide the AAE version, deleting forms of the verb "to be" where necessary, and changing morphological features where necessary.

1. SAE: The Serbian president is gambling that we are going to back down when world opinion turns against us.

AAE:

2. SAE: I understand that this dialect is the way it is for a good reason, and now it makes sense to me.

AAE:

3. SAE: This city's football team is not performing in the way we are hoping they will later in the season.

AAE:

4. SAE: If anyone is aware of what the answer to this question is, he/she is obligated to tell the rest of us even if he/she thinks it is unethical.

AAE:

For SAE sentences #5–7, apply the same rules as in #1–4, but also insert the habitual/invariant "be" where necessary.

5. SAE: The university's students are absent from class frequently, and this problem is on the dean's list of topics to discuss this year.

AAE:

6. SAE: Even if you are absent just one day during the term, it is always a big problem when taking a final exam, especially if the exam includes material from the whole term.

AAE:

7. SAE: Teachers are always presenting important material during class, and that is why this problem is what it is.

AAE:

Glossary

Acronym: A word formed by combining the initials of an expression, such as "scuba."

Adjective: A lexical category whose members can be defined by their function as modifiers of nouns, their ability to take inflections of comparison in English and their tendency to co-occur with nouns (attributive use) or to be part of verb phrases (predicative use).

Adverb: A lexical category whose members have different functions, depending on their subtype (manner adverbs, sentence adverbs, intensifiers), and no inflections.

Affix: A bound morpheme that is attached to roots and stems either before the root or stem (prefix), after the root or stem (suffix) or in the middle of the root or stem (infix).

Affixing: A word formation process in which affixes are attached to roots and stems to create a different form of the same word (inflectional) or a new word (derivation).

Affricate: A type of consonant phoneme that begins with complete obstruction of the air through the vocal tract (stop) and ends with the passage of air in a steady stream through a narrow opening of the vocal tract (fricative).

AAE: An abbreviation for African American English, a variety of English widely spoken in the United States.

Allomorph: A surface level representation of an underlying morpheme that is used in a specific linguistic environment.

Allophone: A surface level representation of an underlying phoneme that is used in a specific linguistic environment.

Alveolar ridge: The ridge on the roof of the mouth just behind the upper front teeth.

Ambiguity: The phenomenon of a given expression having multiple meanings.

Antonyms: Pairs of words with opposite meanings.

Article: A lexical subcategory within the larger category of determiners whose members identify nouns as either definite (the) or indefinite (a/an).

Aspect: In grammar, the internal time of an action or state, such as repetition and duration.

Aspiration: The process of producing a speech sound with a puff of air.

Auxiliary: A lexical category whose members can be defined by their function to add meaning to verbs and their co-occurrence with verbs.

Blend: A word formed by combining parts of two words and pronouncing them as one, such as "motel."

Case: In grammar, the relationship of a noun or pronoun to other elements in a sentence, such as subject and object.

Clause: A syntactic unit consisting of both a subject and a verb.

Coda: An optional element of a syllable, consisting of one or more consonants following the nucleus.

Compound: A word formed by combining two free morphemes in their entirety.

Conjunction: A lexical category whose members can be defined by their function to link grammatically like elements, either coordinately (coordinating conjunction) or subordinately (subordinating conjunction).

Consonant: A type of phoneme formed by obstructing the flow of air as it is passed from the lungs through the vocal tract.

Constituent: A syntactic unit that serves some function in a sentence.

Declarative: A mode of expression with a statement function.

Demonstrative: A subclass of determiners whose members identify the specificity and proximity (literally or figuratively) of nouns.

Derivation: A process of word formation through which affixes are attached to roots and stems to derive new words that have different grammatical functions and/or significantly different meanings.

Descriptivism: An approach to grammar that involves the description of rules after observation and testing of actual language use.

Determiner: A lexical category whose members can be defined by their function as modifiers of nouns and their co-occurrence with nouns and other noun modifiers, such as adjectives and quantifiers.

Diphthong: A vowel phoneme consisting of two sounds blended into one.

Direct object: A grammatical relation (NP) that can be defined by its function as the receiver of a verb's action and by its position directly dominated by a verb phrase node.

Distinctive features: Descriptive characteristics of phonemes, in terms of the place and manner of articulation, that can be used to distinguish sounds from each other.

Fricative: A type of consonant phoneme characterized by the forcing of air in a steady stream through a narrow opening in the vocal tract.

Glide: A type of consonant phoneme characterized by movement of articulators, either the tongue or lips, but very little obstruction of air.

Glottis: A narrow opening in the throat between the vocal cords.

Homonyms: Words that have the same sounds in the same order but different meanings and/or functions.

Homophones: Homonyms with different spellings.

Inflection: A process through which words are changed slightly to indicate some grammatical meaning, such as tense or number.

Intensifier: A subclass of adverbs whose members can be defined by their function, as modifiers of adjectives and other adverbs, and by their co-occurrence with the adjectives and adverbs they modify.

Interference: A phenomenon of second language learning in which the rules of a person's first language are different from those of a second language, and these difference create problems in learning the second language.

Interrogative: A mode of expression with a question function.

Liquid: A type of consonant phoneme characterized by curling of the tongue and very little obstruction of air.

Minimal pair: A pair of words that contain the same sounds in the same order with one exception, with that single difference creatikng a difference in the meaning of the words.

Modal: A subcategory of auxiliary verb whose members can be distinguished from other auxiliaries by their inability to also be used as verbs.

Monophthong: A vowel phoneme consisting of a single sound.

Morpheme: A minimal unit of meaning.

Morphology: The study of word structure and word formation.

Morphophonology: The study of the sound system of word formation (intersection of morphology and phonology).

Nasal: A type of consonant phoneme characterized by the redirection of air through the nasal cavity.

Natural class: A group of phonemes that all share one or more articulatory or acoustic feature.

Noun: A lexical category whose members can be defined by their function as subjects and objects of verbs, by their ability to take number (plural) and case (possessive) inflections in English and by their tendency to co-occur with modifiers such as adjectives and determiners.

Nucleus: The mandatory element of a syllable, its vowel.

Onomatopoeia: The phenomenon in which a word's sounds indicates its meaning, as with the words for animal noises.

Onset: An optional element in a syllable consisting of one or more consonants before the neucleus.

Orthography: A set of written symbols used to represent language by matching the symbols with the sounds they represent.

Palate: The hard part of the roof of the mouth behind the alveolar ridge and in front of the velum.

Passive: A grammatical construction in which the subject of the sentence does not represent the actual doer of the verb.

Person: A grammatical concept that indicates the perspective of the speaker in the event or situation being described (1st, 2nd, 3rd).

Phoneme: A unit of linguistic sound in a language that is recognized as such by a native speaker of that language.

Phonics: An approach to literacy instruction that encourages the learner to sound words out by matching orthographic symbols and sounds.

Phonology: The study of sound systems.

Phonotactic constraints: A set of constraints on the syllable structure a language can have.

Phrase: A syntactic unit consisting of one or more words that lacks one or more of the necessary elements of a clause.

Predicate: The constituent (VP) in a sentence, directly dominated by the sentence node, that makes a statement about the subject.

Prefix: An affix attached to the front of a root or stem.

Preposition: A lexical category whose members can be defined by their function to relate NPs to some other element in a sentence, often in terms of direction or location.

Prescriptivism: An approach to grammar in which rules are assumed ahead of time and speakers are expected to adhere to them.

Pro form: Any word that substitutes for a constituent.

Pronoun: A lexical category whose members can be defined by their function as substitutes for NPs and their ability to take case inflections (subject, object, possessive) in English.

Quantifier: A lexical category whose member can be defined by their function as modifiers of nouns and their ability to co-occur with other noun modifiers (determiners, adjectives).

Relative clause: A clause that is set off by a relative pronoun and embedded within a noun phrase.

Rhyme: The part of a syllable that contains the nucleus and coda (if one is present).

Root: The central morpheme in a word, the one around which multi-morphemic words are built.

Schwa: A mid, central vowel that is used in unstressed syllables in English.

Sibilant: A kind of consonant phoneme characterized acoustically by a hissing sound.

Sonorant: A type of consonant phoneme characterized by little obstruction of air as it is passed through the vocal tract (nasals, liquids, glides).

Stem: A multi-morphemic word to which additional affixes can be added.

Stop: A type of consonant phoneme characterized by a complete blockage of air as it is passed through the vocal tract.

Subject: A grammatical relation (NP) that can be defined by its function as the doer of a verb in a sentence and by its position in the hierarchy of a sentence, directly dominated by the sentence node.

Suffix: An affix attached to the back of a root or stem.

Syllable: A phonological unit consisting of one or more sounds and made up of a mandatory nucleus (vowel) and an optional onset and coda (consonants).

Syllable stress: The relative degree of force with which a syllable is pronounced.

Syntax: The study of phrase and sentence structure.

Transfer: A phenomenon of second language learning in which the rules of a person's first language are similar to those of a second language, and these similarities can facilitate learning the second language.

Transformation: A rule that speakers apply to basic, canonical sentence structures to create non-canonical structures.

Velum: The soft part of the roof of the mouth just behind the palate.

Verb: A lexical category whose members can be defined by their function as the heads of verb phrases and their ability to take tense (past), aspect (simple, progressive, perfective) and person and number (3rd personal singular) inflections in English.

Whole language: A method of literacy instruction in which the use of quality texts is emphasized.

References

Bar-Lev, Zev. 1999. Unpublished workbook.

Barry, Anita. 1998. *English Grammar. Language as Human Behavior*. Upper Saddle River NJ: Prentice Hall.

Cowan, William & Rakušan, Jaromira. 1998. *Source Book for Linguistics*. Amsterdam/Philadelphia: John Benjamins.

Department of Linguistics 1994. *The Language Files*. Columbus: Ohio State University Press.

Finegan, Edward. 1999. *Language. Its Structure and Use*. Fort Worth TX: Harcourt Brace.

Hudson, Grover. 2000. *Essential Introductory Linguistics*. Oxford: Blackwell.

Kaplan, Jeffrey 1995. *English Grammar. Principals and Facts*. Englewood Cliffs NJ: Prentice Hall.

Lester, Mark. 1990. *Grammar in the Classroom*. New York: MacMillan.

Moran, Chris. 2000. Refocusing on Phonics in the Classroom. *SD Union-Tribune*, January 20th.

Whitehall, Harold. 1983. Outline History of the English Language in *Webster's New Universal Unabridged Dictionary*. New York: Simon & Schuster.

Index

T

U

V

W

Y